Gilbert S. Hedstrom
Sustainability

Gilbert S. Hedstrom

Sustainability

What It Is and How to Measure It

DE
G
PRESS

ISBN 978-1-5474-1660-8
e-ISBN (PDF) 978-1-5474-0042-3
e-ISBN (EPUB) 978-1-5474-0050-8

Library of Congress Control Number: 2018955033

Bibliographic information published by the Deutsche Nationalbibliothek
The Deutsche Nationalbibliothek lists this publication in the Deutsche Nationalbibliografie;
detailed bibliographic data are available on the Internet at http://dnb.dnb.de.

© 2019 Gilbert S. Hedstrom
Published by Walter de Gruyter Inc., Boston/Berlin
Printing and binding: CPI books GmbH, Leck
Typesetting: MacPS, LLC, Carmel

www.degruyter.com

Advance Praise

The authoritative book on the most vitally important issue of our day.
— Ken Tierney, Group Vice President, Sustainability
Sims Metal Management

A must read for every business leader who wants an organized, comprehensive summary of sustainability—packed with industry best practices.
— Dave Stangis, Chief Sustainability Officer
Campbell Soup Company

I highly recommend this book to senior leaders who want to understand quickly why sustainability matters to your business and how to measure it. The book also provides a great overview of the current trends around sustainability strategy and governance.
— Karen E. Koster, Executive Vice President
Hexion, Inc.

Building a sustainable enterprise can be a complicated journey, but one made much clearer by Hedstrom's concise primer and valuable roadmap. The book draws on rich examples across industries, and will help boards and executives move faster toward managing risks and harnessing the opportunities of sustainability.
— Jason Jay, Senior Lecturer and Director
MIT Sloan Sustainability Initiative

The challenges facing society and the environment today are unprecedented. Businesses embracing sustainable development will gain competitive advantage and better manage risk. The book provides a balanced, insightful, unbiased review of sustainability—and the Scorecard is a terrific tool to help business leaders gauge how they stack up today.
— Lori Michelin, President and CEO
World Environment Center

DOI 10.1515/9781547400423-202

———

To Peg, for your enduring support.
With special thanks to the sustainability pioneers who lit the flame...
And profound hope for tomorrow's leaders who will carry the torch forward.

About De|G PRESS

Five Stars as a Rule

De|G PRESS, the startup born out of one of the world's most venerable publishers, De Gruyter, promises to bring you an unbiased, valuable, and meticulously edited work on important topics in the fields of business, information technology, computing, engineering, and mathematics. By selecting the finest authors to present, without bias, information necessary for their chosen topic *for professionals*, in the depth you would hope for, we wish to satisfy your needs and earn our five-star ranking.

In keeping with these principles, the books you read from De|G PRESS will be practical, efficient and, if we have done our job right, yield many returns on their price.

We invite businesses to order our books in bulk in print or electronic form as a best solution to meeting the learning needs of your organization, or parts of your organization, in a most cost-effective manner.

There is no better way to learn about a subject in depth than from a book that is efficient, clear, well organized, and information rich. A great book can provide life-changing knowledge. We hope that with De|G PRESS books you will find that to be the case.

DOI 10.1515/9781547400423-204

There is nothing more difficult to take in hand, more perilous to conduct, or more uncertain in its success, than to take the lead in the introduction of a new order of things.

— Niccolo Machiavelli
The Prince (1532)

DOI 10.1515/9781547400423-205

Acknowledgments

When long-time friend and colleague Alex Lajoux suggested I write this book, I thought it would be easy. After all, much of Part 1 existed in my earlier small book (*Sustainability—A Guide for Boards and C-Suites*) and much of Part 2 existed with my Corporate Sustainability Scorecard C-suite rating system. I was, of course, wrong about that. However, Alex provided constant encouragement, invaluable edits and constant inspiration—and for that I am most grateful.

A very special thanks to my editor, Jeffrey Pepper, who not only had a clear vision for this book but also provided constant mid-course corrections. I was incredibly fortunate to have an editor who is as thoughtful, knowledgeable, and even-keeled as Jeffrey. He and the De Gruyter team including Jaya Dalal, have been great to work with.

My Corporate Sustainability Scorecard, on which this book is based, has been influenced and shaped profoundly by conversations I have had in corporate boardrooms. In 1997, two of the Fortune 500 corporate board of directors meetings I participated in sowed the seeds for the Scorecard.

To the long-standing clients who engaged me to work on their behalf, and who entrusted me to meet with their CEOs and present to their boards of directors, I am most grateful. Since 1997, I have had the privilege of working with hundreds of outstanding leaders in large corporations across the globe—at the intersection of business strategy, corporate governance, and sustainability. You have challenged my assumptions, shaped my thinking, and helped create the robust content of the Scorecard, constantly updated on the website (www.thesustainabilityscorecard.com).

The Conference Board has been a strong partner in advancing the business and sustainability agenda over the past two decades. In 2015, they published my article, "Navigating the Sustainability Transformation," essentially an early version of this book's Introduction. A special "thank you" to Conference Board colleagues Thomas Singer, Jim Hendricks, and Uwe Schulte for your constructive partnership.

A core team of Hedstrom Associates colleagues (Beth Tener, Pat Mahon, Justine Pattantyus, Larry Krupp, Nick Braica, Kelsa Summer, and Scott Sousa) has been with me over the past decade, working to create this Scorecard. Your patience and always positive support has kept the Scorecard moving. And I extend a special "thank you" to my colleagues from earlier days at consulting firm Arthur D. Little, especially those with whom I worked closely in Europe for many years: Jonathan Shopley, Richard Clarke, Rick Eagar, and their teams who helped shape the early versions of the Scorecard.

Many colleagues have influenced my thinking about the Scorecard and the subject in general, including Stephanie Aument, Bill Blackburn, Jim Hamilton, Stuart Hart, Andy Hoffman, Jason Jay, Justin Keeble, Peter Lacy, Julie O'Brien, Dawn Rittenhouse, Gwen Ruta, Larry Selzer, Karl Schmidt, Dave Stangis, Ken Tierney, Bob Willard, and Terry Yosie. Thank you! Your insights and broad perspective continue to amaze me.

DOI 10.1515/9781547400423-206

A special thanks to Jeremy Grantham, for your leadership globally, and for alerting investors to the stark realities we face as a society. You are a constant source of inspiration.

Finally, nothing has shaped my thinking about this Scorecard more than the time I have spent in highly confidential sessions with corporate board members. To my long-time friend and mentor, Patrick F. Noonan, I extend my heartfelt thanks.

About the Author

Gilbert (Gib) Hedstrom has over thirty years of experience advising CEOs and board members about how to handle difficult environmental and business challenges. After twenty years at consulting firm Arthur D. Little, where he was vice president and managing director, Gib launched Hedstrom Associates in 2004. Gib provides consulting services to companies about issues that lie at the intersection of corporate governance, strategy, and sustainability.

Gib has reported to full boards of directors or board committees (with oversight of corporate responsibility issues) of major global corporations on over sixty occasions. In his role as independent sustainability advisor, he counsels directors concerning the risks and opportunities, and shares examples of "best practices" globally. He often meets with outside directors in "executive session" (without members of management present).

His clients have included Accenture, AES, Air Products, Alcoa, Ashland, Autodesk, Bayer, Baxter, Boeing, BP, Calvert, Coca-Cola, Conoco, Cytec, Dell, Ford, HP, Honeywell, Kodak, Monsanto, Novartis, Novo Nordisk, Pemex, Raytheon, Sask Power, Shell, United Technologies, USG, and United States Steel, among many others.

For The Conference Board, Gib serves as program director of *Sustainability Council I: Strategy and Implementation, Sustainability Council II: Innovation and Growth,* and the *Chief Environment, Health, and Safety Officers' Council.* These councils provide the opportunity to interact with executives of about 100 leading companies—and to keep his finger on the pulse of current developments.

Gib has authored several books and written dozens of articles related to the environment, governance, strategy, and sustainability. Frequently, he is called upon to speak on business risks and opportunities created by environmental and social trends.

Gib has dual master's degrees from the University of Michigan (MBA Corporate Strategy; MS Natural Resource Management) and a BA (Economics and Geology) from Hamilton College. He welcomes further discussion about governance, strategy, and sustainability issues, and can be reached at gib@hedstromassociates.com.

DOI 10.1515/9781547400423-207

About the Series Editor

Alexandra Reed Lajoux is Series Editor for De|G PRESS, a division of Walter De Gruyter, Inc. The series has an emphasis on governance, corporate leadership, and sustainability. Dr. Lajoux is chief knowledge officer emeritus (CKO) at the National Association of Corporate Directors (NACD) and founding principal of Capital Expert Services, LLC (CapEx), a global consultancy providing expert witnesses for legal cases. She has served as editor of *Directors & Boards, Mergers & Acquisitions, Export Today,* and *Director's Monthly*, and has coauthored a series of books on M&A for McGraw-Hill, including *The Art of M&A* and eight spin-off titles on strategy, valuation, financing, structuring, due diligence, integration, bank M&A, and distressed M&A. For Bloomberg/Wiley, she coauthored *Corporate Valuation for Portfolio Investment* with Robert A. G. Monks. Dr. Lajoux serves on the advisory board of Campaigns and Elections, and is a Fellow of the Caux Round Table for Moral Capitalism. She holds a B.A. from Bennington College, a Ph.D. from Princeton University, and an M.B.A. from Loyola University in Maryland. She is an associate member of the American Bar Association. She is an associate member of the American Bar Association and is certified as a Competent Communicator by Toastmasters International.

DOI 10.1515/9781547400423-208

Contents

Preface

Over the past fifty years, the drumbeat calling for action on corporate environmental and social responsibility (by whatever name) has grown steadily louder. From early concerns about pollution and human rights abuses to more recent angst about impacts of the "throwaway society" and the unintended consequences of the industrial society, the calls for corporate action today rest in the C-suite and boardroom.

The simple reality is that a rapidly growing population—consuming more and more stuff—lives on a fixed planet with limits to nonrenewable resources. This may not seem like the situation in small towns surrounded by thousands of acres of land, clean air, and clean water (such as in Canada or many parts of the central United States). Nevertheless, business leaders increasingly realize that the status quo can not continue. Pressure has increased across the globe at all levels to take action now to make sure the world's health is sustainable. This book is about how corporations gauge where they stand on sustainability as compared to their competitors, peer companies, and global best practices—and what they can do to deliver value to owners as well as to society at large.

Sustainability (known by a plethora of terms) has become a critical CEO and board-level issue. Why? Because customers are asking their suppliers to cut down on energy and water use, hazardous substances in the products, and packaging. Investors want to know that climate-related risks and other key issues are being managed and the company is positioned to reap growth from emerging technologies that solve society's toughest challenges. And young employees care about this stuff; it is hard for companies to attract talent if the company does not live up to the growing expectations to address society's greatest challenges. The "war for talent" is the number one CEO challenge globally—and has been for the past five years.[1]

The Corporate Sustainability Scorecard

So the question all companies—large and small; public and private—are asking is: *How do we stack up?* Double click on that question and others pop up: *Are we thinking about this (sustainability) stuff the right way? Is our company at risk? Are there growth opportunities we are not thinking of? What global best practices can we learn from?*

To help C-suite executives (and those advising the CEO) understand how they stack up today—and how they map a path forward, I developed the Corporate Sustainability Scorecard ™ C-suite rating system. Since the late 1990s, Hedstrom Associates and partners have used the Corporate Sustainability Scorecard with dozens of global corporations. In late 2017 and 2018, we made the Scorecard available to a group of

---

1 The C-Suite Challenge Survey 2018; The Conference Board.

DOI 10.1515/9781547400423-210

clients and companies associated with several Conference Board councils of executives that I run. As we go to press, about sixty-five of the (mostly Fortune 500) companies have submitted data.

This book, which builds on my earlier book (*Sustainability—A Guide for Boards and C-Suites*)—serves two purposes—and is organized into two parts accordingly. The first part gives readers in a wide range of companies—public and private; large and small—an understanding of what sustainability is all about and how companies are addressing the complex set of risks and opportunities sustainability presents. It places the entire sustainability conversation in a simple, business-friendly context.

The second part serves as a "user's manual" for executives at all levels and in particular those who must set the direction for those organizations. It includes a successfully tested "balanced scorecard"—and maturity model—that executives and board members can use to engage in the "right" high-value strategic conversations about sustainability and business growth.

Sustainability is hard work. The first step toward capturing value from sustainability is simply *to learn*. Though initially some business leaders considered sustainability a fleeting trend, such narrow perspectives have changed dramatically. Today, mainstream investors like BlackRock and business leaders understand the essence, scale, and profound global impact of demographic, environmental, and societal mega forces. Such leaders are coming to grips with what sustainability *fully means* to their companies, employees and their families, customers, and supply chain partners. They begin to see the *immense upside business potential from sustainability*.

The Scorecard is published in this book with the hope that it will be used by organizations large and small, public and private across the globe to understand the issues; to gauge how they stack up; and to navigate their path forward during this historic "sustainability transformation" we are witnessing.

—Gib Hedstrom

Introduction

We live in extraordinary times. We can expect unprecedented business and societal change over the coming decade.

Every CEO dreams about having the line of customers outside the store double in size. Well, that is happening—at a global scale. Between 2015 and 2030, the size of the middle class globally will double,[i] which will result in exploding demand for consumer goods and resources.

Yet, already today, the natural systems that provide resources are strained severely.[ii] Across the globe, the rapidly expanding middle class is beginning to crash into constraints caused by the fixed supply of natural resources that support growth. Something has to give.

And with change comes business opportunity as companies navigate the sustainability transformation.[iii]

On the Threshold of Transformation

The last time society experienced such dramatic change was about 150 years ago. In a twenty-year span from 1859 to 1879: oil was discovered in Titusville, PA (1859); the French engineer, J. J. Étienne Lenoir, invented the internal combustion engine (1859); and Thomas Edison invented the electric light bulb (1879). The inventions over those two decades unfolded years later as the industrial revolution of the late 1800s.

Yet, in many ways, very little has changed in the past 100 years. Consider that today we continue to drive oil-fueled vehicles, rely more than ever on light bulbs, and still burn little black rocks to keep our cell phones and iPads running.

Market forces, societal trends, and resource constraints are converging for the first time in history. However, with globalization, the digital transformation, and demands for greater transparency, these changes take place today far more rapidly than the transformation during the late nineteenth and early twentieth centuries.

The entire global economic system is built on a set of assumptions that are eroding in front of our eyes. The century-old model of the industrial era is being shattered—not only by Airbnb, Lyft, and Amazon, but also by more traditional companies such as M&S, Allianz (insurance), Ford, M&S, NextEra Energy, Nestlé, LEGO Group, Philips, Siemens, Unilever, and dozens of other leading companies.

The convergence of global mega forces[iv] (i.e., population growth, urbanization, resource and fresh-water scarcity, ecosystem decline, and more) and business realities that companies face represent the *greatest set of risks and simultaneously, significant business opportunities in a century. That is what sustainability is about.*

DOI 10.1515/9781547400423-211

A CEO and Board-Level Issue

The core business challenge has come into sharp focus for many CEOs. *How can we succeed without consuming too many resources or having a negative societal impact?* That means we need to figure out how to:

– Create a profitable, growing company that approaches zero (negative) and even **net-positive**[1] environmental and social impacts (or **footprint**);
– Help our suppliers and customers to do the same.

Over the next decade, we can expect **environmental, social, and governance (ESG)** factors to increasingly impact how companies choose new businesses to buy, old businesses to reshape, or shed, new offerings to create, and suppliers with which to partner.[2] *Board members and C-suite executives own the sustainability agenda—simply because this subject is inherently long-term, complex, and impactful.* Yet, they continue to struggle with sustainability. I know that from first-hand experience. Over the years, I have been fortunate to meet with Fortune 500 boards and their committees on over sixty occasions—across about twenty companies and many industry sectors.

In every one of the sixty meetings, the board members have asked me some version of a single question regarding sustainability: *How do we stack up?* They want to understand: *Where does our company stand today vis-à-vis sustainability as compared with competitors, peers, and best practices? What are our biggest gaps? What actions should we take now?*

The Corporate Sustainability Scorecard™

The Corporate Sustainability Scorecard builds on my thirty years of experience working in the trenches with executives at over 250 companies in the United States, Europe, and Asia. From 2000 to 2015, my colleagues and I used variations of the Scorecard with executive sustainability teams at dozens of companies across a range of industries. Here are some key points about the Scorecard:

– *By industry; for industry.* This Scorecard—unlike others, has been truly developed by industry—for use by industry. This is not like the hundred odd external sustainability ratings and awards that were developed by some outside group where

---

1 Note: The sustainability topic has its share of jargon and terminology used—words like **net-positive** and **footprint** among many others. We highlight these words or phrases in bold font—and provide definitions in Appendix A.

2 Note: In this book we use the terms **sustainability** and ESG interchangeably. While there are nuances and different areas of emphasis by people using these terms, both terms get at the same thing: building an ethical, resilient, sustainable, and transparent company that is aligned with the needs of society.

they rate you. With this Scorecard, *you rate yourselves* on a set of criteria developed over twenty years by your peers. As a result, the information is confidential if you choose to make it so.

- *It speaks the language of the CEO and board.* This Scorecard has its origins in the boardroom. I started developing it in 1997 after back-to-back meetings with two Fortune 500 boards of directors. The seventeen individual elements that comprise the Corporate Sustainability Scorecard are discussed in the boardroom— and owned by various C-suite executives. Each element (e.g., Culture and Organization; Strategic Planning; Innovation, Research, and Development, etc.) is a major corporate function or activity on which CEOs and boards of directors spend considerable time.
- *It's proven.* The Scorecard has been around for twenty years. In addition to the twenty-five–thirty companies that were involved with the Scorecard prior to 2016, an additional sixty major global companies all completed a company self-assessment in early 2018. These companies found the Scorecard to be easy to use. A common reaction was, "a lot of lightbulbs went on as we completed the self-assessment."
- *A compendium of best-practice company examples.* The Scorecard (and Part 2 of this book) includes several hundred examples of companies that are considered to be global leaders for a particular attribute. In the Scorecard's four-stage rating scale, these companies are Stage 3 or higher.
- *On-line and easy.* While the core Scorecard elements and rating criteria are included in Part 2 of this book, the tool is an on-line rating system that continuously evolves.
- *Continuously improved.* The sixty large global companies using the Scorecard in early 2018 benefited from input from the twenty-five companies that participated in a 2015 pilot. Likewise, these 2018 participants offered suggestions on how to sharpen the rating criteria. Those changes have been made (and are incorporated in Part 2 of this book). While the author expects the core structure, framework, rating criteria, etc., to remain intact, there will be constant improvements going forward.

The Scorecard is intended for corporations globally. The rating system—described in detail in Part 2 of this book, is applicable to companies large and small, public and private.

The initial sixty "founding member companies" that completed a company self-assessment were by invitation only. As we go to press, invitations are being sent out to the next forty global companies.

With the launch of this book—and with a solid presence of the Global 500 already in the database, we expect many additional companies globally, large and small, private and public, to access the benefits of the on-line rating system. While the full rating criteria are included in this book, those criteria are constantly being updated and best practice examples are being added. Moreover, registered Scorecard users are able to access detailed analyses of the results to see how their company compares with all of the others in the database (or just within their industry peer group). To learn more, visit www.thesustainabilityscorecard.com.

Organization of the Book

Sustainability: What it Is and How to Measure it is a business-focused summary of how to think about the risks and opportunities associated with sustainability for your company. The book draws on insights gained from working with hundreds of companies over thirty years—from the boardroom to the shop floor; not only from the approximately sixty board meetings I have participated in, but also from the experiences of over seventy companies that have used the Scorecard over the past twenty years on www.thesustainabilityscorecard.com.

The book is organized into two parts.
- Part 1 provides a full background on the subject from a business practitioner's perspective. It begins with addressing the basics: Why bother with this stuff at all? How do I make sense of all this terminology? What does it mean for my industry sector?
- Part 2 then walks the reader through the seventeen core elements of the Corporate Sustainability Scorecard—organized in the four main parts of the Scorecard: *Governance and Leadership*; *Strategy and Execution*; *Environmental Stewardship*; *and Social Responsibility*.

----

i Homi Charas, *The Unprecedented Expansion of the Global Middle Class: An Update*, Brookings, February 2017.
ii "GEO-5 for Business: Impacts of a Changing Environment on the Corporate Sector," United Nations Environment Program's fifth Global Environment Outlook (GEO-5) Report, June 2012.
iii Gilbert S. Hedstrom, "Navigating the Sustainability Transformation," Director Notes, The Conference Board, January 2015.
iv "Expect the Unexpected: Building Business Value in a Changing World," KPMG/Cutting through Complexity. https://www.kpmg.com/Global/en/IssuesAndInsights/ArticlesPublications/Documents/building-business-value.pdf

Part 1

Part 1 provides an overview of sustainability from a business practitioner's perspective. For those new to the subject, this part begins by answering the basic questions:
- *What's it all about?* How does it really relate to businesses working to increase shareholder value?
- *Why bother with this stuff at all?* Is it required by law? Is it just the new version of corporate philanthropy and environment, health, and safety (EHS)?
- *How do I make sense of all this terminology?* Is sustainability the same as environmental, social, and governance (ESG)? What about carbon footprint—how does that fit in? Some companies talk about becoming "net positive"—what's that about?
- *What does it mean for my industry sector?* I get that the coal industry is under the gun and that Nike and Apple have responsibility for working conditions in their supply chains. But this sustainability stuff must mean very different things for companies in the automotive, chemical, healthcare, and utility sectors—to name a few.

This part then gives an overview of each of the four main "buckets" of sustainability: governance and leadership; strategy and execution; environmental stewardship; and social responsibility. Part 1 ends with a brief overview of how to think about the new ESG requirements being imposed on businesses globally.

Chapter 1
Sustainability in 2020 and Beyond

The transformation of companies—even entire industries—is not new. DHL and FedEx reinvented shipping in the 1970s.[i] Apple created new products seemingly before individuals knew they wanted them.

The transformation happening today is underpinned by a profound realization. Across industries today, companies increasingly recognize that the "take–make–waste" industrial model is no longer viable. That model is being replaced by a new **circular economy** that offers significant business opportunity by creating wealth from waste."[ii]

The Drivers: Economics 101

In a nutshell, here is the problem—and opportunity: *Human society has bumped up against the limits of economic and natural systems.*

Modern industrialism developed in a world far different from the one we live in today: people were few, while natural resources were plentiful. What emerged was a highly productive, take-make-waste system. Take resources out of the earth; make stuff; and throw it away. That system worked for a long time until stuff started to pile up—either visibly or invisibly (like carbon in the atmosphere).

Not anymore. The current model is simply *not sustainable*; that is, not able to be maintained at a certain rate or level, and not able to be upheld or defended.

The basic laws of supply and demand will wreak havoc for many companies while presenting significant opportunities for others. This transformation largely will transpire between now and 2030, driven by the economics of "supply and demand" (as Figure 1.1 illustrates).

DOI 10.1515/9781547400423-001

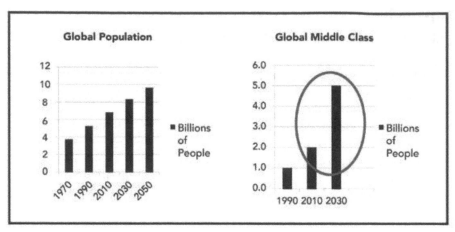

Source: Created from data produced by United Nations, Population Division

Figure 1.1: Growing Demand

- *Demand:* From 2015 to 2030, the global middle class will double in size from 2.5 billion to about 5 billion.[iii] Stop and think about that—particularly if you have spent time in Beijing, Shanghai, Mexico City, or a similar city. Unless things change dramatically, the demand will double for food, cars, soda, diapers, and other "stuff" that today is purchased and discarded.
- *Supply:* Every company and industry requires a baseload supply of a stable physical environment within which to operate. Yet, to support this rapidly growing middle class demand, with a fixed amount of land, forest cover, fresh water, and other nonrenewable resources on the planet, the environmental stability is dwindling.[iv]
- *Prices:* What happens when demand grows while supply is fixed or declining? Economics 101 teaches us that prices increase (at least in the absence of other market forces, such as tax incentives). Unfortunately, the powerful forces of supply and demand have been constrained by inadequate market pricing signals, especially related to carbon and water. (Water is more expensive in Flint, Michigan—adjacent to the Great Lakes which hold one fifth of the global fresh water supply—than it is in the dessert-like conditions around Phoenix, Arizona.)

With respect to carbon, leading companies manage this situation by placing an internal price on carbon. A study by CDP (formerly Carbon Disclosure Project) noted that in 2016, 517 companies were using internal carbon pricing as an accounting and risk management tool (19 percent increase from 2015), and an additional 732 companies planned to implement one by 2018 (26 percent increase from 2015).[v]

Author's advice: In my dozens of meetings in corporate boardrooms, I find that eyes glaze over when executives hear about global population growth (the left side of Figure 1.1). But the right side of this figure grabs their attention. Every CEO is thinking about the next decade.

Sustainability: Four Big Buckets

In the 1990s, sustainability was often characterized as the triple bottom line of people, planet, and profits. A number of years later, the phrase ESG took over, referring to the environmental, social, and governance factors impacting an investment decision. Taken together, these define the four big buckets of the sustainability conversation:
- *Environmental Stewardship*: Reducing waste; cutting carbon and other emissions; managing water quality and quantity; ensuring the materials used in our products are nontoxic, recyclable, reusable, etc.; reducing packaging; owning responsibility for products at the end of their useful life.
- *Social Responsibility*: Taking responsibility for the labor situation that your suppliers (and their suppliers) engage in; eliminating human rights abuses (e.g., child labor, forced labor, etc.); ensuring diversity and inclusion not only in your company but also throughout your value chain; being a good neighbor.
- *Governance*: Defined broadly as "how we run the place"—meaning the organization, structure, culture from the boardroom to the shop floor; the goals and metrics that incent behavior; engagement with internal and external stakeholders; disclosure and reporting.
- *Strategy and Execution*: Determining how our company can actually grow and be profitable while also reducing our full life-cycle (negative) impacts—and helping our customers do the same; creating value for society as well as for shareholders.

The sustainability conversation, as depicted on the left side of Figure 1.2, has been long dominated by environmental and social headlines. Indeed, the vast majority of articles and books written about sustainability over the past thirty years have focused largely on the environment: degradation, resource limits, externalities, climate change, pesticides, toxics, and waste. How depressing!

Dozens of books describe the global environmental challenges, while too many business-oriented books paint a picture that sustainability is all about "win-win" and "green is gold." This is far too simplistic and often just not true. Moreover, not only has the subject been beaten to death, *it is the wrong conversation.*

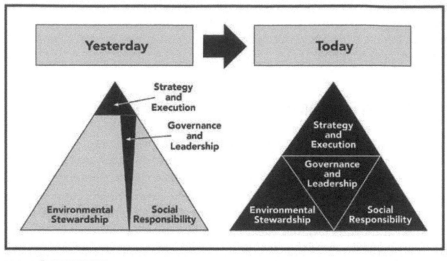

Source: HEDSTROM

Figure 1.2: The Changing Sustainability Conversation

The Huge Business Opportunity

With the supply and demand curves converging, the world is on the cusp of a resource revolution.

This new industrial revolution will enable strong economic growth at an environmental "cost" (in terms of **externalities** such as pollution, CO_2 emissions, etc.) far lower than in the past. *Realistically, achieving high-productivity economic growth to support the 2.5 billion new members of the middle class presents the largest wealth-creation opportunity since the dawn of the industrial revolution.*[vi]

Because sustainability is fundamentally about industry transformation, board members and C-suite executives have found it helpful to assess their company's current corporate sustainability position in terms of four stages—depicted in Figure 1.3. The four-stage transformation model described below refers to Hedstrom Associates' Corporate Sustainability Scorecard™.

The four-stage transformation model helps companies assess and manage progress proactively through the "messy transformation." During the early stages, this involves engaging deeply with (and learning about) sustainability. Toward Stage 3 and Stage 4, it often involves disruptive innovation—in the way that Airbnb, Tesla, and Novelis are transforming their industries.

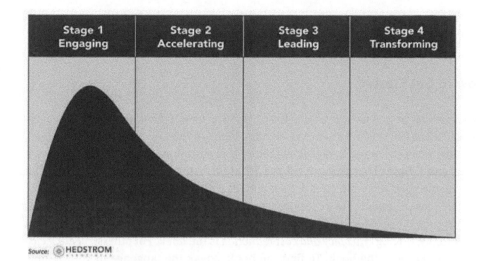

Stage 1 Engaging	Stage 2 Accelerating	Stage 3 Leading	Stage 4 Transforming

Source: HEDSTROM

Figure 1.3: Distribution of Global 500 Companies

Mixed Signals

The industrial economic model launched over a century ago resulted in the one-way, linear "take–make–waste" flow. That worked well for a long, long time. GDP growth has raised billions of people out of poverty.

Today, however, we are in the waning years of that model. The tide has started to turn. Major industrial companies with a decades-long outlook have come to realize they must change. In the meantime, hundreds of young start-up companies recognizing massive new opportunities have tried to position themselves to become the next Google. Some have achieved early success and are still "on a roll."

At the same time, the old linear model chugs along on many fronts. We still often use traditional, carbon-intensive resources to power our iPhones. Detroit still churns out cars and trucks on ever-more efficient assembly lines.

Let's say you are skeptical about all of this. You understand that there is no shortage of highly respected business leaders calling for corporate responsibility—for "doing well by doing good"—but at the end of the day you believe all that truly matters is delivering value to your shareholders.

You may also have seen transformational CEOs who garnered a lot of positive press for their bold sustainability actions—only to find themselves out of a job. Sir John Browne (former CEO of BP) was hailed for his early call for action on climate change. That happened to David Crane of NRG and to Phil Martens of Novelis.

These conflicting signals (continuation of the old "linear" model with ever stronger signals about the new "circular" model) make it tough for companies to know how to respond. That is actually good news!

Smart companies recognize this period for what it is: the transition zone when some undercurrents flow in one direction, while others flow in the opposite direction.

How to Get Started

Sustainability never has been a question of "if." *Sustainability always has been a question of "when."* At this time of mixed signals, here are five "no regrets" actions every company executive working on sustainability issues should be taking.

1. **Speak C-Suite Language; Find the Hook(s).** For every company, a particular "magic hook" on which to drive sustainability becomes critical to propel action. For some companies (e.g., Johnson & Johnson's *Credo*), the hook is *core values*. For others like 3M and GE, the hook is *innovation*. For many companies, at least initially, driving *efficiency and cost reduction* is the hook. For others, *meeting customer needs* is the hook. To find the hook, speak the language of your C-suite executives.

   o *CFO:* Focus on managing risk and driving productivity improvement; and assess the impacts of resource supply disruptions, carbon risk, volatile commodity prices, and **stranded assets**.

   o *Human Resources:* Engage in "the war for talent," knowing that millennials care deeply about unemployment, resource scarcity, climate change/environment, and income inequality."[vii]

   o *Business Leaders:* Intensely focus on creating different ways to meet those needs (as seen with Airbnb)—even if the customer never thinks about them.

   o *R&D/Technology:* Drive to unleash innovation that propels tomorrow's growth.

   o *Investor Relations:* Gather information about the growing interest in ESG among mainstream investors. Assess the impact of ESG-related shareholder resolutions. Learn to tell the story about how the company is seizing growth opportunities, while also mitigating sustainability-related risks.

   Look for "sustainability" and "innovation" in core business publications and media, such as: *Fortune, Business Week, Fast Company, The Financial Times, Sloan Management Review, Harvard Business Review, Wall Street Journal*, and others like these.

2. **Identify Internal Advocates.** This stuff is important to your employees. Assemble a team of high-potential employees across your company's functions, age levels, lines of business, and geographies, especially from Europe. (Many European countries are years or decades ahead of the United States when it comes to sustainability.) The right individual/s may be within the sales organization in Asia or other parts of the world. Perhaps the right internal advocate is within R&D

or new product development. Moreover, the Human Resources recruitment director may be seeking to hire millennial applicants who want to work for responsible companies.

3. **Save Money.** Many hundreds of companies globally have proven that reducing environmental and/or social impacts can save money. The "efficiency" (**footprint** reduction) path to sustainability should be an easy sell. What could be a more natural fit with zero defects than zero waste? The drive toward zero (physical) waste through a company's approaches to procurement, production, assembly, transportation, and sales should align fully with Six Sigma, Lean, or whatever that quality program is referred to within your company.

4. **Uncover Stories from Your Customers and Suppliers—And Their Customers/Suppliers.** Look across your company's full **supply chain**. What are your customers asking about—perhaps related to carbon impact, hazardous materials, packaging, working conditions, etc.)? What are their ESG goals? What technology disruptions are happening in your sector—and how do those disruptions impact the total footprint—negative impacts across the **value chain**?

5. **Collect Data.** Collect data on your company's *baseline resource costs*. Include all forms of energy (fuel, electricity, transport, etc.), materials, water, and other inputs. For the CFO, gather information on the ESG interests of your company's top fifty investors. For discussions with business leaders and sales and marketing executives, collect data on *customer inquiries* or requests for sustainability information. Research your major *customers' sustainability goals*.

Every company in every industry will need to transform in order to survive and thrive. Ask yourself: *If we start a major change now, how many years (decades) will it take to move from the linear model to a more circular one? How long will our "sunk" capital investments in the old linear model play out? Are those smart investments for our stakeholders?*

In the next several chapters, we will address:
- Why bother?
- How to make sense of the terminology.
- What does it mean for my industry sector?

i "Time Flies: The FedEx Timeline." http://about.van.fedex.com/our-story/history-timeline/timeline/
ii *Waste to Wealth: The Circular Economy Advantage.* By Peter Lacy and Jakob Rutqvist, August 2015. https://www.accenture.com/us-en/insight-creating-advantage-circular-economy
iii "Population 2030: Demographic Challenges and Opportunities for Sustainable Development Planning," United Nations, 2015.
iv "Geo-5 for Business," *op cit.*
v "Embedding a Carbon Price into Business Strategy," CDP North America, Inc., September 2016, p. 5.
vi Stefan Heck and Matt Rogers, "Are You Ready for the Resource Revolution?" *McKinsey Quarterly*, March 2014, p. 2.
vii The Deloitte Millennial Survey/Executive Summary/January 2014. http://www2.deloitte.com/content/dam/Deloitte/global/Documents/About-Deloitte/gx-dttl-2014-millennial-survey-report.pdf

Chapter 2
Why Bother?

At its core, sustainability is about building foundations for future success. For company leaders, that requires understanding the trends that will impact your businesses and the buying habits of your customers (and their customers). By shaping your future business offerings to align with those trends, you position your company to win in the marketplace—while helping to solve the world's pressing challenges.

In this chapter, we address the "why bother" question as follows:
- Describe what strategy leaders call the opportunity of the century
- Look globally—at the risks that impact every industry and every supply chain—direct from the annual World Economic Forum (WEF) annual Risk Review
- Look locally—and ask how all this stuff may seem depending if you live in Delhi, Delft, or Des Moines (illustrating different parts of the globe)
- Look at why many companies have pursued environmental, social, and governance (ESG) factors
- Define "the business case" for sustainability
- Examine the growing voice of investors—and then of customers
- End with a discussion of how close we are to the tipping point

Opportunity of the Century

Inherent in any discussion of sustainability is taking a reasonably long-term view. That does not mean trying to anticipate the shape of things ten–twenty years out; today it means looking ahead a few years.

The leading management consulting firms—including Accenture and McKinsey—have argued that sustainability—and the associated **circular economy**—represents *the greatest business opportunity in over 100 years*. That, in short, is why companies *should* bother coming to grips with sustainability.

The biggest business opportunities of the future will be reserved for those companies that realize their long-term competitiveness depends on a healthy planet and society.

Of course, "long-term competitiveness" is relative. Capital intensive industries such as mining, oil, and gas production, or utilities have a planning horizon of many decades. The useful life of a mine or a power plant or a refinery can be thirty to fifty years or more. At the other end of the spectrum, "long term" for a technology company might be a few years.

See Figure 2.1 for the interplay among business, society, and the environment.

DOI 10.1515/9781547400423-002

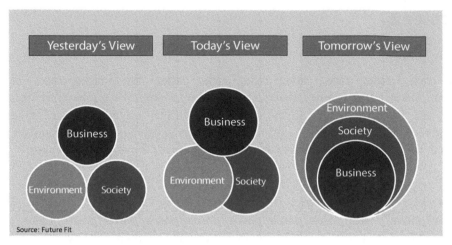

Figure 2.1: Business, Society, and the Environment

Do companies really require a healthy planet and society to win in the marketplace? Increasingly, the answer is yes. Volkswagen learned this the hard way; on June 14, 2018, German prosecutors imposed a €1 billion fine ($1.17 billion) in conjunction with the company's emission-cheating scandal. Prior to this, the company had positioned itself as being among the "more green" auto makers. Apple learned this several years ago when one of their main parts suppliers, Foxconn in China, faced major issues associated with poor and unsafe working conditions.

In looking at Figure 2.1, it is helpful to go back and review the global population growth—and especially the growth of the global middle class—depicted in Figure 1.1. Think of people on a subway car. In "Yesterday's View," the subway cars each have lots and lots of empty seats. If the guy next to you spills a drink, you hardly notice. In "Today's View," there are more people. Most of the seats are full and the center aisle is also packed with people standing. In "Tomorrow's View," the subway cars are jam packed. If one person coughs or sneezes or spills something, half of the car is affected.

When every industry sector looks at its full life-cycle impacts across the value chain, what you increasingly see is that we are already living in "Tomorrow's" world.

- *Yesterday's View.* This aligns with Milton Friedman's dictum that "the business of business is business." Over the past half century, companies have increasingly recognized that the environment and communities are important; however, businesses still operated in their own world. This was basically the situation in most developed economies, certainly in the United States, from about 1950 to 1975.
- *Today's View.* This view acknowledges that business, society and the environment rub shoulders. In today's world, a growing number of CEOs see the important interrelationship between a healthy environment, a robust society and the ability of businesses to remain vibrant for the long term. This has been the situa-

tion between about 1975 (the onslaught of environmental, health and safety laws, and regulations) and about 2015.
- *Tomorrow's View*. This view, in many ways, simply states the obvious: business operates within society at large—which in turn operates on the planet and within the basic natural rules of the environment.

Some day soon, we will look at the picture in Figure 2.1 and ask ourselves, "Why didn't we see this obvious fact sooner?"

Global Risk Review—WEF

The WEF (World Economic Forum) produces a widely read and highly respected annual *Global Risks Report*. (Note that this is a business and *economics* group—not an *environmental* group.) The report examines a wide range of global risks and ranks them on two dimensions: likelihood and impact.

The headline for 2018 is telling: "Climate and tech pose the biggest risks to our world in 2018." The report states that environmental risks have grown in prominence over the 13-year history of the *Global Risks Report*, and this trend continued in 2018. The latest WEF report looks at five categories of environmental risks:
- Extreme weather events and temperatures
- Accelerating biodiversity loss
- Pollution of air, soil, and water
- Failures of climate change mitigation and adaptation
- Risks linked to the transition to low carbon

All these risks ranked highly on both dimensions of likelihood and impact. The WEF report summarizing The Global Risks Landscape 2018 does not impose requirements on industry; however, it is widely read by CEOs and board members and it describes the broad landscape companies will need to succeed in during the coming years. (We discuss this in more detail in Chapter 9: The New ESG Regulators.)

But Wait—Delhi, Delft, Des Moines

The way you view all this sustainability stuff varies dramatically based on where you live. Using the subway car analogy, if you live in Delhi (India) the car is overflowing with people sitting on top of one another. If you live in Delft (Netherlands), the car is very crowded even though there are fields of open space out the windows—but the train tracks are below sea level. And if you are in Des Moines (Iowa) with few people in the car looking out at wide, open spaces, you are wondering what this stuff is all about.

The toughest business conversations about sustainability I have had in over thirty years working with hundreds of major companies around the world have been with companies headquartered in the Midwest of the United States. Think about it: the air is clean; the water is clean; there are relatively few people around for hundreds of miles. And if you were to travel those hundreds of miles, all you would see—especially looking north to Canada—is more open space, clean air, and clean water. So, what's the big deal about all this sustainability stuff?

The answer lies in your supply chain. If your company sources raw materials from Delhi (or any highly populated, rapidly developing economy) and/or if your sell your products to customers in Delft (or anywhere in Europe for that matter), you are hearing the growing sirens for action.

Why Have Companies Pursued ESG?

Looking back over the past forty years, companies have invested in environmental stewardship and/or social responsibility initiatives for one of two reasons:
- *The Values Case.* Acting because "it is the right thing to do"—perhaps because it aligns directly with the company's core values or business principles.
- *The Business Case:* Actions that are very likely to result in traditional business benefit—such as reduced cost, reduced risk, sales growth, etc.

The "values case" has been well-documented. Companies that come to mind are Patagonia, Body Shop, Johnson and Johnson, and Interface Carpets, among others. In all cases, a visionary CEO became personally committed to driving transformational change in the company and its industry sector. Ray Anderson, the founder and CEO of Interface Carpets was one such individual. Ray led the charge, speaking at hundreds of events, until his unfortunate death.

In a growing number of industry sectors, one company has led the charge where its visionary CEO essentially broke ranks with industry peers. And, breaking ranks with the industry often brings risks as well as the spotlight. Paul Polman (Unilever) certainly stands out. As discussed elsewhere in this book, shortly after becoming CEO, Polman famously told investors not to expect quarterly financial reports and, in 2010, launched Unilever on a bold path (completely unchartered territory) of doubling the size of the business (sales revenue) while cutting its footprint in half.

In some cases, the visionary CEO moves too fast—at least faster than the board wanted. This happened at NRG and Novelis. David Crane, CEO of NRG (the U.S. power company) from 2012 to 2015 put the company on a transformational path to renewable energy. He ultimately resigned—reportedly after a disagreement with the board. Similarly, Phil Martens, CEO of Novelis (the leading global rolled aluminum manufacturer) from 2009 to 2015, committed the company to transforming its supply chain. Martens set a goal to move from 20 percent raw material from recycled content to 80 percent recycled content. This bold goal set in motion a massive industry restructuring. But perhaps Martens moved too fast. He and the Novelis Board decided to part ways. Nevertheless, the company continues this aggressive industry transformation pathway.

The Business Case for Sustainability

The business case for sustainability is well established. The original study defining the business case was conducted by Arthur D. Little under contract with Shell (see Figure 2.2).

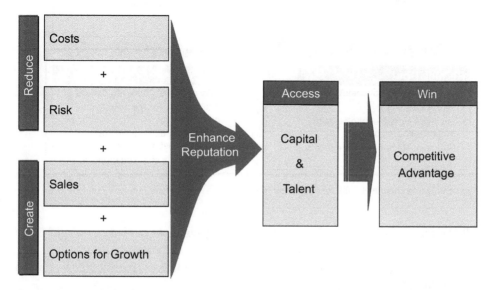

Figure 2.2: The Original Business Case for Sustainability

The business case story reported back in 2000 went like this:
- Reduce cost and risk by cutting energy, water, waste, materials, and negative social impacts.
- Drive revenue growth by either launching a separate line of sustainably advantaged products, services, and solutions or by embedding ESG features into your full product lines.
- Invest in technologies and businesses that create options for future growth— which may also involve helping your customers reduce their footprints.

Together, these actions will strengthen your brand and reputation, giving you better access to capital and talent—resulting in competitive advantage.[i]

Over the past two decades, various research studies about the "sustainability business case" have come to the same conclusion. A slightly different graphical depiction of the business case—used by Accenture among others—is a two-by-two matrix as shown in Figure 2.3.

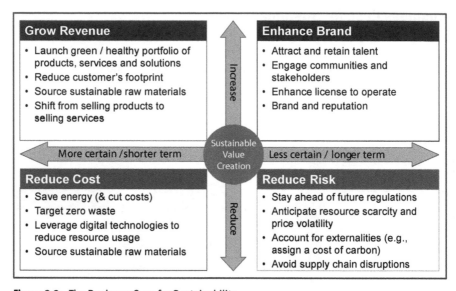

Figure 2.3: The Business Case for Sustainability

What do these four "buckets" of the sustainability business case mean to you? Every company should do the following:
- Make a long list of all your company's current initiatives that somehow relate to sustainability/ESG.
- Map those initiatives into these four buckets.
- Try to quantify the benefits of all sustainability-related initiatives.
- Unless an activity falls into one of the four quadrants, think hard about whether your company should be doing it.

Investors Speaking Up

There is a growing call for action coming from mainstream investors. BlackRock, State Street, Vanguard, and other large institutional investors are beginning to exert pressure on companies to articulate their social purpose. This point was made clear by BlackRock CEO Larry Fink in his January 16, 2018 letter to CEOs:

Society is demanding that companies, both public and private, serve a social purpose...To prosper over time, every company must not only deliver financial performance, but also show how it makes a positive contribution to society. Without a sense of purpose, no company, either public or private, can achieve its full potential.

Investors Change their Views. Fink's words reflect an important shift in how society views the role of business. Indeed, the words above contrast starkly with the traditional view.

– *Traditional View = Deliver Value to Shareholders.* Milton Friedman declared that "The business of business is business" in his 1970 *New York Times Magazine* article. For most of the ensuing 50 years, this view has held dominant.
– *New View = Deliver Value to Shareholders + Society.* Society increasingly expects companies to play a constructive role in addressing some of its biggest challenges (such as income inequality, climate change, natural disasters, water crises, cyberattacks, etc.).

Rather than dismissing these challenges as distractions to core business, CEOs who plan to steer their companies to be 21st century leaders recognize that tackling society's most pressing issues can represent an opportunity for growth, and not a burden.

Analyzing Your Company's Investors. What do your company's owners think about ESG issues? For privately held companies, the answer may vary dramatically depending on whether the owners are long-standing, perhaps family members on the one hand, or hedge fund owners out to flip the company for a profit on the other hand.

For publicly-held companies, an analysis of your "top 50" investors may surprise you. Do the largest investors that own stock in your company care about ESG? A good way to evaluate this is to find out whether those investors are signatories to the CDP and/or the UN Principles for Responsible Investing (UNPRI).

A mid-size chemical company recently did this investor analysis and found that thirteen of their top twenty investors (65 percent) were signatories to CDP and/or UNPRI. At the time they did this analysis (early 2018), these thirteen companies comprised 47 percent of the ownership of the company.

Shareholder Resolutions. Investors are demanding that companies disclose the likely impact of global warming. In its 2017 report on shareholder resolutions, The Conference Board notes that shareholder resolutions on ESG issues now represent more than 43 percent of all voted resolutions, up from 34 percent in 2013.

Shareholder proposals asking companies to disclose the business risks related to climate change continue to gain significant momentum. In 2017, eighteen proposals on climate risk disclosure were brought to a vote, up from thirteen in 2015. These proposals have now reached historically high levels of support: an average support of 39.2 percent of votes cast in 2017, up from 16.7 percent in 2015.[ii]

In a historic (and surprise) vote on May 31, 2017, ExxonMobil's shareholders voted *for* a resolution (*against* Exxon's management) to report clearly how climate change impacts Exxon's business.

More on Investors. Because of the growing importance of investors on ESG issues, we discuss the topic in Chapter 5 (Governance and Leadership—the "G" in ESG) and Chapter 9 (The New ESG Regulators).

Customers Speaking Up

CEOs focus intently when a key owner or investor asks about ESG. They also pay careful attention when a key customer speaks up. That has been happening for over twenty years. In fact, this has been a dominant factor driving many of today's "leading companies" to engage with sustainability. In recent years, the volume and significance of customer ESG requests have been growing rapidly.

During the 1990s and into the early 2000s, the trigger for many companies was one or more key European customers asking for information—about, for example, chemical substances in the raw materials or products delivered; carbon footprint, etc. Then, Walmart (the "elephant in the room") spoke—and the tide turned.

In 2005, Walmart's (then) CEO Lee Scott, announced three aspirational goals: to create zero waste, operate with 100 percent renewable energy and sell products that sustain our resources and the environment. Five years later, Walmart used its size and scale to impact its massive supply chain. The company placed stiff requirements on its suppliers—starting with a focus on energy and removing the equivalent of 3.8 million cars from the road for a year.[iii]

Approaching the Tipping Point

Sustainability has never been a question of "if"—it has always been a question of "when." After all, we live on a fixed planet with fixed land mass and nonrenewable resources. With the rapidly growing population, sooner or later society must come to grips with figuring out how to "live within our means."

How close are we to "the tipping point"—that time when there is no longer any debate about the vital importance of ESG? When that happens, an onslaught of companies will race to differentiate themselves from competitors on their ESG excellence.

Renowned economist and former Harvard University President Lawrence H. Summers noted that the late economist Rudiger Dornbusch was fond of remarking that: "In economics, things take longer to happen than you think they will, and then they happen faster than you thought they could." So, it has been with the build-up of pressures on companies to treat sustainability as a board and C-suite agenda and start transforming the company to align with ESG principles.

There is a growing global consensus that the only way society can evolve to a point where thriving economies grow within the confines of the environment and resource base is if *business takes a lead role.* We can not rely on global institutions (like the United Nations) or on governments to do the job.

Markets can be powerful agents for positive social change. And this is not an "either-or" situation. Companies are proving that they can take significant steps to lower the overall negative impacts on the planet and society—while still making a decent profit. Increasingly this will be the only way to go.

Business leaders who embrace long-term value creation over opportunistic short-term results will earn: (1) the capital to grow from investors; (2) ongoing revenue from customers; and (3) the license to operate and grow from society at large.

---

i Gilbert S. Hedstrom, Jonathan B. Shopley, and Colin M. LeDuc, *Realizing the Sustainable Development Premium*, Prism, 2000.

ii "Environmental and Social Proposals in the 2017 Proxy Season," The Conference Board, September 2017.

iii https://www.nytimes.com/2010/02/26/business/energy-environment/26walmart.html

Chapter 3
Terminology—What Does Sustainability Really Mean?

If you are confused about all this sustainability stuff—you are in good company—and for good reason. This chapter:
- Gives an overview of the terminology used to characterize the subject
- Provides some definitions
- Recaps the two broad waves of development—triple bottom line and environmental, social, and governance (ESG) factors
- Describes the "two sides of the sustainability coin"—risk and opportunity
- Gives an overview of the full supply chain or value chain aspect that is core to any discussion of sustainability
- Summarizes the four big buckets of sustainability (which are also the four main parts of the Corporate Sustainability Scorecard)
- Describes how the sustainability conversation is changing—to finally be what smart CEOs have seen all along

The Jargon

What is sustainability—in the context of business? And how—if at all—is sustainability different from *corporate responsibility; corporate social responsibility*; or a host of other terms used to convey some degree of responsible behavior? On the environmental side we hear companies use *environmental sustainability* or various versions of the term *green*. On the social side, there is plenty of gray area. Does corporate social responsibility (CSR) really mean "just" social responsibility—or does CSR also include the environmental dimension?

In addition to the generic terms used across industry, individual companies use their own terminology: *Ecomagination* (GE), *Eco-premium solutions* (Akzo Nobel), *Smarter Planet* (IBM), *ECO+ Solutions* (DSM), *Accelerator Solutions* (BASF), and many more.

Then there are all the "supporting" terms that are often used. Among the more common is **footprint** meaning all the (positive and negative—though it is normally used to mean the negative) environmental and social impacts throughout your value chain. At a basic level, your company's footprint is the buildings and land owned and operated. But the life-cycle view of footprint includes all the energy, water, and materials used throughout the supply chain to source, produce, transport, use, and ultimately dispose of those products.

As noted earlier, definitions of key terms are provided in Appendix A.

DOI 10.1515/9781547400423-003

What Is Sustainability?

At the end of the day, all the different terms used to describe this boil down to the same thing: "building a more ethical, resilient, sustainable, and profitable company."[i] In lay terms, sustainability is about running a successful business without messing up the place we live for our kids—and doing so in a manner that respects the communities within which we operate.

A widely used business definition is that used by The Conference Board—which defines sustainability as "...the pursuit of a business growth strategy that creates long-term shareholder value by seizing opportunities and managing risks related to the company's environmental and social impacts."[ii]

Note that this definition incorporates two sides of the coin: opportunity and risk. We will discuss these two sides of the coin—but first a quick look back.

ESG and the Triple Bottom Line

Over the past two decades, corporate sustainability has evolved in two waves, discussed below.

First Wave—Triple Bottom Line: During the late 1990s and early 2000s, sustainability was characterized as the "triple bottom line" of environmental stewardship, social responsibility, and economic performance—sometimes referred to as *People–Planet–Profits*. Here is the rub: the "triple bottom line" does not mention governance (see Figure 3.1). Furthermore, the "profit" leg of sustainability has been given short shrift and rarely has been discussed in a comprehensive way.

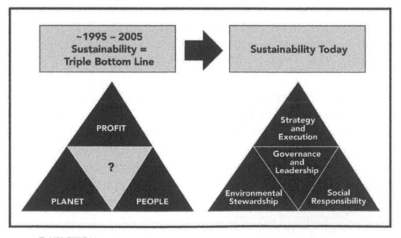

Source: HEDSTROM

Figure 3.1: Where Is the "G" in the Triple Bottom Line?

Second Wave–ESG: Around 2005, the mainstream investment community began to focus on carbon risk in particular, while starting to use the term "ESG" (referring to the environmental, social, and governance factors impacting an investment in a company) to characterize these risks. However, in looking a bit deeper, Hedstrom Associates finds that investors focus almost entirely on governance *data*, such as gender diversity of the board and executive ranks, or CEO compensation as a multiple of average employee compensation. ESG analysis often does not look at governance *processes*. We discuss this further in Chapter 5 (Governance and Leadership—The "G" in ESG) in the section called "Investors Dilemma: Failing the 80/20 Rule."

So where are we today? A quick review of the two waves shines a spotlight on the major problems:

- *No Governance in the Triple Bottom Line*: The "People, Planet, Profits" way of characterizing sustainability helped bring focus to the environment and social responsibility. But it completely missed the boat when it comes to governance—which is the glue that holds everything together.
- *No Strategy in ESG*: When Wall Street started focusing on sustainability—characterizing it as ESG, they too missed the boat. ESG does capture most of the "risk" aspect of sustainability; however, ESG misses what today is the most important part—strategy.

Both points are serious problems—and reinforce directly the rationale behind the Corporate Sustainability Scorecard rating system.

Two Sides of the Coin: Stop and Go

As The Conference Board definition suggests, there are two sides to the coin:

- *Seize Opportunities*: Sustainability represents massive growth opportunities for those innovative companies that *create value* by reducing their own footprints and helping customers reduce their footprints dramatically.
- *Manage Risks:* Climate risk, resource supply disruptions, and water shortages increasingly will result in volatile commodity prices, stranded assets, restrictions on license to operate, and reputational harm. Today's leaders *protect value* by managing those risks very well.

Sustainability is not about the "limits to growth" or just a bunch of tree-huggers wanting to save the planet. It is true that for most of the past twenty-five years (from the first Earth Summit in Rio de Janeiro, Brazil in 1992 to the Paris Accord in 2015), the dominant theme has been "STOP." Stop polluting. Stop emitting carbon. Stop sending waste to landfills. Stop depleting our aquifers of fresh water. Stop your suppliers from poor working conditions that might include child labor. Stop. Stop. Stop.

Give credit to General Electric. While the company is going through some tough sledding in 2018 (what company does not go through this?), GE's launch of *Ecomagination* in 2005 opened a lot of eyes. The logic behind (then CEO) Jeff Immelt's big bet was simple: if GE supplies the same or better products to its customers at the same or cheaper cost—and those products also are more energy efficient that those of GE's competitors—customers will save money in the long run (and likely remain customers of GE).

GE was not the first company to position itself as selling greener or healthier products. Back in the early 1990s, Xerox moved from selling copiers to leasing them. The company tag line at the time was "zero waste products from zero waste factories." Xerox was ahead of its time.

As GE's Ecomagination initiative unfolded, it included a strong balance of both growing product sales and reducing the company's footprint. But *GE led with the opportunity story*. Since that time, many other companies have started to follow suit.

From Farm to Fork

Inherent in any conversation about sustainability is assessing the impacts across its full **value chain**.

Today, like it or not, every company is responsible for its full life cycle impacts. Nike learned this in the late 1990s when the company ran into human rights abuses in its supply chain. The issue ultimately made it to the U.S. Supreme Court in 2003 (Nike v. Kasky). Apple learned it when its supplier Foxconn in China was accused of terrible working conditions.

Bill Ford, a well-known environmentalist, bluntly noted in Ford's 2003–2004 **sustainability report** that approximately 90 percent of a vehicle's lifecycle greenhouse gas emissions are attributable to CO_2 emitted during customer vehicle use."[iii] A company's responsibility does not end at the factory gate. Coca-Cola and Pepsi are not only responsible for the energy and water used to make their products; they are also responsible—in a growing way—for the obesity epidemic and the litter of used soda cans and bottles that end up on roadsides or in the Great Pacific garbage patch (a collection of garbage in the central North Pacific Ocean twice the size of Texas). Likewise, Ford and General Motors and BMW bear some responsibility for the carbon footprint of all of us driving their vehicles throughout our lifetime. And let's face it: auto companies also bear responsibility for not having been (and being) as effective as they could in minimizing the overall impact of cars and trucks on society globally.

Over the past several decades, a growing number of companies have sold off their "dirty businesses" perhaps as part of their transformation to becoming more sustainable companies. But selling off your dirty businesses, especially to owners in countries that are not strictly regulated, does not help the global ecosystem. Responsibility for legacy businesses can have a long tail, as U.S. companies have found with their former contaminated ("Superfund") sites.

The opportunity for chief sustainability officers and those communicating with the C-suite and board about sustainability is to frame and discuss environmental issues in the context of the supply chain or the value chain, defined below.

– **Supply Chain:** Manufacturing companies manage their business activities across the supply chain: defined as the movement and storage of raw materials, work-in-process inventory, and finished goods from point of origin to point of consumption.

– **Value Chain:** Companies in the service sector focus particularly on the value chain; those steps along the chain where value is created as distinct from steps where material is moved.

Regardless of industry, many companies are organized around key functions that include sourcing, production, distribution, sales, and customer service. It is very common in companies across industries today to have senior officers in charge of supply chain, procurement, operations, marketing, sales, etc.

Figure 3.2 illustrates key stages of a typical industry supply chain. (For purposes of simplicity, this figure assumes that "transportation" in or out of each step of the supply chain is incorporated into those steps.)

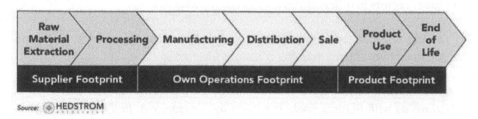

Source: HEDSTROM

Figure 3.2: Typical Industry Supply Chain

Supply chains and value chains can be complex and business-specific. To simplify, most companies operate predominantly in one or more of the following major value chains:

– *Agricultural Value Chain*: Think of all the renewable resources on the planet: air, water, soil, trees, fish, food. Industry sectors here are food and beverage, forest products, water management.

– *Metals Value Chain*: Think of everything your company uses or produces that is composed of metals (as opposed to petrochemicals or renewable resources). Mining companies mine the ore and then refine it into various metals. Many metals are highly recyclable. Thus, the metals value chain has the benefit of oper-

ating highly recyclable materials—but the downside of being very capital intensive with very long-time horizons.
- *Petrochemicals Value Chain*: Virtually everything in day-to-day living involves
  use of chemicals. And industrial chemicals, for the most part, are derivatives of
  petroleum-based products.

The point is that regardless of which of these value chains are responsible for your
company's "top five" material impacts, *your company is responsible for the behaviors
of your business partners across the value chains.*

Today's Sustainability Conversation

*The "right" conversation about sustainability focuses on corporate positioning and strat-
egy.* It begins with a deep examination of the megatrends impacting every company.
As reported by the World Economic Forum in its annual (2017) update,[iv] *several of the
highest-risk megatrends are not only sustainability related but also focused squarely
on climate change.* Four of the top five risks are: extreme weather events, failure of
climate change mitigation and adaptation, water crises, and large-scale involuntary
migration. These risks—interwoven with other societal challenges (e.g., inequality,
technology impact of digital transformation on job creation, etc.)—will impact different industry sectors in different ways.

With the robust understanding of the ESG trends in hand, board members, CEOs, and
other top executives should examine questions like these:
- *As the sustainability transformation unfolds, how are we positioning ourselves?*
- *Are we at risk of "missing the boat" by doing business as usual?*
- *Will we, as with Borders Books overcome by Amazon.com, find ourselves saying,
  "Whoops. We missed that!"?*

In the next chapter, we discuss what sustainability means for your industry.
    Then, the following four chapters tackle the four major buckets of sustainability:
governance and leadership, strategy and execution, environmental stewardship, and
social responsibility.

i Dave Stangis and Katherine Valvoda Smith, *The Executive's Guide to 21st Century Corporate Citizenship*, Emerald Publishing, 2017.

ii Charles Mitchell, Rebecca L. Ray, PhD, and Bart van Ark, PhD, The Conference Board CEO Challenge® 2015: "Creating Opportunity out of Adversity—Building Innovative, People-Driven Organizations." https://www.conference-board.org/topics/publicationdetail.cfm?publicationid=2888

iii Email to Gib Hedstrom from Jon Coleman, Ford Motor Company; May 11, 2018.

iv "The Global Risks Report 2017, 12th Edition," World Economic Forum, 2017, p. 4. http://www3.weforum.org/docs/GRR17_Report_web.pdf.

Chapter 4
What Does Sustainability Mean to Your Industry?

Many company executives are asking: "How can our company become more sustainable?" The answer to that question involves assessing items that are common across all industry sectors and those that vary from sector to sector.

In this chapter, we:
- Look from 30,000 feet and characterize sectors in three broad groups
- Define the common denominator across industry sectors
- Outline tomorrow's industry sectors—as they are quickly evolving
- Provide examples of how companies are transforming themselves today (and in some cases have been for over two decades)
- Offer a counterpoint—sharing the view of climate change deniers and other skeptics who may think all this sustainability stuff is counter to economic growth
- Share some parting thoughts on how every company can position itself for growth

The 30,000 Foot View

Every industry is undergoing disruption. Some sectors are changing more rapidly and visibly than others—but all are transforming.
- *Well Under Way.* The forest products and fisheries industry sectors provide very visible examples of how companies and industries have handled basic limitations on their historic raw material base. Virgin timber is still being cut and converted into lumber and paper products; however, the move to sustainable-yield forests is well established. Today, a growing percentage of paper and wood products are sourced from certified sustainable yield forests—defined as those managed to ensure replacement of the part of the forest harvested by regrowth or reproduction before another harvest occurs. The lumber industry offers a very simple example. If forest products companies cut down all the trees, there would no longer be a business. This has been repeated through world history; buffalo hunting and the whaling industry are old examples of society's inability to monitor its consumption for the benefit of all.

    Likewise, around 90 percent of global fisheries today are depleted or overfished according to the United Nations. As a result, many countries and regions have placed restrictions on fishing. This in turn has spawned new industries. Aquaculture is now forecast to overtake wild-caught fish as the source of most fish consumption in 2021, for the first time.[i]
- *Early Stages.* The automotive and energy sectors are examples where disruption is happening; however, the old business models still predominate. Major

DOI 10.1515/9781547400423-004

companies in these sectors are forced to "play on both sides of the street." Their core businesses (selling vehicles or petroleum products) still generate the clear majority of company sales and profits; however, leaders in these sectors see the writing on the wall.

- o In the auto sector, the future (whether it is thirty years from now or just a few years off) will reflect a variety of forms of "sustainable mobility" (ride sharing, electric and autonomous vehicles, etc.)—increasingly powered by various forms of renewable energy.

- o In the energy sector, while society still relies heavily on oil and gas (and coal) to power society, renewable technologies are moving quickly down the learning curve, experiencing rapid disruption. A key challenge looking ahead is the area of storage technology—finding better ways to efficiently harvest alternative technologies including wind and solar.

Companies undergoing transformation—and having one foot on each side of the street—are in a bind. They tend to lobby governments to maintain the status quo—while also investing in tomorrow's growth technologies and businesses.

- *Awaiting Disruption*. Other industry sectors are arguably still awaiting disruption. The chemical industry comes to mind. Leading chemical companies like BASF have very advanced methodologies for evaluating their more "sustainably-advantaged" products; however, the sector is virtually entirely based on petroleum feedstocks.

The point is that transformation is under way. This is not tomorrow's opportunity. The signals of change are all around us today. The trick is to get the timing right.

The Common Denominator: More Profit—Less Stuff

The core premise of sustainability is simple: how companies can generate more profit while having less use of materials and energy that have unintended consequences (waste, toxics, greenhouse gas emissions). This is the shorthand challenge for every company: "How can we grow our company, make money, satisfy a growing customer base providing products, services and solutions they want—all with a far lower impact on the planet?"

Today's companies can be tomorrow's successful companies if they can *decouple growth from resource consumption across the full value chain*. That is the core premise behind sustainability and the circular economy.

For individual companies, this is an opportunity to completely rethink your value proposition to existing customers. Philips is selling lighting as a service. Zipcar launched ride-sharing. Many companies are working hard to eliminate the very concept of waste, starting by achieving zero waste to landfills.

Tomorrow's Industry Sectors

We noted above that virtually every industry is undergoing disruption. But let's be clear: simply because a company transforms itself in a way that aligns with sustainability principles does not mean the driving force behind a newer start-up company or the transformation of an established one has much to do with sustainability. Uber and Lyft are not trying to save the planet. But their **sharing economy** model is a strong sustainability story.

Table 4.1 (Industries in Transformation) lists a group of many of today's major industry sectors and offers a brief description of how that industry is in the early stages of transformation. Some might look at the right side of Table 4.1 and say it is an idealized view; a long-shot, something far into the future. But in every case, the signals of transformation and change exist today.

For most industry sectors that rely heavily on use of materials to generate profit, the transformation involves a gradual shift:
- *From* yesterday's **linear economy** focus where long-term growth has been tied directly to growth in resource consumption across the full supply chain...
- *To* tomorrow's **circular economy** focus where growth in sales and profitability is decoupled from growth in resource consumption.[ii] In the circular economy, resources remain in use for as long as possible; and at the end of a product's useful life, materials are recycled, reused, or regenerated rather than discarded as waste.

Some companies will be driven heavily by sustainability principles. This has clearly been the case with Unilever and Novelis. In addition to the companies mentioned above, long-time companies like BMW, DSM, DuPont, Marks and Spencer, Desso, Michelin, and Total are busy shedding their "old economy" businesses to create tomorrow's growth businesses.

In contrast, companies that cling to the "old economy" core businesses face significant pressures. ExxonMobil found this in 2017 when shareholders voted for a shareholder resolution (and against Exxon's management) to report how climate change impacts the company's business.

Table 4.1: Industries in Transformation

Industry	Yesterday's (Linear) Focus	Tomorrow's (Circular) Focus
Aerospace	More flights; more fuel; more carbon	More connection; less carbon
Apparel	Sell clothing	Sell; lease and take back clothing
Automotive	Sell cars and trucks	Sell mobility solutions
Chemicals	Make chemicals from hydrocarbons	Sell solutions; source biomaterials & recycled products
Energy	More energy; more carbon	More energy; more efficiency; less carbon
Food & Beverage	More food and drinks that taste good	More healthy food; less water; less waste
Hotels & Leisure	Sell lodging from a facility	Sell lodging solutions – including from a host
Industrial	Make; sell; and forget	Make; lease; take back; remanufacture
Information Technology	Sell equipment and services	Solve the world's toughest challenges
Metals & Mining	Mine ore	Mine landfills and warehouses (take back); recycle
Pharmaceuticals	Sell drugs	Sell health solutions
Paper & Forest Products	Source from virgin forests	Source from sustainable-yield forests
Retailing	Sell "stuff"	Sell solutions
Utilities	More electricity; more carbon	More electricity; less carbon
Waste Services	Haul & dispose of waste in landfills	Sell, recycle, reuse; eliminate waste

HEDSTROM ASSOCIATES

Other companies—especially start-ups and new technology plays, may align with the industry transformation we outline—but their motivation may have little to do with climate change, resource constraints or ESG issues. This is arguably the situation with Airbnb, Lyft, and Uber.

Tomorrow's Industry Sectors—Today

Each of the following examples illustrates how one or more companies in an industry sector is transforming how its industry provides goods or services.

– *Automotive: Pure (Green) Play or Dual Track.* The Tesla story is well-known. CEO Elon Musk positions the company as a "green play" (though of course electric vehicles can be powered by coal as well as solar). The financial markets have rewarded Tesla. The company sold about 0.5 percent as many vehicles as General Motors did in 2015 (50,580 for Tesla compared with 9.8 million by General Motors). Yet, Tesla's market capitalization in July 2018 was ~$54.02 billion (as compared with General Motors at ~$54.78 billion).

Meanwhile, talk with executives at BMW, Ford, or General Motors and you will hear that the companies are changing faster in the current five-year period than at any time in the last century. Former Ford CEO Mark Fields aggressively pursued a sustainability agenda. In a bold move, he re-engineered ("light-weighted") the company's profitable product (F-150 trucks) by shifting from steel to aluminum. Fields launched the company on a "dual track" of sustainable mobility coupled with the traditional selling of vehicles. Yet, in 2017 he was replaced with a new CEO charged with moving even *faster* into sustainable mobility. Incremental improvements are yesterday's solution.

- *Chemicals: Use Bio-Based Chemicals.* The industry churn has been going on for decades; however, little has changed. The industry awaits disruption. Monsanto spun off its chemical business (Solutia) and focused on "Food, Health, Hope" back in 1997. DuPont transformed from an explosives company in the 1800s to a chemical company in the 1900s to a biology and science company before its merger with Dow Chemical. AkzoNobel Chemicals, DSM, and BASF are slowly but deliberately figuring out how to move away from the heavy hydrocarbon footprint, using bio-based chemicals and other innovations.

- *Consumer Products: Reduce the Environmental Impact of Consumer Products.* Unilever, many years into its Sustainable Living Plan, aims to double the size of its business, while cutting in half the environmental impacts (footprint) of its products across the full value chain. Procter & Gamble is striving to use "100 percent renewable or recycled materials for all products and packaging, having zero consumer waste go to landfills and designing products to delight customers while maximizing the conservation of resources."[iii]

- *Food and Beverage: Transform How Water Is Sourced and Used.* For Coca-Cola, water is the company's lifeblood. The company still churns out sugary drinks that are part of the obesity epidemic; though its portfolio of less sugary beverages has grown. The company has a goal of being water neutral by 2020, replenishing, or balancing, the water used in its finished beverages.[iv]

- *Hospitality: Upend the Hotel Industry.* Airbnb (founded in 2008) has become one of the world's largest hotel chains—*without owning a single hotel room.* They are disrupting the entire industry; it took Airbnb less than a decade to accomplish what it has taken other hotel chains almost a century to achieve. Let's be clear: Airbnb was not launched to "save the planet." Furthermore, Airbnb's "sharing economy" business model brings with it a variety of negative societal consequences. (Key issues include trash, parking problems, fights, unprofessional supervision, theft, damage, and noise. Furthermore, taxes paid by Airbnb owners arguably do not compensate the local government for extra police work and insurance claims.) Nevertheless, Airbnb's industry disruption is a positive sustainability story: it drives efficiency in the marketplace—utilizing the vast pool of existing underused bedrooms (rather than building new hotels).

– *Metals & Mining: Close the Metals Loop.* Novelis, a world leader in rolled aluminum products, has shifted its business model from a traditional linear one-way production model to a closed-loop model in which materials are reused rather than discharged as waste. The company is on track to achieve 80 percent recycled inputs by 2020, an increase from 33 percent in 2011. Meanwhile, Boeing and Alcoa formed (2013) a **closed-loop** program to significantly increase the recycling of internal aluminum aerospace alloys used during the production of Boeing airplanes.[v]

– *Paper and Forest Products: Drive Sustainable Forestry.* For decades, the pulp and paper industry has been moving from the old model (cutting down virgin forests) to sourcing primarily or only from "sustainable yield" forests. The Forest Stewardship Council (FSC) is an international, nonprofit, multi-stakeholder organization established in 1993 to promote responsible management of the world's forests. FSC is the best-known of the roughly fifty such certification schemes globally. While it is difficult to assess the results, between 2012 and 2017, an area roughly the size of Sweden was newly certified by FSC. A similar organization, the Sustainable Forestry Initiative (SFI), operates in the United States and Canada and likewise reports considerable progress.

– *Utilities: More Electricity; Less Carbon.* This sector is characterized by two key factors: the very long investment cycle (a power plant lasts over fifty years) and the continuous reduction in the cost of wind and solar energy over the past decade. Many utilities have been making the shift toward renewables as they retire older, less efficient coal plants. Duke Energy has brought five new natural gas combined-cycle plants on line since 2011—and retired older, less efficient coal units. Natural gas emits about half the carbon dioxide of coal.[vi]

– *Waste Services: Turn Waste into a Resource.* Faced with a growing number of large customers with goals to approach zero waste, Waste Management is a decade into transforming from its old economy business (hauling trash) to its new economy business (providing waste services).

Counterpoint: The Skeptics …

Let's say you read this stuff and just think it all sound like a noble goal: make money while saving the planet. But you look around and you just do not see the change.

You see people using Swiffers instead of brooms. Everyone has cell phones that they replace every year or two—instead of land lines that lasted fifteen years. Cars are outmoded in four years. Christmas and Hanukkah lights to decorate the house will need to be replaced (very inexpensively) next year.

What ever happened to diaper services? And remember that Maytag commercial about products that lasted so long the repair man (it was man in those commercials) had nothing to do?

Recycling waste is far from commonplace—and varies dramatically by country and region. In the United States, a handful of states are fairly advanced but the rest of the country has plenty of room for landfills.

And then there are TV sets. If it has a problem, toss it. If anything short of a computer breaks, toss it because you can not fix it yourself any more.

The point is that this is complex. The sustainability transformation is messy! When a "leading company" sells off a "dirty business," these businesses simply do not go away. A company like Waste Management that truly transforms itself (creating new growth businesses in waste solutions and tackling a real problem) makes greater inroads than companies that simply sell off a dirty business that continues under different ownership.

Table 4.1 may paint a bit of an idealistic picture; however, in every industry sector, the disruptions and transformations are happening. You do not turn an ocean liner on a dime.

Positioning for Growth

As noted in Chapter 2, the late economist Rudiger Dornbusch was fond of remarking that: "In economics, things take longer to happen than you think they will, and then they happen faster than you thought they could."

That is the situation here. In a very real sense, sustainability is about economics. It is about the laws of supply and demand—at a "planet" level. When demand grows and supply is fixed, something must give. (In economics, the result is that prices rise.)

So, it has been with the build-up of pressures on companies to treat sustainability as a board and C-suite agenda and start transforming your company to align with ESG principles.

The exciting sustainability conversation is about *growth*. As these mega forces play out in the coming decades, opportunities exist for each company to position itself for sustained growth and profitability. Across a range of industries, *traditional* and *next-generation* companies have begun to unleash that "power of innovation" to transform how to do business.

The reality is that, to survive, *many traditional companies across industries will have to change more in the next ten–fifteen years than in the past 100 years*.

The challenge in all of this is to get the timing right: to invest in new technologies and business models just ahead of when they will reap rewards.

Who will innovate and ultimately win in the marketplace, thereby profiting from the convergence of these mega forces? Will it be old-line players, new start-ups, or some of each? Ask yourselves these questions: "Who are the top few start-up companies in our industry that potentially could disrupt the entire sector over the next five to ten years? What technologies and business models will provide them competitive advantage?"

Over the next decade, society can expect to see trillions of dollars in value created and destroyed. Markets are driving disruptive change.

---

i https://www.theguardian.com/environment/2016/jul/07/global-fish-production-approaching-sustainable-limit-un-warns

ii Gilbert S. Hedstrom, "GEMI Quick Guide: Sustainability 101," Global Environmental Management Initiative, October 2015.

iii P&G/Environmental Sustainability/New Long-Term Vision. http://www.pg.com/en_KE/sustainability/environmental_sustainability.shtml

iv Sustainability at Coca-Cola. http://assets.coca-colacompany.com/a3/4b/a3e7d93f4232a8ac16ed519cde76/sustainability-at-coca-cola-pdf.pdf

v Boeing and Alcoa form "closed-loop" program to boost recycling of aluminum aerospace alloys. http://www.airframer.com/news_story.html?release=22343

vi Duke Energy/Low-Carbon Technologies. https://www.duke-energy.com/environment/advanced-tech.asp

Chapter 5
Governance and Leadership: The "G" in ESG

Sustainability Stories from the C-Suite and Boardroom ...

Consider the story of one company that is *"getting sustainability governance right."*

> At the request of the CEO of a major North American utility, I recently led a one-hour discussion titled "Sustainability and the Future" with the full board of directors. The conversation continued over dinner that evening. The next morning, I participated in a three-hour scenario planning exercise with the full board and executive team.
>
> The purpose of the exercise was to determine how the company would respond to future disruption in its industry while meeting increasing stakeholder demands. The board members and leadership team "rolled up their sleeves" and dove into carefully developed scenario exercises. The executives explored how the company would fare in potential future worlds involving the two extremes of: (1) global attention to climate change and carbon reductions, and (2) technology developments (e.g., with renewables and storage technology). Groups of directors and executives (four–six per group) explored how to succeed in four very different futures.
>
> Quite honestly, I was astonished at how energetically and deeply the board members engaged! For several hours we had small group exercises, report-outs, and open discussion—quite the opposite of the "normal" highly orchestrated board meeting.
>
> At the end of the morning, the board met in executive session as the rest of us left the room. When we returned, the board chairman said that the sustainability conversations had been the best use of time he could remember at any board meeting. (That was quite a statement!) The board had decided to add an extra half-day to their next full board meeting. The chairman summarized some instructions for the next steps.
>
> Postscript: In the months since that meeting, the board has increasingly taken leadership of the sustainability agenda. The chief sustainability officer (CSO) was moved to the strategic planning team; and the CEO changed the corporate planning approach from the traditional "one-shot" annual event into a series of 12 monthly sessions over the year.

The core message to take away from this story is this: *it is possible for a sustainability director to change the boardroom conversation—and to do so dramatically.* The story above is notably different from traditional boardroom sustainability discussions, where many boards may spend only 30–60 minutes per year on the subject. In a recent Conference Board poll, 69 percent of companies responded that their board committee (or full board) typically spends two to four hours per year on sustainability—including environment, health, and safety (EHS) issues.[i]

DOI 10.1515/9781547400423-005

The Situation: Governance and Sustainability

Governance is one of the four main components of sustainability—as described in Chapter 3. And, of the four buckets (governance, strategy, environment, social), *governance is the most important. It is the glue that holds the others together.*

Without "getting governance right," a company finds it difficult to get anything else right. This is true with creating successful products and services, creating robust brands, delivering consistent and strong financial results, and earning a reputation as "a good company to work for." *Increasingly, companies understand that this is true with sustainability too.*

Governance for a corporation essentially defines "how we run the place." It consists of the leadership structures, policies, processes, and practices affecting the way the CEO, board, and senior management team run a corporation. It includes the goals, the culture and organization, and the relationships among the various **stakeholders**, including: shareholders, employees, suppliers, customers, banks and other lenders, regulators, the environment, and the community at large.

The third landmark report on corporate governance (King III) by the Institute of Directors in South Africa (the King Committee on governance)—the bellwether of corporate governance—states ...

"Sustainability is the primary moral and economic imperative of the 21st century. It is one of the most important sources of both opportunities and risks for businesses. Nature, society, and business are interconnected in complex ways that should be understood by business decision-makers. Most importantly, current incremental changes towards sustainability are not enough—we need a fundamental shift in the way companies and directors act and organize themselves."[ii]

King III goes further than previous guidance. The report urges that the disclosure of sustainability performance be done through integrated financial and sustainability (environment, social, and governance) reports, which are overseen and evaluated by the audit committee of the board.

Governance: The Key Elements

In the Corporate Sustainability Scorecard, we break down the (admittedly sometimes fuzzy) subject of governance into seven specific elements, listed in Table 5.1.

Table 5.1: Elements of Governance and Leadership

Governance and Leadership
– **Vision, Mission, Values:** The *public statements* articulating a company's *raison d'être* (reason for existing); the less formal but critically important *private actions* a company takes to reinforce its values, mission, and vision; and the *external recognition* received from credible organizations.
– **CEO Leadership:** The way in which the CEO *personally engages with ESG and* drives sustainability throughout the company; *manages the board of directors' agenda*; and *structures the sustainability organization and initiatives* within the company.
– **Board of Directors Leadership:** The *structure and resources* of the board committee(s) providing oversight of sustainability; the *assurance processes* that report on sustainability risks and opportunities to the board; and the *board's commitment of time* to learning about sustainability issues, best practices, and trends.
– **Goals and Metrics:** The overall approach to establishing and tracking performance against sustainability goals, including the *goal-setting process*; the *time horizon* for framing the goals and metrics; and the *content and impact* of the individual targets that are set, measured, and reported on.
– **Culture and Organization:** The *accountability for and attention to* sustainability by the CEO and executive team; the *key culture indicators related to sustainability* in place that define the actual culture (including the "unwritten rules of the game"); and the *sustainability organization* (structure and people) leading the charge.
– **Stakeholder Engagement:** The quality and impact of engaging with external stakeholders on sustainability: *why engage*; *with whom to engage*; *what issues to engage on*; and *how and when to engage*.
– **Disclosure, Reporting and Transparency:** The information that is *disclosed* to stakeholders related to own operations, suppliers, and the full supply chain sustainability impacts; the way in which sustainability data and information is *reported*; and the extent to which the company has earned a reputation for *transparency*.

The opportunity for companies today is to build robust governance processes that drive the full integration of sustainability/environmental, social, and governance (ESG) into the core of the company.

So how do board members rate their effectiveness at sustainability? The National Association of Corporate Directors (NACD) tracks this in their annual survey of over 600 corporate board members.

The 2017–2018 NACD Public Company Governance Survey reinforces the need for board action. A strong majority of respondents in every industry sector ascribed importance to improving ESG strategy over the next twelve months, only a small minority saying that improving ESG was "not at all important." Responses varied by industry; improving board oversight of ESG is viewed as being most important in materials, utilities, energy, and healthcare—and least critical in information technology. [iii]

Investors' Dilemma: Failing the 80/20 Rule

As noted in Chapter 2 (Why Bother?), investor interest in ESG and sustainability is growing rapidly. Many companies are reporting that investor calls and roadshows regarding sustainability have dramatically increased in the last two years. Chief sustainability officers are now often involved in calls or presentations on a monthly, quarterly, or biannual basis. Investors have increased their own expertise and resources in the areas of sustainability and corporate governance. They do not particularly focus on sustainability rating agencies groups like RobecoSAM that publishes the Dow Jones Sustainability Indices.

In the opinion of Hedstrom Associates, ESG, as practiced today, suffers from the 80/20 rule.

– *Data—The 20 Percent*: Investors love data. Indeed, at a recent meeting of Conference Board executives, one mainstream investor said, "ideally, we want everything in an Excel file." As a result, they focus on those (relatively few) aspects of sustainability governance for which there are data. Examples include: diversity of the board and senior management, compensation information, etc.

– *Processes—The 80 Percent*: Anyone who has participated actively in C-suite and board of directors' meetings knows that the clear majority of what constitutes "robust governance" is driven by robust governance *processes*. How are ESG risk gathered and discussed among executives and the board? How is sustainability incorporated into the strategic planning processes? What assurance mechanisms are in place?

Historically, many companies examine the "governance" part of ESG with their annual Dow Jones Sustainability Index (DJSI) application. DJSI is constructed as a tool to help with investment decisions. However, by design, DJSI is not particularly focused on long-term strategy. Hedstrom Associates works with a client on its DJSI submittal. We find that while DJSI makes some attempt to address corporate governance and business issues, DJSI heavily reflects the left side of Figure 3.1 The DJSI application focuses primarily on past data and correlations; the Index has relatively little focus on the connection between sustainability and corporate strategy. The governance section of DJSI (and other external sustainability ratings) focuses almost entirely on areas where there is *data* about governance.

The buzz today among investors seems to be asking public companies to report following the structure of the Task Force on Climate-Related Financial Disclosures (TCFD). At a meeting the author ran in February 2018, about 100 chief sustainability officers (or equivalent) heard a candid conversation with executives of BlackRock and Nuveen Investments (a subsidiary within TIAA-CREF). They had a simple message to companies: follow the TCFD guidance—not only for climate-related risks but for all material ESG risks.

Interestingly, *the TCFD framework aligns almost exactly with the structure of the Corporate Sustainability Scorecard*:
- TCFD is structured into: governance, strategy, risk, and metrics.
- The Scorecard is structured into governance, strategy, environment, and social. (In the Scorecard, goals and metrics are included in governance; we simply break out the two main sources of risk into environment and social.)

The Corporate Sustainability Scorecard squarely addresses this "80/20 gap" in today's investor approach to governance. Most of the Scorecard's governance attributes are reflected in robust business *processes*—not in *data*.

Governance at a Glance: Tomorrow's Leaders Today

Ironically, "getting governance right" is not difficult, nor does it require navigating unchartered waters. In a word, it is about *leadership*. Companies that are Stage 3 on the Scorecard today in sustainability governance have made initial, significant steps toward transformation.

Below is a brief snapshot of how a few leading companies are addressing the seven key elements of sustainability and corporate governance:

1. **Vision, Mission, Values:** Companies wanting to move beyond Stage 2 often start with *rethinking their vision, mission, and values.* Intel amended its corporate charter in 2010 to include sustainability. Total, the French oil giant, sensing peak demand for crude oil, declared in 2017 that "electricity is the energy of the 21st century." Total is transforming its portfolio and building tomorrow's cleaner, less carbon-intensive businesses alongside its traditional business.
2. **CEO Leadership:** Tomorrow's leaders have *very strong, often bold leadership from the CEO* regarding sustainability. Current or past CEOs of DuPont, GE, IBM, Kingfisher, Marks & Spencer, Nike, Novelis, NRG, Unilever, and Walmart, for example, have singlehandedly staked out a transformative position on sustainability. In some cases, the CEO moved too fast toward fully embracing sustainability. Phil Martens, former CEO of Novelis, embraced an "ethos of disruption" requiring a whole new way of thinking and operating. NRG's former CEO David Crane wanted to "transform our company, our industry, and society." In other companies' situations, the CEO may not be moving fast enough to integrate ESG into the core of the company. Ford's former CEO Mark Fields was pushed out in 2017; the new CEO, James Hackett, had been leading Ford's sustainable mobility businesses.
3. **Board Leadership:** The boards of directors of Stage 3 companies *engage deeply with sustainability—and then they respond.* Sims Metal Management, the world's largest metal recycling firm, is positioned as a model circular economy company.

The board and CEO decided to demonstrate further commitment at the top by having the board of directors personally sign a commitment to sustainability.

Having a strong sustainability voice on the external board of directors is one of the best ways to learn about sustainability. Notable examples have included: Ashland (Patrick Noonan, followed by John Turner), International Paper (Patrick Noonan), DuPont (Bill Riley), and Nike (Jill Ker Conway).

Absent a sustainability expert on the board, external sustainability advisors play a big role in informing the CEO, board, and leadership team, while also serving as a sounding board for many aspects of strong governance, such as long-term goals, stakeholder relations, and reporting.

4. **Goals and Metrics:** Stage 3 companies *set bold, long-term sustainability goals directly addressing their top one, two, or three material issues* (such as Coca-Cola and water). These bold goals often stand in stark contrast to their industry peers. Stage 2 companies typically have a dozen or more ESG goals based on their materiality assessment; however, the goals are not particularly bold. As Stage 3 examples, BT, Coca-Cola, Kingfisher, IKEA, Interface, Sony, and Tesco all have goals of **net neutral** or **net positive** impact (at least in some material issues like carbon or forests).

5. **Culture and Organization:** Stage 3 companies *drive a culture of innovation and sustainability through employee benefits and incentives.* 3M's "15 percent time" was launched in 1948 giving all employees the opportunity to pursue creative ideas in the workplace. Increasingly, that time is devoted to tomorrow's sustainability solutions. Google provides a host of sustainability-related incentives. Intel calculates each employee's bonus, in part, on sustainability results. Walmart engages its 2.2 million employees through My Sustainability Plan.

6. **Stakeholder Engagement:** Stage 3 companies typically *engage in deep partnerships with one or more leading nongovernmental organizations (NGOs).* Walmart has worked closely with the Environmental Defense Fund, as did SC Johnson, McDonald's, and Starbucks in prior years. JPMorgan Chase has provided major funding to NatureVest, which is The Nature Conservancy's impact investing program supporting water markets, green infrastructure, climate adaptation, sustainable agriculture, and more.

7. **Disclosure, Reporting, and Transparency:** Issuing a sustainability report is fine, but in the Corporate Sustainability Scorecard C-suite rating system, that puts a company in Stage 1. It is the content of the report that matters, as well as the extent to which the report's key audience appreciates it. As companies move from Stage 1 through Stage 2 to Stage 3 and beyond, the audience for the sustainability report changes. For Stage 3 companies, a *primary audience is Wall Street.* Investors want short, concise, purely business-focused reports that demonstrate how the company plans to capture value from sustainability trends in the coming years. Stage 3 companies are moving rapidly toward integrated reporting as they incorporate ESG issues into traditional financial reporting.

The Scorecard: Governance and Leadership

This chapter has provided a general overview of Governance and Leadership, the first main section of the Scorecard. As noted above, this section of the Scorecard contains seven elements.

In Part 2 of the book, a separate chapter (chapters 11 through 17) addresses each of these seven elements in detail. Each of those seven chapters aligns with the rating criteria on the web-based tool that had been used by sixty companies by February 2018 and by a growing number since then.

In addition to providing the detailed scoring templates for each element of Governance and Leadership, the Part 2 chapters also provide dozens of company best practices—which are defined as being in Stage 3 or higher.

---

i "The Seven Pillars of Sustainability Leadership," The Conference Board, 2016, p. 19.
ii "King Report on Governance for South Africa 2009," King III, last modified September 7, 2009, p. 11. http://c.ymcdn.com/sites/www.iodsa.co.za/resource/resmgr/king_iii/King_Report_on_ Governance_fo.pdf
iii "2017-2018 NACD Public Company Governance Survey," National Association of Corporate Directors, 2018.

Chapter 6
Strategy and Execution: The Missing "S" in ESG

Sustainability Stories from the C-Suite and Boardroom ...

The first time I met with Ashland's Board of Directors Committee overseeing the company's corporate responsibility issues, the company looked very different than it looks now. In the late 1990s, Ashland owned the specialty chemical business that defines the company today. At the same time, the company also owned Arch Coal, Ashland Petroleum Company, Ashland Distribution Company, APAC (an asphalt paving company), and Valvoline. Ashland was a holding company—holding not only diverse businesses but also extensive environmental and social risks.

Over a period of years as an outside advisor, I met with the Board Committee eight or ten times. At each meeting, I participated in the full meeting (normally two hours). Then, at the end, I often met in executive session with the outside directors. The Committee Chair was long-time environmental leader Patrick F. Noonan, former President of The Nature Conservancy and Chairman of The Conservation Fund.

Without divulging confidential conversations, imagine the boardroom conversations in the late 1990s regarding Arch Coal and the long-standing practice in the coal industry of "mountain-top removal," essentially stripping off the top of mountains to access the coal seams below. Imagine too the conversations about Ashland's petroleum business, when BP (then) CEO John Browne had just spoken publicly about the need for oil companies to adopt a precautionary approach to climate change.

Working alongside the company's vice president, environment, health and safety, I gave the CEO and the executive team a primer on climate change in the late 1990s. We were not advocating any position, but rather summarizing the science and business risks and opportunities as best we knew at the time. Not surprisingly, the president of Arch Coal took strong exception to our remarks, quoting "experts" who denied climate science. At the end of that presentation, the Arch Coal president was the first one to ask for a copy of our slides.

Postscript: Fast forward 20 years and we see a story of transformation. Today the company's vision is "to make a better world by providing creative solutions through the application of specialty ingredients and materials."

[Note: the author's conversations with company executives—and especially his participation in board meetings—are strictly confidential. Every comment in this book about my interactions with a specific corporate board has been shared publicly by corporate executives of that company.]

The key message from this story is for companies to *"Lyft yourself before you get Kodak'd."* This requires C-suite and board conversations about how to transform the company to be leaner, more fit, and a less carbon-intensive twenty-first century winner.

DOI 10.1515/9781547400423-006

The Situation: Beyond ESG

When the mainstream investment community finally began to latch on to sustainability in about 2005, it was through the lens of environment, social, and governance (ESG). Today, it is striking that ESG, as a descriptor of sustainability, remains inherently silent on corporate strategy and execution. Somehow, the "economic leg" of the *People–Planet–Profits* sustainability stool was simply replaced with governance. As Figure 6.1 illustrates, the ESG characterization of sustainability misses the vitally important dimension of weaving ESG issues into corporate strategy and execution.

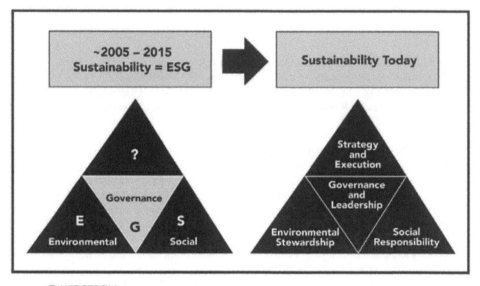

Source: HEDSTROM

Figure 6.1: Where Is Strategy in ESG?

As many CEOs and board members have underscored in their discussions with Hedstrom Associates, a company can not be "sustainable" unless it generates sustained profits. Companies achieve that by executing a robust strategy. It does not matter whether environmental or social drivers are the main reason for key business decisions (e.g., portfolio changes; buying and selling companies). In the experience of Hedstrom Associates, if a board pays careful attention to ESG issues alongside other business issues in a balanced and thoughtful way, the company is likely positioned well for future (sustainable) growth and profitability.

Embedding sustainability into strategy is the *single most significant place* where companies fall short vis-à-vis sustainability. Importantly, CEOs recognize this gap. In The Conference Board CEO Challenge 2016 survey, four of the top five strategies mentioned by CEOs globally for meeting the sustainability challenge relate directly to *embedding sustainability into corporate strategy*.[i]

Strategy: The Key Elements

In the Corporate Sustainability Scorecard, we break down strategy and execution into four elements, listed in Table 6.1.

Table 6.1: Elements of Strategy and Execution

Strategy and Execution
– **Strategic Planning:** The company's *overall sustainability strategy and positioning*; the *business drivers* that frame how the CEO and CFO think about sustainability; and the sustainability inputs into the corporate (operational and capital) *planning processes*.
– **Innovation, Research, and Development:** The *role innovation plays* in the business and the extent to which sustainability is connected to innovation; the *processes and methodologies* for embedding sustainability into innovation, research, and development; and the output of *innovation investments*.
– **Customers and Markets:** The *sustainability linkage to customers*; the *core approach* a company takes to address customer needs; and the role sustainability plays in *shaping future market opportunities* the company is pursuing.
– **Products, Services, and Solutions:** The *basic product positioning* of the company; the integration of sustainability into *the product development process*; and the extent to which sustainability principles are incorporated formally into *existing products, services, and solutions*.

The Opportunity: Strategy and Sustainability

As noted earlier, there are two sides to the sustainability coin. Companies can drive ESG considerations into their core business and strategy by *reducing cost or risk* and by *growing sales and options for future growth*. Examples abound:
– *Reducing Cost*: 3M, Dow Chemical, and DuPont have cut waste and saved millions for decades. Herman Miller has committed to zero waste by 2023 with 50 percent of its power from renewables. Dell achieved a 95 percent "recycle and reuse" rate in 2014.
– *Reducing Risk*: The potential risk presented by climate change caught the attention of Swiss Re and Munich Re over a decade ago. It caught ExxonMobil's attention in May 2017 when 62 percent of Exxon shareholders voted against management and for the company to be more open about the impact of climate change

on its business. ExxonMobil executives sought to head off the proposal, which was backed by 38 percent of shareholders in 2015 (and therefore failed).

– *Growing Sales*: Over the past decade, a dozen or more very large multinational companies have demonstrated that they can grow revenue through a defined set of products, services, and solutions that are environmentally or socially preferred over the typical products in that product family. (See Table 6.2 and access a recent Conference Board report for more information.[ii])

– *Creating Options for Future Growth*: Avis purchased Zipcar to position itself for growth in the sharing economy. Cisco and other companies view the "smart grid" as representing a $400 billion market by 2020. Croda (UK) considers sustainability a key differentiator and growth driver. Terracycle CEO Tom Szaky has built the company by working with large customers to recycle/upcycle their waste packaging into reusable products.

Provided in Table 6.2 are examples of how a range of industry leaders are transforming their product and service offerings toward tomorrow's circular economy focus.

The place to start always is to reduce cost and risk: the low-hanging fruit. Many companies have used these savings to fund investments in other areas of sustainability.

The exciting sustainability conversation is not about "doing less bad" by reducing impacts; instead, it is about growth. As the mega forces of middle class population growth, climate change, resource scarcity, and impact of externalities play out in the coming decades, companies can position themselves to grow and profit from these trends. Across a range of industries, *traditional* and *next-generation* companies have begun to unleash the power of innovation—driven by ESG issues—as a way to drive sustained profitability and growth.

Table 6.2: Company Sustainable Product, Service, and Solution Portfolios

Examples of Company Sustainable Product, Service, and Solution Portfolios
– *BASF's* Accelerator Solutions accounted for 27 percent of BASF's relevant sales in 2017, or about €15.5 billion.
– *Caterpillar's* portfolio of sustainable products generated almost $10 billion in 2014 and accounted for 18 percent of the company's total revenue.
– *Dow's* portfolio of products that are highly advantaged by sustainable chemistry reached sales of $12.4 billion in 2015, accounting for 25 percent of total 2015 revenue.
– *DSM's* ECO+ solutions accounted for 57 percent of the company's total sales in 2015, with an average annual growth rate of about 10 percent. Across several of DSM's businesses, ECO+ sales have higher margins than do non-ECO+ sales. Today, ECO+ and People+ are combined into the "Brighter Living Solutions" portfolio, which in 2017 accounted for 62 percent of total sales.
– *GE's* Ecomagination portfolio generated $36 billion in revenue in 2015, up from $18 billion in 2010. Ecomagination now accounts for one-third of GE's industrial segment revenue.
– *Johnson & Johnson's* Earthwards® portfolio grew from 9 products in 2009 to 100 products in 2017. This portfolio represented over $11 billion in revenue and about 15 percent of the company's 2017 revenue.
– *Kimberly-Clark's* ecoLOGICAL portfolio accounted for 52 percent of the company's revenue in 2014 (up from 10 percent in 2010), or more than $10 billion.
– *Kingfisher* (the UK-based home improvement company) derived 28 percent of sales from eco products in 2016 with a target of 50 percent by 2020.
– *Philips's* "green products" accounted for 64 percent of the company's overall revenue in 2016.
– *Siemens's* Environmental Portfolio accounted for almost €36 billion (47 percent of the company's overall revenue in 2017).
– *Toshiba's* sales of "Excellent Environmentally Conscious Products" rose from $3.6 billion in 2011 to $24 billion in 2015 (accounting for 42 percent of 2015 revenue).

Strategy and Execution at a Glance: Tomorrow's Leaders Today

When surveyed, most CEOs say they have a sustainability strategy. Yet dig a little deeper and that "strategy" likely includes sustainability reporting, some basic footprint reduction goals, a materiality assessment, and a host of programs and initiatives. In the experience of Hedstrom Associates, *the vast majority of companies lack a process that hard-wires the most material ESG issues to its corporate strategy.*

Below is a brief snapshot of how a few leading companies are addressing the four key elements of how sustainability is factored into corporate strategy and execution:

- **Strategic Planning:** Stage 3 companies *do not have a separate sustainability strategy; they have embedded sustainability squarely into their core business strategy*. They use a robust scenario planning process (as Shell is famous for and companies like Nike and PepsiCo have emulated). Importantly, they factor ESG issues into **key business decisions,** defined as the handful of major decisions a company makes each year that typically require board of directors to "sign-off." 3M did this in 2000 when the company decided to phase out chemicals PFOA and PFOS in Scotchgard. Swiss Re and Munich Re did this with climate change more than a decade ago.
- **Innovation, Research, and Development:** Stage 3 companies *see innovation as core to their future. They see sustainability as the main driver of innovation.* Tesla was created to accelerate the advent of sustainable transport. Akzo Nobel is developing products that use CO_2 as a source material. Dell is using recycled ocean plastics in packaging. Philips is using drone technology for wind farm inspection. Toyota is using pollution-reducing billboards in California. XL Hybrids retrofits vans and trucks into hybrids, thereby reducing emissions and fuel use by 20 percent. Walmart convened over a dozen CEOs of major companies and CEOs of leading NGOs to sign new commitments accelerating innovation in sustainable agriculture and recycling.
- **Customers and Markets:** Stage 3 companies *work in new and different ways with customers.* GE launched Ecomagination purely in response to meeting customer needs (lower life-cycle energy costs) in the face of emerging mega-trends (environmental degradation and climate change). Unilever holds "Big Moments" events to make *sustainable living* commonplace. Waste Management's transformation from waste disposal to waste services was driven by a combination of attention to early signals of a customer trend and a CEO's major strategic thrust to respond to those needs (to move toward zero waste). Allianz (Brazil) home insurance provides a range of green services: energy and water efficiency; solar power; and recycling—including home collection service. Natura Cosmeticos (Brazil) launched Programa Amazonia, a 1.7-million-square-meter closed-cycle industrial complex in the Amazon region. Novo Nordisk's (Denmark) Changing Diabetes program in China educated 280,000 patients, trained 55,000 physicians, and grew its market share in insulin by 23 percent. NTT Docomo (Japan) aims to be a "Smart Life Partner" for its customers, deploying a wide range of health-related services (e.g., monitor their customers' exercise and diet).
- **Products, Services, and Solutions:** Stage 3 companies *decouple "product resource intensity" from sales*. They drive revenue growth through sustainable products and services—without growing the full life-cycle product footprint.[iii] They shift from selling products to selling services and solutions. Ashland's new vision is to sell solutions (not chemicals). Michelin is moving to sell "distance" (a service), not only tires. Today's leaders are selling sustainable products, services, and solutions to existing markets (e.g., Campbell Soup, Siemens, Philips,

GE), to new markets (e.g., Cisco with smart grid; Schneider Electric and IBM with smart cities), and into emerging markets. Many people think of Apple as primarily selling products. However, Apple reported in August 2017 that revenue from services (as opposed to products) accounted for more than $27.8 billion for the 12 months ending July 1, 2017—making their "services" the equivalent of a Fortune 100 company.

The Scorecard: Strategy and Execution

This chapter has provided a general overview of Strategy and Execution, the second section of the Scorecard. As noted above, this section of the Scorecard contains four elements.

In Part 2 of the book, a separate chapter (chapters 18 through 21) addresses each of these four elements in detail. Each of those four chapters aligns with the rating criteria on the web-based tool that has been used by sixty companies by February 2018 and by a growing number since then.

In addition to providing the detailed scoring templates for each element of Strategy and Execution, the Part 2 chapters also provide dozens of company best practice examples—which are defined as being in Stage 3 or higher.

---

i "The Conference Board CEO Challenge 2016," The Conference Board, Research Report 1599, January 2016, p. 67.
ii Thomas Singer, "Driving Revenue Growth through Sustainable Products and Services," The Conference Board, Research Report 1583, June 2015. https://www.conference-board.org/publications/publicationdetail.cfm?publicationid=2975
iii Singer, "Driving Revenue Growth," *op cit.*

Chapter 7
Environmental Stewardship: The "E" in ESG

Sustainability Stories from the C-Suite and Boardroom ...

In 2001, I was almost *"kicked out"* of Oklahoma for mentioning climate change. In my final year at consulting firm, Arthur D. Little, I was leading a high-profile consulting assignment for the CEO of Kerr McGee. (Since that time, the oil and gas and chemical company sold its chemical operations by IPO as *"Tronox"* in 2005. The balance of the company was purchased by Anadarko Petroleum Corporation in 2006. The company no longer exists today.)

The CEO had five business transformation teams that each focused on a major corporate function. I was the senior advisor to the environment team comprising six senior executives from across the company. Our team identified four areas that could have a significant cost or risk impact on the company. One of those areas was captured as "environmental strategy." Taking pride in its strong compliance posture, the company wanted to be a leader.

Interviewing the Senior Vice President of Strategy, I asked what he thought a leadership posture on climate change might look like. I set the context with the company's North Sea oil and gas competitor, BP, whose public posture on climate change was quite aggressive. BP's CEO at the time, John Browne, publicly stated his position that it was reasonable to take a precautionary approach to limiting greenhouse gas emissions.

Sitting in a corner office on the executive floor of the Kerr McGee Building in Oklahoma City, I realized that this SVP was the CEO's right-hand advisor. Along with the presidents of the oil and chemical businesses and the CEO, they comprised the executive leadership team. I asked the senior vice president a few strategic questions about carbon-related risk and opportunity. He looked me in the eye and said, "Don't ever mention climate change around here" (implying in this company or this city).

Postscript: Six weeks later, our team was able to have a business-focused conversation about climate change and environmental strategy. A Kerr McGee UK production manager from the North Sea operations was in Oklahoma and joined one of our presentations to the executive leadership team. He was the one who brought up climate change. Furthermore, he completely surprised the CEO and C-suite executives when he stated that Kerr McGee UK actually had a position statement (similar to BP's) on climate change.

As this story shows, *sustainability involves tough—and evolving—conversations.* If a company is not having those conversations, those in charge probably are dancing around the edges of the core ESG issues.

DOI 10.1515/9781547400423-007

The Situation: Overdose on Environmental Issues

Environmental stewardship depicted in Figure 7.1 (see also Figure 1.2 in Chapter 1) has long dominated the sustainability headlines in the United States. The vast majority of articles and books written about sustainability over the past thirty years have focused largely on the *environment*: degradation, resource limits, externalities, climate change, pesticides, toxics, and waste. (The sustainability conversation in the United States has often had a lighter emphasis on the social dimension of sustainability (human rights issues, etc.) The conversation in Europe, in contrast, has often been fairly evenly balanced between environmental and social issues.

We mentioned in Chapter 3 that sustainability is two sides of a coin: one side represents *risk*, and the other represents *opportunity*. Every company must focus first and foremost on risk: reducing the "bad stuff" not only in your own company's operations, but also throughout the supply chain. However, Stage 3 companies also see sustainability as a *source of innovation* to drive top-line revenue growth.

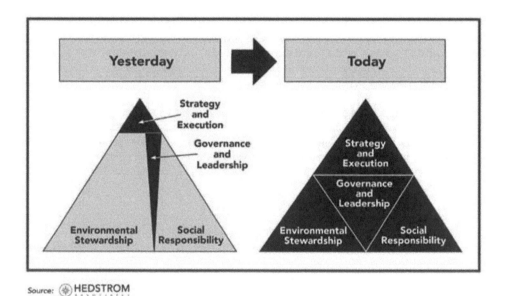

Source: ⊛ HEDSTROM

Figure 7.1: The Changing Sustainability Conversation

Materiality Assessment

In Chapter 2 (Why Bother?), we introduced the Global Risk Review—a report published annually by the World Economic Forum. Over the past thirteen years of that report, environmental and social issues have grown steadily. Today, they dominate the "upper right quadrant" of the risk profile—indicating the risks of greatest impact and greatest likelihood. So that is the backdrop for every CEO to figure out what issues are most significant (**material**) to his or her company.

The starting point for every company's approach to environmental stewardship should be to conduct a robust **materiality** assessment. A materiality assessment should be the basis for considering sustainability goals and metrics, as well as the associated programs, initiatives, and performance incentives that drive actions to meet those goals.

However, this is where things go amiss for so many companies. The Global Reporting Initiative (GRI) uses the term "materiality" in a way that actually reinforces the lopsided sustainability conversation depicted on the left side of Figure 6.1. GRI defines materiality in a far broader way than investors do.[1]

– GRI defines materiality as a threshold for what they believe is *important* to be reported: "The report should cover aspects that reflect the organization's significant environmental and social impacts; or that substantively influence the assessments and decisions" of the various stakeholders.

– Investors define materiality as a key threshold for making investment decisions.

As a result of this GRI definition, the vast majority of sustainability reports today include a materiality matrix. (Figure 7.2 shows one example format.) Many companies include as many as thirty or fifty ESG issues on their reported materiality matrix. Though these issues are *important*, the vast majority of them are not truly *material* (in the financial sense of the word).

An excellent report from Germany identifies the top three material ESG indicators for each of 68 different industries. This report, titled "Sustainable Development Key Performance Indicators (SD-KPIs),"[1] was initially developed for the German Environment Ministry. The report aligns with the author's view that the vast majority of companies have only a small handful (typically just one to four) environmental or social issues that are truly *material*. For example, Chevron, Duke Energy, and General Motors are essentially "single issue" companies (and industries): the material issue is carbon/GHG. The material issues of BASF or Dow Chemical are typically safety, toxins, and carbon/GHG. For Coca-Cola or Pepsi, the material issues are water usage, obesity, carbon/GHG, and packaging waste.

---

1 This statement is not intended to in any way diminish the importance of GRI over the years. True confessions: I was one of the seventeen individuals (invited by Bob Massie, then CEO of Ceres in October 1997) who conceived of and crafted GRI over the ensuing eighteen months.

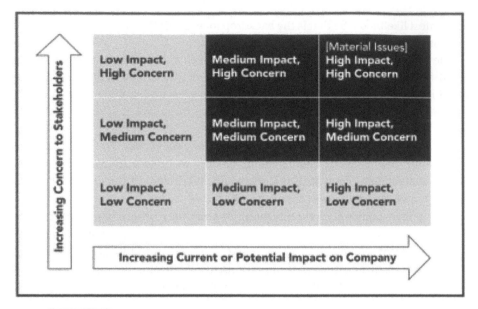

Figure 7.2: Example Materiality Matrix

The Sustainability Accounting Standards Board (SASB) is an independent, private-sector standards setting organization based in San Francisco, California. SASB is working to develop and disseminate sustainability accounting standards that help corporations disclose information to investors. SASB standards address the ESG topics that are "reasonably likely" to have material impacts on the financial condition or operating performance of companies in an industry. SASB recognizes that each company is responsible for determining what information is "material" and what information should be included in filings with the U.S. Securities and Exchange Commission (SEC). In identifying sustainability topics that are reasonably likely to have material impacts, SASB applies the definition of "materiality" established under the U.S. securities laws.[ii]

When companies define ESG materiality narrowly—as only a handful of truly material issues or impacts—they facilitate a conversation with the C-suite about strategy. Indeed, shortly after Jeff Seabright (current Chief Sustainability Officer at Unilever) arrived at Coca-Cola as VP Environment and Water and launched a major water initiative, the CEO added "water" as one of the company's major strategic thrusts.

Environment: The Key Elements

NGOs and many chief sustainability officers tend to think of sustainability by issue (carbon, water, waste, etc.). Ask C-suite executives about environmental stewardship and they think about the way they run the company across the supply chain.

CEOs realize that *every company is responsible today, like it or not, for the full environmental footprint of its products, services, and solutions across the supply chain.* The days are over for a company to own responsibility only for its wholly-owned or majority-owned operations.

For example, Ford, GM, and Toyota own the carbon impact of consumers as they drive their cars and trucks. (Of course, if these companies did not create cars and trucks, someone else would; therefore, their impact is relative to what might be thought of as a standard of excellence.) McDonald's and PepsiCo own their contribution to the obesity epidemic. Starbucks is responsible for how much water and pesticides are used to grow its coffee beans—as well as the labor practices involved. Tesco and Walmart own the ecological impact of producing the food and beverages they sell.

In the Corporate Sustainability Scorecard C-suite rating system, the many environmental issues are organized into three buckets aligned to the supply chain: your own operations footprint; your supplier footprint; and your product footprint (see Table 7.1).

Table 7.1: Elements of Environmental Stewardship

Environmental Stewardship
– **Environmental Footprint—Operations:** Environmental Impacts associated with wholly owned or partially owned operations, including *managing purchased resource inputs* (chemicals, energy, materials, water); *managing own physical footprint* (buildings, equipment, land); and *managing non-product outputs* (emissions and wastes).
– **Supply Chain Environmental Impacts:** Managing the environmental impacts of the company's supply chain, including the *posture and management processes* governing supplier interactions; the means of *addressing the most material supplier environmental impacts*; and the *nature and extent of supplier sustainability partnerships*.
– **Environmental Footprint—Products:** Managing the environmental impacts of the company's products, including the *overall product stewardship approach*, the *product design process*, and *end-of-life product management* following retail, consumer use, and disposal.

For most companies, the large majority of the full life-cycle environmental impacts occur in only:
- One or two areas of environmental impact, for example, carbon/GHG; toxics, water, etc.

- One key part of the supply chain, for example, their supplier, their own operations, product use, and disposal

For example, Ford, GM, and Toyota have the vast majority of their impact in *product use* and *energy/carbon*. (As mentioned in Chapter 3, Ford has stated that approximately 90 percent of a vehicle's lifecycle greenhouse gas emissions are attributable to CO_2 emitted during customer vehicle use.)

Environmental Stewardship: Tomorrow's Leaders Today

Below is a brief snapshot of how some leading companies are addressing the three key elements of environmental stewardship: their own operations, their suppliers, and their products.

- **Environmental Footprint—Operations:** Today's leaders are *driving relentlessly toward "zero waste" in managing their own operations*. They are reducing or eliminating hazardous waste, achieving or working toward zero waste to landfills (Caterpillar, P&G, and Subaru), and working toward becoming **carbon neutral** (Adobe Systems, Google, IKEA, and small companies like Curtis Packaging). Companies as diverse as General Mills and Novelis are committed to sourcing their raw materials sustainably. Kering (France) and Nike have committed to phasing out all hazardous chemicals. IKEA and Kingfisher (UK) are following a roadmap to become "forest positive" (creating more forest than they use). Johnson Controls and Telus (Canada) manage their buildings for zero impact.
- **Supply Chain Environmental Impacts:** Stage 3 companies have taken bold steps to *green their supply chains*. Walmart, since 2005, relentlessly has driven "green" forward by demanding, for example, that suppliers reduce their packaging, hazardous materials, and water use. P&G and Kaiser Permanente followed Walmart's lead and made similar demands on suppliers. Natura Cosmeticos (Brazil), Compass Group (UK), Hershey, and Rio Tinto (UK) demanded that their suppliers protect biodiversity. Baxter, HP, and Owens Corning led their industries in setting supply chain sustainability goals. Dell is using certified closed-loop recycled plastics in its computers. Adidas, Anvil Knitwear, and Nike (among others) put in place processes to verify the performance of their suppliers.
- **Environmental Footprint—Products:** Stage 3 companies have, for years, *systematically reduced the environmental footprints of their products*. SC Johnson was an early leader: its Greenlist program evaluates material components of the company's products, and systematically phases out more hazardous ones. In the 1990s, Electrolux and Ikea offered a green product line. Desso (Netherlands) adopted a cradle-to-cradle approach in 2007. Today, many companies clearly are Stage 3 in at least one sustainable product attribute. Leaders in selected product attributes include: energy efficiency (EMC and HP), traceability (Hershey and

Patagonia), material use (Adidas and Herman Miller), durability (Autodesk and DuPont), and recyclability (Electrolux and Shaw Industries). Finally, leaders in diverse industry sectors have staked out a leadership position in end-of-life product responsibility, such as BMW for vehicles and Sprint for cellphones.

Of course, one company's products are often another company's material inputs. If Walmart imposes a requirement on Dell, HP, Proctor & Gamble, and other suppliers that are required, for example, to reduce or take back their packaging material, that is a supplier issue for Walmart but a product issue for its suppliers.

The Scorecard: Environmental Stewardship

This chapter has provided a general overview of Environmental Stewardship, the third section of the Scorecard. As noted above, this section of the Scorecard contains three elements (own operations, supply chain, products).

In Part 2 of the book, a separate chapter (chapters 22 through 24) addresses each of these three elements in detail, aligned with the rating criteria on the Scorecard website, used by 60 companies by February 2018 and by a growing number since then.

In addition to providing the detailed scoring templates for each element of Environmental Stewardship, Part 2 also provide dozens of company best practice examples—which are defined as being in Stage 3 or higher.

------

i "SD-KPI Standard 2016-2021," SD-M GmbH, September 2016.
ii "SASB Conceptual Framework," Sustainability Accounting Standards Board (SASB), February 2017.

Chapter 8
Social Responsibility: The "S" in ESG

Sustainability Stories from the C-Suite and Boardroom ...

I had the opportunity to spend two weeks in Papua New Guinea in the late 1990s. This was a starkly different physical and social setting from anything I had yet experienced. As a member of a high-level executive audit team, we were charged with assessing the environmental status of the controversial Ok Tedi mining operation for BHP Billiton (then BHP).

The Ok Tedi mine was critically important to BHP. One of the largest copper mines in the world, the mine was (at the time of our visit) about 15 years through its useful life of 30 years. Moreover, the mine was facing considerable pressure for environmental reasons. Despite being located in one of the most remote places in the world, Ok Tedi was in the crosshairs of NGOs in Asia. The mine was located about 6,000 feet above sea level, in a rainforest area on geologically "new" soil, which was easily eroded (the opposite of granite).

The environmental issues at Ok Tedi were mind-boggling, so much so that BHP actually had a staff of about 30 full-time environmental scientists and experts at the site. They had commissioned major ecosystem studies examining the impacts of mining waste runoff into the Fly River—one of the most fertile fishing grounds in the South China Sea.

For two weeks, we reviewed compliance records; took helicopter rides up and down the river systems; and met with local community groups. Then we came to a surprising conclusion: on paper, the Ok Tedi mine appeared to be largely or completely in compliance with PNG laws and regulations.

Yet, late one evening sitting around a conference room table, I stood up and went to a copy of the Corporate Environmental Policy hanging on the wall. I set it on the table so that all of us could read the words. The company's environmental policy, like that of most peer companies, included a general statement about "commitment to protecting the environment." We zeroed in on the actual words in the policy statement. After some heated discussions, our team developed a list of findings and recommendations.

Postscript: In the end, our report made it to the highest levels of the company. Not long after, BHP began divesting itself of the Ok Tedi mine and taking major financial charges against operations.

The message from this story: *Social issues are complex, intertwined with environmental issues, and owned not only by the parent company but also throughout the value chain.* Nike owned the child labor issues in the late 1990s that led to a Supreme Court lawsuit; Apple owned the Foxconn labor and environmental abuses a decade ago; and every company that purchased copper sourced at Ok Tedi owned the social and environmental issues in Papua New Guinea.

DOI 10.1515/9781547400423-008

The Situation: Looking Back—Not Looking Ahead

From its beginning, the socially responsible investing (SRI) movement has had social issues at its core—as the name implies. Assets invested using SRI strategies have continued to grow, doubling between 2012 and 2014. Furthermore, one third of millennials consider socially responsible factors when they invest.[i]

The "social dimension" of sustainability has grown in importance across many industry sectors as they take responsibility for environmental, social, and governance (ESG) issues across their supply chains. The Nike, Inc. v. Kasky lawsuit that reached the U.S. Supreme Court in 2003 brought to the forefront how major corporations are responsible for far more than their own operations. Moreover, that lawsuit also raised visibility for human rights and related conditions. Supply chain issues pushed the social dimension of sustainability to a point of "roughly equal" weighting as the environmental issues—although this varies significantly by industry sector and by geography.

Globally, the environmental and social dimensions of sustainability tend to receive roughly equal focus. However, for many U.S. industry sectors, social responsibility (as depicted in the left-hand triangle of Figure 8.1) has long been overshadowed by the environment.

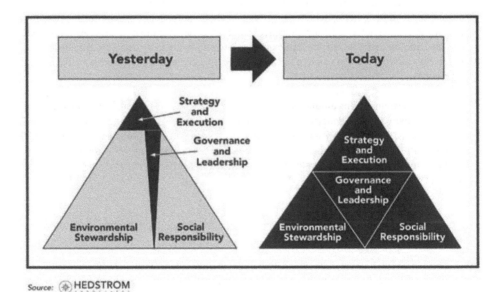

Source: HEDSTROM

Figure 8.1: The Changing Sustainability Conversation

Unfortunately, it is not nearly as clean as Figure 8.1 depicts. *The line between what is an environmental issue and what is a social issue is often blurry.* Availability of fresh water may be seen primarily as an environmental issue in many parts of Arizona in the U.S., while it is considered a social issue in the 37 countries that the World Resources Institute rates 4.01 or higher on a 1-to-5 scale of water-stressed countries.

The emerging social responsibility agenda is vast and complex. To name a few, the issues of social injustice, economic inequality, and the impacts of digital transformation place social issues squarely in the C-Suite. A very simple way to segment the issues is depicted in Figure 8.2.

Source: HEDSTROM

Figure 8.2: Social Spheres of Influence

Social Responsibility: The Key Elements

In the Corporate Sustainability Scorecard, we break down social responsibility into three elements, depicted in Figure 8.2 and listed in Table 8.1.

Table 8.1: Elements of Social Responsibility

Social Responsibility
– **Own Operations: Workplace:** The *general workplace environment* established by management and seen by the employees; the *core workplace programs* to promote safety, health, and employee wellbeing; and the *sustainability capability-building initiatives* in place.
– **Supply Chain Social Impacts:** The *posture and management processes* implemented by the company across its supply chain; the processes and programs in place to address the most material supply chain social impacts; and the *supply chain partnerships* that drive change.
– **Community Investment:** The company's *community policies and programs*; the *community investments* made by the company; and the *benefits to society* from those initiatives and investments.

The Opportunity: Glass Half Full

The exploding middle class globally and all that it represents is at the core of significant business opportunities over the next decade—and beyond. Every company, even those sourcing from and selling to suppliers and customers locally in the United States or Canada (where populations are fairly stable and the environment is clean) ignores these changes at its peril.

Think back to this list of major global risks reported by the World Economic Forum (WEF) in its annual Global Risks Report. As mentioned in Chapter 2 (Why Bother?), the latest WEF report looks at five categories of environmental risks:
- Extreme weather events and temperatures
- Accelerating biodiversity loss
- Pollution of air, soil, and water
- Failures of climate change mitigation and adaptation
- Risks linked to the transition to low carbon

All of these risks ranked highly on both dimensions of likelihood and impact.

So why are we talking about these environmental risks in the chapter on social issues? The reason is that global environmental issues (such as climate change and fresh water shortages) can have profound societal impacts. They can also be a threat multiplier, as they contribute to economic and political instability.

With that backdrop, consider two scenarios:
- *Scenario #1 is the "glass half empty."* From a societal point of view, the addition of 2.5 billion middle class consumers represents a massive threat in one sense. With society bumping up against ecosystem limits today (fresh water availability, atmospheric carbon, etc.), future regional wars will be fought over water rights, agricultural land, mineral rights, and the like. (At a local level, wars have been fought over such limits for generations.) In addition, populations are migrating to cities, most of which are already full of smog, vehicles, and congestion.
- *Scenario #2 is the "glass half full."* Doubling the number of people globally represents massive growth markets: in renewable energy; in transportation (sustainable mobility, ride sharing, tomorrow's car-sharing); in food (grown without use of hydrocarbon-based fertilizers and pesticides—and without depleting aquifers); in housing (zero energy, zero impact urban housing, etc.); in affordable health care (access to medicines, water, and food); and in consumer products. Clearly, providing products, services, and solutions to meet these future needs will not be the same as today. *The future simply can not look like it does today.* Realistically, one can not even envision a world with twice the number that we have today of cars in cities, big-box stores in suburbia, and CO_2-spewing power plants—and much, much more.

Undoubtedly, both scenarios will play out in various ways, in different sectors and parts of the world, and in pockets of time. Yet the common thread through both scenarios is making a business out of solving the world's most pressing challenges.

As the world becomes more volatile, boards and C-suite executives must make their companies more agile to deal with the increasing disruptive developments. That will require thinking about solutions in very different ways than companies have been thinking over the past few decades.

Data suggests that the next generations of consumers, entrepreneurs, and business leaders are ready to pitch in and do their part to solve the world's pressing challenges (see Table 8.2).

Table 8.2: Next Generations of Consumers, Entrepreneurs, and Business Leaders

Responses by age to the question: "We should do what is right for the planet, even if it harms the U.S. economy."		
Generation Descriptor	**Born**	**Percentage**
Matures	Before 1946	48%
Boomers	1946–1964	53%
Xers	1965–1978	62%
Millennials	1979–1996	72%
Centennials	After 1997	74%

Source: 2016 U.S. Yankelovich MONITOR.

Social Responsibility at a Glance: Tomorrow's Leaders Today

The vast majority of companies that might be considered "leading" today tend to have Stage 3 or Stage 4 practice(s) in one or a few dimensions of social responsibility. One company may be a leader on diversity, another company on supply chain monitoring and verification, and another on community volunteerism. In some cases, the leading initiative is tied directly to a particular passion of the CEO.

Below is a brief snapshot of how a few leading companies are addressing these three key areas of social responsibility:

- **Workplace:** Stage 3 companies have a *workplace environment and supportive core programs that make the company a* "great place" *to work.* They set an inclusive and supportive culture at the top (Cisco, Kimberly-Clark, and SAS); have highly diverse leadership (Kaiser Permanente, PwC, and Sodexo); have great benefits (Adobe, Facebook, and Salesforce.com); have outstanding safety culture and performance; or have leading health and wellness programs (Goldman Sachs,

Intuit, and Sprint). Leaders invest in personalized training and staff development related to sustainability.

- **Social Supply Chain:** Stage 3 companies *actively drive social responsibility culture and initiatives throughout their supply chain.* They set high standards and work closely with suppliers to create open and trusted collaboration (ASML Holding NV and Nike) and incorporate this philosophy into their procurement practices (Baxter and Siemens). Many leaders today have established a comprehensive supplier sustainability performance measurement system (Kaiser Permanente and Walmart) and provide strong independent oversight, assurance, and verification of performance (HP, Intel, and Siemens). Importantly, Stage 3 companies are boldly out in front of their peers on the most material social impact issue in their value chain, as seen by: Nike (human rights), Unilever and REI (labor relations), and Patagonia and Cisco (child and forced labor).

- **Community:** Stage 3 companies *take philanthropy to a new level as they rethink their company relationship to the global community and the local communities where they operate.* Leading companies focus squarely on initiatives that will help attract tomorrow's best and brightest employees, who will help them produce outstanding competitive advantage. Intel's annual Science Talent Search has a global and inspiring reach. Danske Bank (Denmark) helps the growing population of elderly citizens bridge the "digital divide." IBM developed an app to allow students to catalogue rainforest biodiversity—a program that squarely addresses both the environmental and social "legs" of sustainability. JPMorgan Chase exceeded its initial $100 million investment in the city of Detroit in just three years and now expects to invest $150 million by 2019. The company's goal is to prove the concept: *As more people move up the economic ladder they share in the rewards of a growing economy.*

The Scorecard: Social Responsibility

This chapter has provided a general overview of social responsibility, the fourth and final section of the Scorecard. As noted above, this section of the Scorecard contains three elements (workplace; supply chain; community).

In Part 2 of the book, a separate chapter (chapters 25 through 27) addresses each of these three elements in detail. Each of those three chapters aligns with the rating criteria on the web-based tool that has been used by sixty companies by February 2018 and by a growing number since then.

In addition to providing the detailed scoring templates for each element of social responsibility, the Part 2 chapters also provide dozens of company best practice examples—which are defined as being in Stage 3 or higher.

---

i https://www.kiplinger.com/article/investing/T041-C009-S002-7-great-socially-responsible-mutual-funds.html

Chapter 9
The New ESG Regulators

Back in the 1970s, 1980s, and 1990s, if companies wanted to read about the latest developments in pending environmental, health, and safety (EHS) requirements, the vice president of EHS tracked regulatory developments from the U.S. Environmental Protection Agency (EPA)—and similar agencies globally. The core business issue was *managing risk* and the responsibility was squarely in the hands of corporate executives managing EHS.

Today, the issue is increasingly about *business opportunity* (while paying close attention to risk). The company's vice president of strategy reads Bloomberg New Energy Finance and similar news feeds from mainstream investors.

So who are the new regulators? Who sets the basic environmental, social, and governance (ESG) expectations that companies need to follow? This chapter describes "the new ESG regulators" in four buckets:
- Investors: The new EPA
- The global regulatory landscape
- Private sector collaborations
- The power of millennials

Investors: The New EPA?

A June 26, 2018 Special Supplement to *The Wall Street Journal* titled "Investing with Purpose" sums it up. The ten-page First Wealth and Asset Management Group Special Report reviews the rapidly changing landscape of ESG investing.

The subtitle of *The Wall Street Journal* June 26 piece says: "Larry Fink's Mission: How the BlackRock CEO is leading a sustainable revolution on Wall Street." (In Chapter 2: Why Bother?, we mentioned the letter sent to CEOs in early 2018 by BlackRock CEO Larry Fink. BlackRock is the world's largest investor.)

The key messages in *The Wall Street Journal* supplement reinforce those shared during a Conference Board webinar where leaders from BlackRock, MSCI, and ISS-Oekom Americas shared their views of how mainstream investors are reacting to ESG. The MSCI representative said this:

> ESG is coming up in virtually every conversation with institutional investors. Everything is getting scaled up very quickly. ESG is the fastest growing part of MSCI. Our investors are looking at ESG across the entire portfolio (equities, fixed income, large cap and small cap; global and U.S.; emerging markets).

DOI 10.1515/9781547400423-009

Why Do Mainstream Investors Care?—Bill Davis, CEO of Stance Capital (an emerging leader in responsible investing) describes today's youngest investors as "The Impact Generation, referring to Gen Yers (millennials) and Gen Zers, some of whom are still in high school."[i] A few key points about these emerging investors:

- Millennials future will be driven by a combination of their unique values and worldview, unparalleled access to information, and the tools to use it, sheer size (nearly 80 million people), and an estimated $24 trillion of accessible wealth by 2024.[ii]
- Millennials care about the environment and social issues; they are entering the investment space; and poised to inherit considerable wealth as the baby boomer generation passes on.
- Historically, when wealth is transferred, the younger generation changes investment managers or advisors over 60 percent of the time.

The megatrends of population growth, climate change, pressure on resources, and social inequities are mainstream news today. They are not far away ideas; they actually affect people we may know—through adverse weather events, and the like. Tomorrow's investors are soaking up this news; they are developing a world view where climate change and societal inequities may well influence their career choices and their investment preferences.

What Do Mainstream Investors Want?—In August 2017, Vanguard joined Black-Rock, State Street and other mainstream investors to vote *against management* and for shareholder measures on climate change at ExxonMobil and Occidental Petroleum. This was a watershed moment, since historically the large institutional investors including those listed above tended to vote *with management* the vast majority of the time. Here are a few data points from 2018:

- In 2018, more than 400 shareholder resolutions were filed on ESG issues. Eighty resolutions demanded that companies address *climate risk rated highest* (tied with political activity spending) there were seventy resolutions about equal treatment for women.[iii]
- BNP Paribas and HSBC were among sixty investors, collectively managing over $10 trillion in assets, have urged oil companies to set clear targets on climate change, cut investments in fossil fuels, and be more transparent about plans to support a low carbon future.[iv]
- New York City will divest $5 billion in its pension funds from holdings in fossil fuel companies.[v]

Investors want value creation. Short term investors want to make money quickly; longer-term investors including pension funds want to preserve and grow their capital over many years.

What Are Key Market Drivers?—The Trump administration has reportedly proposed a 72 percent cut in clean energy research funding in fiscal 2019.[vi] But the likely impact is minimal. The "horse is out of the barn"; investment in clean energy is growing globally. Here are a few data points from the 2018 news:

- *Impact of weather events on earnings.* An analysis by S&P Global Ratings that analyzed public research and earnings call transcripts between April 2017 and April 2018 found that the average impact of weather events on S&P 500 company earnings was 6 percent.[vii] The same study noted that during FY17, seventy-three companies (15 percent) on the S&P 500 publicly disclosed an impact on earnings from weather events; however, only eighteen companies (4 percent) quantified the impact.
- Global investment in renewable energy and energy-smart technologies reached $333.5 billion in 2017, up 3 percent from 2016. China invested a record $132 billion into clean energy technologies while the United States invested the second most—$56 billion.[viii]
- Global corporate funding in solar reached $12.8 billion in 2017, up from $9.1 billion in 2016 (a 41 percent increase).[ix]
- The global annual revenue for energy storage for renewable integration is projected to exceed $23 billion by 2026.[x]
- The global emission monitoring systems market is projected to reach $4.4 billion by 2025, nearly double the size in 2017.[xi]
- The global fuel cells market is projected to reach nearly $14 billion in 2017.[xii]

The above list provides just a snapshot of the size and scale of the market changes that are happening as the sustainability transformation rapidly unfolds.

The picture for green investments is not all rosy. In fact, the bankruptcy rate among solar companies is significant. A May 2017 article noted that bankruptcies in the solar industry show signs of weakness but could ultimately lead to a more profitable industry.[xiii] The sustainability transformation is messy; it is not simple and clean.

The Global Regulatory Landscape

This book does not attempt to assess the highly fragmented and complex legal and regulatory landscape associated with environmental and social issues. However, a brief, "30,000 foot" overview is important to complement the other forces driving corporate change with respect to ESG.

Global Standards—Most global standards in the ESG space are not strict requirements; they are more likely characterized as voluntary guidance. Companies then decide how to respond.

The most dominant global ESG development in recent years is the launch of the United Nations **Sustainable Development Goals (UN SDGs).** The SDGs are a collection of seventeen global goals set in 2015, under the formal name: "Transforming our World: The 2030 Agenda for Sustainable Development."

It has been interesting to watch how companies have responded to the SDGs over the past three years. Initially, it is fair to say most companies went on about their business and did not pay much attention to the SDGs. Many took the easy first step of simply comparing the seventeen SDGs with the material ESG issues the company (and its industry sector) faces. This basic "mapping" exercise often resulted in a statement on the company website or in its sustainability report about which SDGs are most relevant.

While it is still early days for the SDGs, many leading companies are paying greater attention to them. One key reason is that investors are asking! A logical step for companies is to identify the major countries where they operate and the dominant SDG issues in that country—and then to find ways to partner with peer companies or nongovernmental organizations (NGOs) to make a positive contribution to addressing those issues.

National/Country Standards—Many countries have set standards for sustainability reporting and for specific actions to address national and global environmental and social issues. Several examples from the recent news are:

- China announced plans in early 2018 to create the world's largest carbon market to limit the amount of CO_2 emissions Chinese power companies can emit. The market is expected to manage over three billion tons of CO_2 annually.[xiv]
- China has created a new Ministry of Ecology and Environment to lead the nation's fight against climate change—and to drive implementation of aggressive goals in the country's latest five-year plan.[xv]
- A coalition of businesses and investors, representing over €21 trillion in assets, sent a letter to European Union Heads of State and Government calling for increased levels of action to deliver on the Paris Agreement carbon objective of 1.5 degrees Celsius (growth over pre-industrial levels).[xvi]
- India has pledged to ban all single-use plastics by 2022. And the European Union has proposed a similar ban.[xvii] Where alternatives are readily available and affordable, single-use plastic products will be banned from the European market. For products without straightforward alternatives, the focus is on limiting their use through a national reduction in consumption; design and labelling requirements and waste management/clean-up obligations for producers.[xviii]
- France plans to retire all of its coal power plants by 2021[xix] and voted to ban all oil and gas exploration and production in the country and its overseas territories by 2040.[xx] In a related move, the French government plans to support sustainable aviation biofuel industries and help them grow in the country.[xxi]
- Ireland plans to phase out the use of coal power by 2025.[xxii]

- The UK government plans to eliminate all avoidable plastic waste by 2042[xxiii] and plans to cut the energy use of new buildings by 50 percent by 2030.[xxiv] In addition, the UK and Saudi Arabia have agreed to work together to develop more low-carbon technologies.[xxv]

Starting in the 1970s, the United States became a global leader addressing what are commonly referred to as "point source" environmental impacts—specifically with laws and regulations addressing air pollution control, water pollution control, and solid and hazardous waste management.

At the same time, many European countries stepped out front in addressing full life-cycle product environmental and social impacts. Think about automobile recycling and contrast the United States with Europe:
- At the end of 1999, ten European Union member countries (Austria, Belgium, France, Germany, Italy, the Netherlands, Portugal, Spain, Sweden, and the United Kingdom) had specific regulations and/or industrial voluntary agreements addressing the recycling of what they call "end of life vehicles."
- In the United States, roughly twenty years later, no such law exists, even at the state level. There are some requirements for certain automobile parts (such as nickel cadmium batteries), but no requirement for cars and trucks themselves.

So, looking back at the last thirty to forty years, as a broad generalization the United States has been far out front of many European (and other) countries on conventional air, water, and waste pollution. At the same time, Europe has been roughly twenty years ahead of the United States on product-related environmental, health, and safety requirements.

Europe has also been far out front on climate change. As the decades passed, China and other Asia countries have tended to follow Europe's lead on global issues including climate change, while gradually addressing the point-source air, water and waste issues.

Regional Standards—Individual states or groups of states within a country often take the lead. In the United States, California and a handful of other states have long played this role.
- A group of seventeen U.S. states including California, New York and Massachusetts have filed a lawsuit against the EPA for its decision to cut Obama-era fuel economy standards.[xxvi]
- California, Quebec, and Ontario conducted their first joint cap and trade auction of carbon allowances in early 2018, generating sales of $725 million for California and over $500 million for Quebec and Ontario combined.[xxvii]
- California Governor Jerry Brown signed an executive order in early 2018, increasing the number of zero-emission vehicles to five million by 2030, adding 250,000

vehicle charging stations and 200 hydrogen fueling stations by 2025. The state will also invest $1.25 billion in cap-and-trade auction proceeds.[xxviii]

These are just a few sound bites, but the picture is becoming clear.

City and Local Standards—The phrase "all politics is local" is commonly associated with former Speaker of the United States House of Representatives Tip O'Neill. The same can certainly be said for ESG issues that acutely impact local communities.

Think about the Flint Michigan contamination that hit the news in 2015. In 2014, in an effort to save money, Flint began drawing water from the notoriously dirty Flint River instead of relying on water from Detroit. Residents complained of smell, taste and appearance, and raised health concerns. Later in 2015, a group of doctors urged residents to stop using the water after finding high levels of lead in the blood of children. Many were left wondering, "How could a country and state with stringent water pollution control standards in place since the 1970s allow the Flint water issues to happen?"

Several current examples of ESG issues being addressed at the state or regional level include:
- Cape Town, South Africa's second largest city, was initially projected in February 2018 to run out of water by June, four months later. The date of "Day Zero" as it is called—the date the city taps shut off—has since been pushed back to 2019 following rains.[xxix]
- The American Cities Climate Challenge (launched by Bloomberg Philanthropies) provides $70 million to help U.S. cities achieve the Paris Agreement carbon reduction goals.[xxx]
- Ford, General Motors and other automakers sent a letter to the Trump administration reaffirming their strong support for continued alignment between California mileage standards and those set by the federal government.[xxxi]
- Of the 570 plus global cities reporting, over 100 now get at least 70 percent of their electricity from renewable sources such as hydro, geothermal, solar, and wind.[xxxii]

In the United States, cities are stepping up to address ESG issues. From 2014–2017, the U.S. Sustainable Cities Initiative supported SDG achievement strategies, serving as models for cities worldwide. New York City, Baltimore (Maryland), and San Jose (California) are lauded as global pioneers.[xxxiii]

Private Sector Collaborations

So far in this chapter we have discussed the impact of investors and of governments in pressuring business to address ESG issues. A third source of pressure actually comes from companies themselves, in the form of partnerships. In some cases these are industry-only collaborations; in other cases they are partnerships among companies and one or more NGOs.

- RE100, a campaign to source 100 percent of power from renewable energy, was launched in 2014. Since then, over 125 major companies from twenty countries have joined. Most have set a target date of 2030 to achieve the 100 percent renewable energy goal.[xxxiv]
- A group of twenty-five UK retailers signed onto the British Retail Consortium's Better Retail Better World initiative to address climate change, responsible production and consumption, and other global challenges.[xxxv]
- The Closed Loop Ocean Initiative, sponsored by Coca-Cola, Dow Chemical, and Kimberly-Clark along with Closed Loop Partners, will fund initiatives in Southeast Asia to help prevent plastic from entering the oceans.[xxxvi]
- The AgWater Challenge, sponsored by Diageo, General Mills, Kellogg, PepsiCo, DanoneWave, and other companies, is a partnership with Ceres and the World Wildlife Fund to develop stronger, more transparent water stewardship commitments in the agricultural value chains.[xxxvii]

The Impact of Millennials

Earlier in this chapter we spoke about the impact of the younger generation, specifically millennials (born between 1979–1996) on the mainstream investment community. That is one key source of impact on companies. Another source that is often felt more acutely is when companies seek to hire young talent to fill open positions.

Chapter 8 (Social Responsibility) discussed how younger generations (millennials and centennials (born after 1997) believe that "we should do what is right for the planet, even if it harms the U.S. economy" (see Table 8.1).

At a recent Conference Board meeting I ran in June 2018 of about 50 sustainability executives from the same number of major corporations, a group of Villanova University engineering students shared what's on their minds as they enter the workforce. We asked a group of five students what they believe and what they hear from their peer students. Some key messages:

- Students are dead serious about working to address society's ills.
- They are bright, ambitions, driven, sincere, and keen to get on with work.
- They will be extremely selective when choosing a company to work for. They read through the glossy photos in sustainability reports and zero in on how *sincere* the company truly is about ESG.

Summary

These four sources of pressure on companies—from investors, regulators, peer companies, and young prospective employees—are aligned. The message is increasingly clear: companies need to step up and address global challenges while also returning value to shareholders. The race is on.

---

i "Investing in the Impact Generation," Davis, Bill (2018), Manuscript submitted for publication in "Millennials Are Not Aliens" by Gui Costin.

ii "Millennials—The Global Guardians of Capital." www.ubs.com, 22 June 2017, www.ubs.com/global/en/wealth-management/chief-investment-office/key-topics/2017/millennials.html

iii https://www.asyousow.org/press-releases/2018/3/8/climate-politics-and-women-top-shareholder-issues-for-proxy-season-2018

iv http://www.climateactionprogramme.org/news/major-investors-call-for-oil-and-gas-groups-to-step-up-climate-action

v https://www.theguardian.com/us-news/2018/jan/10/new-york-city-plans-to-divest-5bn-from-fossil-fuels-and-sue-oil-companies

vi https://www.washingtonpost.com/business/economy/white-house-seeks-72-percent-cut-to-clean-energy-research-underscoring-administrations-preference-for-fossil-fuelsv/2018/01/31/c2c69350-05f3-11e8-b48c-b07fea957bd5_story.html

vii https://www.spratings.com/documents/20184/4918240/The+Effects+of+Weather+Events+on+Corporate+Earnings+Are+Gathering+Force_Revised/6f654f4a-2be2-475f-a1cb-096f5b70201a

viii https://about.bnef.com/clean-energy-investment/#toc-download

ix https://globenewswire.com/news-release/2018/01/10/1286735/0/en/Solar-Industry-Corporate-Funding-Surges-Up-41-Percent-With-12-8-Billion-in-2017-Reports-Mercom-Capital-Group.html

x https://www.navigantresearch.com/newsroom/total-annual-revenue-for-energy-storage-for-renewables-integration-expected-to-exceed-23-billion-by-2026

xi https://www.marketsandmarkets.com/PressReleases/emission-monitoring-systems.asp

xii https://www.prnewswire.com/news-releases/global-fuel-cells-market-forecasts-2018-2023-market-to-reach-138-billion-in-2023-from-31-billion-in-2017-300603980.html

xiii https://www.fool.com/investing/2017/05/19/bankruptcies-continue-in-solar-industry.aspx

xiv https://www.nytimes.com/2017/12/19/climate/china-carbon-market-climate-change-emissions.html

xv https://www.bloomberg.com/news/articles/2018-03-13/as-beijing-s-smog-war-rages-china-rearms-environmental-watchdog

xvi http://www.caneurope.org/docman/climate-energy-targets/3356-statement-of-the-coalition-for-higher-ambition/file

xvii http://time.com/5302732/india-ban-single-use-plastic/

xviii https://ec.europa.eu/commission/news/single-use-plastics-2018-may-28_en

xix https://www.independent.co.uk/news/world/europe/france-coal-power-station-emmanuel-macron-davos-shut-2021-a8176796.html

xx https://www.huffingtonpost.com/entry/france-oil-gas-ban_us_5a3a608be4b025f99e138aaf

xxi https://www.webwire.com/ViewPressRel.asp?aId=217860

xxii https://www.dccae.gov.ie/en-ie/news-and-media/press-releases/Pages/-Minister-Denis-Naughten-announces-Ireland-to-join-Powering-Past-Coal-Alliance.aspx

xxiii https://www.edie.net/news/11/25-year-Environment-Plan—Green-business-reaction/

xxiv https://www.euractiv.com/section/energy/news/theresa-may-unveils-plan-to-halve-building-energy-use-by-2030/

xxv https://cleantechnica.com/2018/03/13/uk-saudi-arabia-sign-clean-energy-partnership/

xxvi https://www.reuters.com/article/us-autos-emissions/17-us-states-sue-trump-administration-over-vehicle-emissions-idUSKBN1I241H

xxvii http://blogs.edf.org/climatetalks/2018/02/28/ontario-california-quebec-joint-carbon-auction/

xxviii http://www.latimes.com/politics/essential/la-pol-ca-essential-politics-updates-gov-brown-california-will-put-5-1516999162-htmlstory.html

xxix https://www.reuters.com/article/us-safrica-drought/cape-town-day-zero-pushed-back-to-2019-as-dams-fill-up-in-south-africa-idUSKCN1HA1LN

xxx https://www.bloomberg.org/press/releases/american-cities-climate-challenge/

xxxi https://www.bloomberg.com/news/articles/2018-05-21/carmakers-tell-white-house-that-climate-change-is-real-in-letter

xxxii https://www.cdp.net/en/cities/world-renewable-energy-cities

xxxiii http://unsdsn.org/what-we-do/solution-initiatives/usa-sustainable-cities-initiative-usa-sci/

xxxiv https://www.bloomberg.com/news/articles/2018-03-01/it-ll-take-94-billion-for-these-companies-to-go-100-green?cmpId=flipboard

xxxv https://brc.org.uk/news/2018/retail-industry-launches-ground-breaking-action-plan-to-advance-sustainability-development-and-equality

xxxvi http://www.plasticsnews.com/article/20180307/NEWS/180309918/dow-coke-others-join-effort-to-fight-plastic-marine-litter-in-asia

xxxvii https://www.ceres.org/news-center/blog/ceres-wwf-expand-agwater-challenge-drive-water-stewardship-ag-supply-chains

Part 2

As mentioned in the Introduction, Part 2 of this book walks the reader through each key element of the Corporate Sustainability Scorecard. The Scorecard enables you to rate your own organization's level of sustainability maturity using a number of metrics, so that in the end, you have a better sense of how the organization stacks up.

As depicted in the figure below, the Scorecard:
- Is organized into four broad sections that collectively address seventeen elements of how companies manage various aspects of sustainability.
- Provides a four-stage rating scheme, whereby stages one and two define the vast majority of how companies globally manage environmental, social, and governance (ESG) issues and stages three and four define the more advanced approaches to ESG management.

The first chapter in Part 2 (Chapter 10) sets the stage, providing a detailed overview of the Scorecard. Read this chapter and visit the website (www.thesustainabilityscore-card.com) to have a good starting point.

Then, starting with Chapter 11, Part 2 walks through all seventeen elements of the Scorecard, one element per chapter. Within each chapter, eight to twelve specific rating criteria (called **key sustainability indicators—KSIs**) are defined, along with many examples of leading practices.

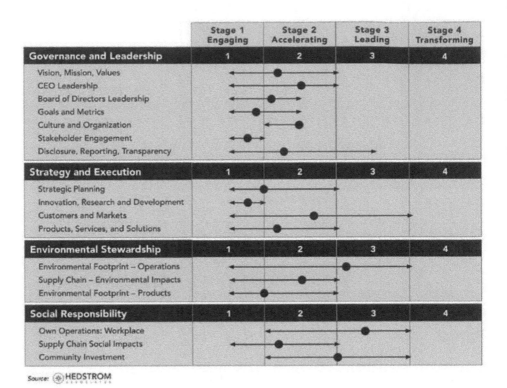

	Stage 1 Engaging	Stage 2 Accelerating	Stage 3 Leading	Stage 4 Transforming
Governance and Leadership	1	2	3	4
Vision, Mission, Values				
CEO Leadership				
Board of Directors Leadership				
Goals and Metrics				
Culture and Organization				
Stakeholder Engagement				
Disclosure, Reporting, Transparency				
Strategy and Execution	1	2	3	4
Strategic Planning				
Innovation, Research and Development				
Customers and Markets				
Products, Services, and Solutions				
Environmental Stewardship	1	2	3	4
Environmental Footprint – Operations				
Supply Chain – Environmental Impacts				
Environmental Footprint – Products				
Social Responsibility	1	2	3	4
Own Operations: Workplace				
Supply Chain Social Impacts				
Community Investment				

Source: HEDSTROM

The example Scorecard above is repeated and discussed in the next chapter.

Chapter 10
Introduction to the Corporate Sustainability Scorecard—C-Suite Rating System

This chapter serves as an introduction to the Corporate Sustainability Scorecard. We encourage readers to also visit the website (www.thesustainabilityscorecard.com) to visualize the on-line tool.[1]

However, all of the detailed elements of the on-line rating tool (the back-end) are described in detail in the following chapters. In other words, as of the time of writing, Part 2 of this book (the following seventeen chapters) actually includes *more* detail than is in the back-end of the website.

This chapter outlines:
- What is the Corporate Sustainability Scorecard?
- Why this Scorecard?
- Who is the Scorecard intended for?
- How is the Scorecard structured?
- How do companies progress through the four stages?
- How should the Scorecard be used?
- Will the Scorecard change over time?
- How is Part 2 of this book organized?

What Is the Corporate Sustainability Scorecard?

The Corporate Sustainability Scorecard™ is a rating system developed by industry, for industry—to facilitate discussions in boardrooms and executive offices. The Scorecard is an on-line rating tool available to registered users. Visit: www.thesustainabilityscorecard.com for more information.

The Scorecard is designed to help companies answer the same question many CEOs and board members have asked the author: "How do we stack up today vis-à-vis sustainability as compared with competitors, best practices, and where leading companies are heading?" The Scorecard also helps executives map out where they want their companies to be tomorrow—given the competitive landscape, each company's ambitions, and the speed needed to win in the marketplace.

---

1 The website has a "front end" that is visible to all and a "back-end" that is visible only to registered users of the Scorecard. Unless you are a registered user, you will not see the back-end at this time.

DOI 10.1515/9781547400423-010

An example of a summary scorecard for a typical company is depicted in Figure 10.1.

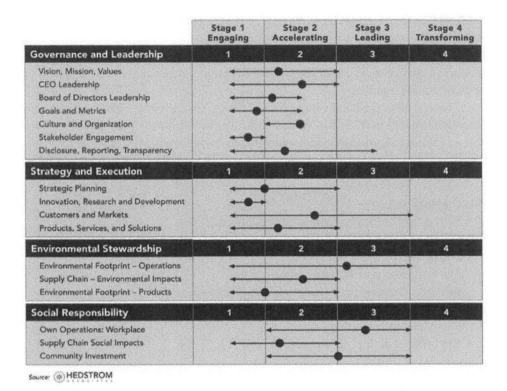

Figure 10.1: Example Corporate Sustainability Scorecard

Why this Scorecard?

There is no shortage of scorecards out there that companies are barraged by. Walmart has its scorecard. Dow Jones Sustainability Index and the various other corporate sustainability rating organizations each have some kind of template or methodology or scorecard to rate companies.

In stark contrast to the over 100 sustainability rating schemes in existence today, this Scorecard is focused on the aspects of running a business that matter most to boards of directors and C-suite executives. And, you rate your own company.

So why this one? Four reasons:

- *By Industry; for Industry.* The Scorecard has been used with the following companies in recent years: 3M, Air Products, Akzo Nobel, Anheuser-Busch, Ashland, Campbell Soup, Coca-Cola, Cytec, Deere, Dell, DuPont, Ford, Honeywell, HP, International Paper, Johnson & Johnson, Novartis, Novelis, Novo Nordisk, Pemex, Raytheon, SC Johnson, Shell, Sims Metal Management, UPS, USG, and Xerox. (Note: In some cases, the Scorecard was used as part of a Hedstrom Associates client assignment for the company; in other cases, the company used the Scorecard on its own.)
- *Full of Best-Practice Company Examples.* Several hundred examples are provided of companies that are considered to be in Stage 3 or Stage 4 for a particular attribute.
- *It Speaks the Language of the CEO and Board.* The seventeen individual elements that comprise the Corporate Sustainability Scorecard are purely business-focused. Each element (e.g., Culture and Organization; Strategic Planning; Innovation, Research and Development, etc.) is a major corporate function or activity on which CEOs and Boards of Directors spend considerable time.
- *Proven.* The Scorecard has been around for twenty years. In addition to the twenty-five to thirty companies that were involved with the Scorecard prior to 2016, an additional sixty major global companies all completed a company self-assessment in early 2018. These sixty companies found the Scorecard to be easy to use and applicable. They also provide some improvement suggestions that have been adopted in the on-line tool and are reflected in this book.

Who Is the Scorecard Intended for?

The Corporate Sustainability Scorecard™ C-suite rating system is designed for use by corporations—especially large corporations.

Though the Scorecard can be used by various individuals and groups within a company, the tool is designed primarily for use by (and discussions with) the executive team. Typically, use of the Scorecard is led by the officer who oversees internal sustainability efforts and reports to the CEO and Board of Directors (or Board Committee) about sustainability posture, programs, performance, and plans. The Scorecard places the entire sustainability conversation in a simple board-friendly context.

Corporate executives use the Scorecard to map their company's current position on a one-to-four maturity scale so that they can know with confidence:

- Where their company stacks up vis-à-vis sustainability (in other words, where they are on the maturity path)
- How their company compares with competitors and peers
- What "best practice" (defined as a Stage 3 or Stage 4 practice) looks like today

How Is the Scorecard Structured?

The Scorecard's summary table (depicted in Figure 10.1) is supported by a robust methodology. It is organized into:
- **Four Parts.** The four main sections of the Sustainability Scorecard include: *Governance and Leadership, Strategy and Execution, Environmental Stewardship*, and *Social Responsibility*.
- **Seventeen Elements**. Within the four parts described above, seventeen topics (elements) comprise the overall Corporate Sustainability Scorecard.
- **~150 KSIs.** For each of the seventeen elements of the Scorecard, executives rate the company on eight to twelve "sub-elements" "KSIs." (Note: The current version of the Scorecard has 147 KSIs. The precise number may vary slightly over time based on feedback from registered users of the Scorecard.)
- **~600 Descriptors.** In each of the following 17 chapters, small tables define the four stages of performance for each KSI.

The Four-Stage Transformation Model

Engaging, Accelerating, Leading, and Transforming

The Scorecard rating scale is deliberately tough. This is not your traditional rating scale where Stage 4 is the top quartile of companies today. The bell curve on this Scorecard is skewed left, reflecting the fact that the vast majority of companies today are early in their sustainability transformation (see Figure 10.1).

As depicted in Figure 1.3, the vast majority of companies today are in Stage 1 and Stage 2. The fundamental premise behind this Scorecard is that sustainability is about transformation; that is, virtually every old-school company must transform itself to survive and thrive.

A brief synopsis of the characteristics of the four stages of transformation follows.

Stage 1: "Engaging"—*Stage 1 companies engage with sustainability issues in a variety of ways, although they do not change their company or their businesses fundamentally.* These companies undertake important efforts to reduce impacts and drive environment, health, and safety (EHS) and social responsibility excellence. Sustainability efforts are often driven by the chief EHS officer in collaboration with the officer leading philanthropy and corporate citizenship initiatives. Environmental stewardship and social responsibility are considered the "right thing to do." Environmental management is largely about risk management. Social responsibility is about worker safety and health, diversity, community responsibility, and philanthropy.

Stage 1 companies are committed to compliance—not just with laws, regulations, and internal company standards, but also increasingly with industry codes of practice and de facto requirements, including the **Global Reporting Initiative (GRI)** sustainability reporting guidelines and other nongovernmental organization (NGO) expectations. Stage 1 companies implement strong programs to reduce energy use, greenhouse gas (GHG) emissions, and waste in their own operations. They also respond to environmental and social pressures throughout their supply chain.

Stage 1 companies tend to interact primarily with their industry peers; and they typically support positions endorsed by their major industry associations. These companies may partner with external stakeholders on selected initiatives. Many, but not all, Stage 1 companies publish external EHS and/or sustainability reports (or the equivalent on their websites).

In summary, Stage 1 companies do many good things. However, when viewed in hindsight from those who are leaders, Stage 1 companies essentially "dabble in sustainability," while they continue to make the same products they traditionally produced. For example, many chemical companies continue to churn out the same chemicals while cutting energy use; consumer products companies keep selling the same products while "tweaking around the edges"—cutting a little water use or packaging content; oil companies continue to produce oil while driving operational efficiencies.

Stage 2: "Accelerating"—As a key characteristic of Stage 2 companies, *the CEO explicitly recognizes the potential significance of sustainability—and launches a few key initiatives to position the company as a leader on a business-critical aspect of sustainability.* In some cases, the CEO sees sustainability issues not only as a source of risk, but also as a source of potential opportunity.

What separates Stage 2 companies from their Stage 1 counterparts? Notably, the CEO of a Stage 2 company personally stakes out a position that addresses a "material" environmental or social issue faced by the company and its industry. A **material** issue (Appendix A: Definitions) is much more than an important issue. Many Stage 1 and Stage 2 companies publish a "materiality assessment" that may identify twenty to forty or more important issues. Yet, in virtually every case, a company has only a small handful of truly material ESG issues. (See Chapter 8: Environmental Stewardship for a further discussion of materiality.)

In some cases, Stage 2 companies set forth CEO-driven and bold sustainability positioning and goals. Many companies (e.g., Alcoa, AT&T, Campbell Soup, FedEx, Ingersoll Rand, and J&J, among others) have done this with their GHG reduction goals. The CEO and other senior executives may weave sustainability into public statements and speeches. In other situations, the company achieves a breakthrough position on a key issue facing its industry. For example, many Stage 2 companies took a lead role in addressing key industry challenges such as electronic waste. As Stage 2 companies advance, they build a culture that values sustainability-related innovation. For example, they may focus on stakeholder partnerships on a major social or ecosystem issue.

Stage 2 companies have well-defined environmental and social management systems, though those processes tend to be *"bolted onto"* (rather than *"woven into"*) core business processes and business decisions. These companies have not changed their business models fundamentally.

Those in the manufacturing or process industries still largely operate in the traditional, linear, "take-make-waste" model, as contrasted with the new circular economy model. Those in the lighter footprint and service sectors remain focused on traditional customers, rather than also focusing on emerging middle class customers (at the bottom of the economic pyramid).

Stage 3: "Leading"—*Stage 3 companies begin to transform their business portfolios to leverage sustainability opportunities.* Moving beyond the few key CEO-driven sustainability initiatives of Stage 2 companies, the Stage 3 companies embody economist Joseph Schumpeter's concept of "creative destruction." They make strategic choices to divest "old economy" businesses and to invest in cleaner, greener, and more society-friendly enterprises.

Stage 3 companies take a longer-term view. They see the clean technology sector growing at double-digit rates—including products and processes that improve environmental performance in the construction, transport, energy, water, and waste industries. These companies want to be part of the "clean technology" revolution. They see massive growth opportunities in stabilizing atmospheric carbon concentrations, providing access to fresh water, and investing in smart cities. For example, more than any other major oil company globally, the French oil company, Total, sees electricity as a hedge against oil's eventual decline. Total is building a new business (akin to Ford's sustainable mobility business) around green energy, including batteries, solar, and other renewables.

Companies moving significantly into Stage 3 consider sustainability key to their organizations' long-term viability and value-creation. For example, NextEra Energy has made such a choice with its investments in renewable energy. Sustainability represents one or more platforms for top-line growth. Siemens sees the transition to a low-carbon economy as the biggest industrial challenge of this century. The company's *Environmental Portfolio* grew to almost half (46 percent) of the company's annual revenue in 2016. Stage 3 companies have a clear, focused strategy that places global environmental and social drivers at the core. They anticipate customer needs and future differentiators, as Toyota did with the Prius many years ago. A Stage 3 company is viewed internally and externally as open, transparent, innovative, and critically aware of risks and opportunities (e.g., SC Johnson and Nike have been systematically removing toxic materials from their products).

In making the decision to implement such significant changes, CEOs of Stage 3 companies begin the hard work of *weaving material ESG issues into the fabric of every critical business process, key business decision, and investment.* The key here is *material* as opposed to *important* ESG issues. For example, it is not likely material for a bank to reduce its water consumption, while it is material to change its investment criteria or lending policy to better reflect the ESG risks of its customers. This turns out to be a massive effort, as anyone close to the transformation of Novelis or Unilever can attest.

Stage 4: "Transforming"—*Stage 4 companies are evolving rapidly as models of twenty-first century corporations.* Those in the manufacturing or process industries (historically reliant on physical resources) live in the circular economy. For a pharmaceutical company, the issue is less about the circular economy and more about how many lives are improved as a result of access to medicines.

Sustainability is incorporated fully into the Stage 4 company's vision, mission, culture, business model, and goals. Each of these companies has a clearly defined roadmap for sustainable growth and profitability, which explicitly reflects the firm's responsibility to future generations. This commitment extends far beyond the CEO. In Stage 4 companies, *sustainability is integrated fully within all aspects of the business* as they move toward 100 percent renewable energy, closed-loop manufacturing, shifting from product to service to solution, and enhancing employee and community health.

The focus of these companies remains steadfast on long-term profitability and growth, while also helping to solving the world's toughest problems. Tesla CEO Elon Musk embodies many of these attributes, though not without some controversy. He points to Tesla's huge "gigafactory" in Nevada as a model for one way to *transition the entire world to sustainable energy.* At the same time, Musk may not have sufficiently addressed the disposal of lithium batteries and he also is criticized for focusing on space exploitation while there are giant problems on our planet crying for attention.

Though *no major company today is solidly in Stage 4,* a growing number of companies have some Stage 4 attributes. They fall into two groups: young, innovative, sharing-economy companies, such as, Google, and Tesla; and old-line companies, such as BASF, Philips, Siemens, Unilever, and Waste Management.

How Should the Scorecard Be Used?

As you consider where your company (as well as your competitors and customers) sits across the four-stage model, keep these points in mind:

– *There is no inherently right or wrong place to be on this continuum.* The Corporate Sustainability Scorecard focuses on progressing through various stages. "Right" or "wrong" depends on timing. Certainly, examples exist of Stage 3 and Stage 4 companies that have faltered, and of Stage 1 and Stage 2 companies that have looked wise in hindsight.

– *Don't be surprised if your company is largely in Stage 1.* The majority of companies find that many attributes of their company are in Stage 1 today—or were until fairly recently. Even if your company is predominantly in Stage 2 or above, the

chances are that you have many internal activities and core business processes that remain in Stage 1.
- *Moving at the right speed at the right time is essential.* Companies move at different speeds. DuPont began early and moved systematically from Stage 1 to Stage 3. *GE* decided in 2005 that it was "behind the game" and needed to leapfrog beyond competitors and peers as it moved very quickly from Stage 1 to Stage 3.
- *A key point to keep in mind.* While it is convenient to express a company as being "in Stage 1" or "a Stage 2 company," in reality, most companies exhibit a range of attributes that fall across several stages of maturity on this scorecard.

The Scorecard is designed not only as a tool, but also as a collaborative learning process. Companies have successfully used it in facilitated meetings of the C-suite, board, or a senior cross-functional team. Having identified very clearly how their company "stacks up" today, C-suite executives use the Scorecard to engage in a typically deep and profound discussion of how they want to position the company for future growth—leveraging the mega-trends impacting society.

Individuals can gain access to the online rating tool by visiting www.thesustainabilityscorecard.com and reviewing the various "Join" options. Individuals who meet the join criteria become a "registered user" and receive a username and password, providing access to the "back end" of the website with the full rating system.

Will the Scorecard Change over Time?

A final point: While the Hedstrom Associates team does not expect the fundamental structure of the Scorecard to change, we do anticipate that over time the individual KSIs—and the descriptors of those KSIs for Stages 1–4—will evolve. Moreover, we expect the hundreds of best practice company examples to change on a continuing basis. Users are encouraged to submit their own suggestions of a Stage 3 or Stage 4 practice (of their own company or of a company they admire). The Hedstrom Associates team will continue to update the downloadable scorecard templates periodically and provide those to registered users on www.thesustainabilityscorecard.com.

Organization of Part 2

The seventeen chapters that follow present the seventeen elements of the Scorecard. These chapters follow a similar structure:
- A definition of what is meant by the Scorecard element, the key question it aims to address, and an example of a company best practice
- A brief overview of how the individual key sustainability indicators (KSIs) are grouped under several headings

-   Descriptions of the eight to twelve KSIs—including a small table defining the KSI and including brief descriptors of Stage 1 through Stage 4
-   Bulleted lists of "best practice company examples" (which we define as being in Stage 3 or beyond) for each KSI
-   Final thoughts on what the data shows from the initial group of companies completing the Scorecard

---

NOTE: The KSI numbering is off by ten, meaning that the next chapter is Chapter 11, dealing with the first element of the Scorecard. Thus, the KSIs in Chapter 11 and in each subsequent chapter are off by ten.

Chapter 11
Vision, Mission, and Values

The Scorecard begins by examining (in the Governance section) the essence of any corporation or enterprise: its stated vision, mission (or purpose), and core values. This is the starting point for any company (its reason for existing)—and thus a logical starting point for the Scorecard.

Ashland recently revised its corporate vision and mission statements to align more directly with the realities of twentieth-first century growth. Ashland's *old vision* was "To be viewed as the best specialty chemical company in the world." *The company's new vision is* "To make a better world by providing creative solutions through the application of specialty ingredients and materials."[i]

Having some strong reference to a sustainability-related issue in a company's publicly stated corporate vision or mission statement—or statement of core values—can be incredibly powerful. This type of reference is not only for "tree-hugging companies" like Patagonia or Toms of Maine, as the Ashland example above illustrates. The key question for every company is this:

Key Question: How are sustainability and the drive to deliver long-term value to society integrated into our company's vision, mission and core values?

To help answer this key question, the Scorecard analyzes how companies manage and perform in three areas:
- The public statements articulating a company's *raison d'etre* (reason for existing)
- The less formal but critically important private actions to reinforce sustainability in the company's vision, mission, and values
- External recognition for sustainability programs and performance

Within each of these areas, executives evaluate their company performance from Stage 1 to Stage 4 on several key sustainability indicators (KSIs).

Public Statements

When some commitment to the role your company plays in "making the world a better place" is set in stone in a company's guiding public documents, this can be a powerful hook on which to hang many sustainability initiatives. The references to ESG matters can be quite subtle—yet still powerful.

The Scorecard addresses these public statements with four KSIs—dealing with how the CEO views the role of the company in society; the words used in the vision

DOI 10.1515/9781547400423-011

and mission statements as well as the core values; and public support of international sustainability charters.

KSI 1.1: CEO's View Regarding Role of Company in Society. What the CEO says—either publicly to external audiences (investors, customers, community groups, etc.) or internally to employees (all hands meetings, videos to staff, etc.) is often the most important indication of where sustainability stacks up on the list of important priorities. And, when a CEO repeats a key message (or fails to), this also sends a message.

The table below, describing a range of industry responses, depicts the rating criteria on the website (as of publication). For each KSI, I will summarize the KSI and provide a brief description of the four stages companies use to rate themselves. Each description of the stage is based on my review of leading company practices globally over the past twenty years. Thus, the rating criteria are based on actual industry practices of pioneer companies leading the way.

KSI	Stage 1	Stage 2	Stage 3	Stage 4
CEO's View Regarding the Role of the Company in Society	Typical of most industry peers over the past ten years; role is to create shareholder value	Sustainability ("S") is part of how the company sees its role in society	"S" is near the core of how the company sees its role in society	"S" is at the core of how the company sees its role in society; aligned with **circular economy**

Listed below (and throughout the rest of this and subsequent chapters) are individual company examples. In each case, the example is one that would be characterized as Stage 3 or higher.

- **Interface:** The carpet company founder, Ray Anderson's early vision was to lead the way to the next industrial revolution by becoming the first sustainable corporation, and eventually a restorative enterprise. This led to "Mission Zero® promise to eliminate any negative impact the company has on the environment by 2020."[ii]
- **Patagonia:** Founder Yvon Chouinard has built the company challenging conventional wisdom, aiming to create a profitable company without losing your soul. The company's mission statement is "Build the best product, cause no unnecessary harm, use business to inspire and implement solutions to the environmental crisis." He first codified his view of how a company can do good in the publication, "Let My people Go Surfing."[iii]

KSI 1.2: Sustainability in Corporate Vision and Mission. Virtually every company has a publicly stated vision and mission statement. Though the names vary, the *vision* statement describes what the company aims to create; the *mission* or purpose statement articulates the company's core reason for being.

Companies address this in a range of ways depicted below:

KSI	Stage 1	Stage 2	Stage 3	Stage 4
Sustainability in Corporate Vision and Mission	**Sustainability principles** are not explicitly embedded; vision / mission can enable sustainability	Enables, facilitates, and encourages "S"– it is "part of what we do"	"S" is integral to vision and mission; bold "S" statement; requires significant investment	Transforming the corporation to drive the **circular economy**; goal of being **net neutral** (ultimately restorative) impact

Listed below are some examples of Stage 3 or higher practices:
- **DuPont:** While the company has merged with Dow Chemical and is in the process of spinning into three separate companies, DuPont's long-stated mission is worth remembering for its simplicity: "Our mission is sustainable growth."[iv]
- **Zipcar:** The company aims "to enable simple and responsible urban living."[v]

KSI 1.3: Sustainability in Core Values and Corporate Policies. For some companies, the most powerful point of leverage for its sustainability initiatives—and especially for potentially contentious **key business decisions (KBDs)**—is not in its vision or mission but in its core values. The range of approaches is depicted below.

KSI	Stage 1	Stage 2	Stage 3	Stage 4
Sustainability in Core Values & Corporate Policies	Formal business ethics policies & controls are broadly communicated	Employees, customers, and investors view company as committed to "S"	Robust ESG posture is fully woven into core values and policies	A balance in creating economic value and value for society

Here are some highly regarded references to sustainability principles in company statements of core values:
- **Johnson & Johnson:** The venerable company has long had its culture rooted in "Our Credo."[vi]
- **Lloyds of London:** Generally known simply as Lloyds, the organization is not actually an insurance company, but rather operates as a marketplace. Regarding environmental, social, and governance (ESG), Lloyds excluded coal companies from its investment strategy by April 2018.[vii]
- **Ricoh:** The company's Values statement: "To be one global company, we must care about people, our profession, our society, and our planet."[viii]

- **SC Johnson:** One of the world's leading producers of household products, the (more than a century old) company summarized its business principles as "This We Believe" articulating the company's "values in relation to the five groups of stakeholders to whom we are responsible and whose trust we have to earn."[ix]

KSI 1.4: Support of International Sustainability Charters or Commitments. Over the years, there have been a variety of global ESG-related charters or "codes of conduct" that companies could—at their choosing—decide to subscribe to. Perhaps the best known is the United Nations Global Compact—an initiative launched in 2000 to encourage businesses worldwide to adopt sustainable and socially responsible policies, and to report on their implementation. Perhaps not surprisingly, many of the initial signatory companies to United Nations Global Compact (UNGC) were European-based ones.

Companies today address this in a range of ways:

KSI	Stage 1	Stage 2	Stage 3	Stage 4
Support of International Sustainability Charters or Commitments	Conform to common industry guidelines (e.g., Responsible Care or Global Reporting Initiative)	Conform to highest industry "S" initiatives (e.g., green chemistry)	Support leading global charters (e.g., UNGC) as signatory or equivalent	Leading corporate efforts to drive growth and value from the Sustainable Development Goals (SDGs)

A report issued in April 2018 identified which global companies lead in strategic lobbying for the ambitions of the Paris Agreement. The study rated companies on the extent to which they exhibit leadership within their sector, the "engagement intensity" of their efforts, and their overall posture toward ambitions climate policy. The "A-List of 20 Climate Policy Leaders included: Tesla, AkzoNobel, Royal DSM, Unilever, Coca-Cola, Nestlé, GSK, ABB, and Siemens, among others.[x]

Some additional examples of Stage 3 or higher practices include:
- **Marriott:** Now the largest hotel chain in the world, Marriott is working to address a set of 17 sustainable development goals (SDGs) to end poverty, fight inequality and injustice, and tackle climate change by 2030. Working to address UN SDGs, it achieved 13.2 percent energy intensity reduction in 2015.[xi]
- **BASF, Bayer, Deutsche Bank AG, Deutsche Telekom AG, Nike, Nestlé, Novartis, Rio Tinto, SAP, Shell, Statoil, UBS, and Unilever:** Among the inaugural signatories to the United Nations Global Compact.[xii]

- **Amgen, Campbell Soup, CVS, Hess Corporation, DuPont, Intel, Kimberly-Clark, Johnson Controls, and Lexmark:** Among U.S. companies that since became signatories to the United Nations Global Compact.[xiii]
- **Unilever:** The company endorsed the UN Guiding Principles on Business and Human Rights.[xiv]

Private Actions to Reinforce Sustainability in Vision, Mission, and Values

All the stuff above relates to public actions. Where the rubber meets the road is what happens internally within the company. Actions by CEOs to reinforce sustainability principles in the vision mission, and values run the gamut.

The Scorecard addresses these private actions with two KSIs: one dealing with managing the long-term viability of the core businesses and a second that looks at how ESG principles are factored into KBDs.

KSI 1.5: Managing the Long-Term Viability of Core Businesses. The concept of creative destruction—coined in the 1950s by economist Joseph Schumpeter—is core to sustainability. How do leading companies systematically invest in new technologies and businesses that will drive tomorrow's growth—while at the same time exiting those "old" businesses that may not be aligned to tomorrow's customer needs?

The range of industry responses follows:

KSI	Stage 1	Stage 2	Stage 3	Stage 4
Managing Long-Term Viability of Core Businesses	May or may not align with **sustainability principles**	Aligned with sustainability principles— either as is or by reframing	Fully aligned with sustainability principles	Driving the global sustainability agenda

Two good examples of leading practices include:
- **Waste Management:** The waste services company has transformed itself from simply hauling away customer's waste to helping its customers *reduce* waste.[xv]
- **Novelis:** The leading producer of flat-rolled aluminum products and the world's largest recycler of aluminum has made a commitment to sustainability that is core to our business operations and extends to how the company partners with stakeholders across the aluminum value chain.[xvi]

KSI 1.6: KBDs tied to Core Values. We define *KBDs* as the handful of major decisions the CEO and **board** make each year—typically involving mergers, acquisitions or divestitures; large capital expenditures; new product launches; major research and development expenditures, etc. The range of ways ESG elements are incorporated into KBDs follows.

KSI	Stage 1	Stage 2	Stage 3	Stage 4
Key business decisions (KBDs) tied to Core Values	ESG elements in core values remain "on the conference room wall"	ESG elements in core values openly discussed and they "rule" during crises	ESG elements in core values drive KBDs	ESG elements in core values are the basis for "all" business decisions

It is instructive to look back into history a bit for some KBDs that were affected by what today we call sustainability principles.

- **BHP Billiton:** One of the world's largest coal companies, BHP Billiton announced plans to end its relationship with the World Coal Association due to the international lobby group's stance on climate change. BHP is also reviewing its relationship with the U.S. Chamber of Commerce in light of the Trump administration's decision to withdraw from the Paris climate accord. The company stated that "the warming of the climate is unequivocal, the human influence is clear and physical impacts are unavoidable."[xvii]
- **Johnson & Johnson:** In 1982, seven people died after Tylenol capsules were laced with cyanide; J&J recalled 31 million bottles helped J&J maintain their 30 percent share of the market.[xviii]
- **Disney:** Employees all know the core values of: Safety, Courtesy, Show, and Efficiency.[xix]
- **IBM:** The company decided in 2003 to undertake the first disciplined reexamination of the company's values in nearly 100 years. They ran a Values Jam—to define the essence of the company.[xx]

In each of these examples, the company directly embedded ESG issues into the core values that employees often hear about.

External Recognition

The author conducted a detailed review of third party sustainability ratings and rankings. Companies obviously try to put their best foot forward in presenting data for such ratings; as a result, they sometimes should be taken with a grain of salt. However, since the leading rating agencies do have robust methodologies for analyzing companies, we have included them in our Scorecard.

The Scorecard addresses external recognition with two KSIs: one dealing with ratings specific to sustainability; and a second that looks at ethics and trust ratings.

KSI 1.7: *Sustainability Ratings and Rankings.* There are currently over 100 sustainability-related ratings, rankings, and awards. Each of these has its origin in a different set of circumstances; each ranking owner has its own agenda. A number of these are well-established, global ratings, supported by a reasonable methodology with varying degrees of transparency. Among the most common are:

- Barrons launched its *100 Most Sustainable Companies* list in 2018, which ranks companies according to their performance in five categories: shareholders, customers, employees, planet and community.
- Bloomberg *ESG Scorecard* uses publicly available information to assess transparency (not performance).
- CDP (formerly Carbon Disclosure Project) invites companies to respond to a detailed questionnaire and provides a score for each module (climate, forests, water).
- Corporate Knights *Global 100* index ranks the world's most sustainable companies based on fourteen ESG indicators (released annually in conjunction with the World Economic Forum in Davos).
- *CR Magazine* annual list of *100 Best Corporate Citizens*, ranks Russell 1,000 companies on ESG performance.
- EcoVadis invites companies to respond to a survey to assess overall CSR performance.
- ECPI operates primarily in Europe to assess company and country level information that is publicly available.
- FTSE4Good assesses circa 4,000 companies on 300 ESG indicators across 14 themes
- MSCI provides an overall company ESG rating (AAA to CCC) based on a review of publicly available information.
- Newsweek's *Green Rankings* evaluates the 500 largest global and U.S. companies based on sustainability performance.
- Oekom takes a hybrid approach (publicly available information and company interviews)
- Reprisk, a research organization (not a rating agency) uses publicly available information to provide risk research
- RobecoSAM publishes the *Dow Jones Sustainability Indices* based on responses to a very detailed questionnaire; invitations are sent to about 3,400 companies (of which roughly 25–30 percent respond).
- ShareAction, introduced in 2017, invites FTSE 50 companies (plus another twenty-five companies) to respond to a detailed questionnaire.
- STOXX Global ESG Indices uses ESG indicators provided by Sustainalytics.

- Sustainalytics assesses over 7,000 companies globally on a comprehensive set of ESG indicators (both core and industry-specific).
- Thomson Reuters uses publicly available data to assess over 6,000 companies globally on ESG.
- Vigeo Eiris (and Euronext Vigeo), an independent provider of global ESG research and services, uses publicly available data to assess thirty-eight ESG criteria.
- Workforce Disclosure Initiative, piloted in 2017, reviews information based on a questionnaire response

Many large companies are involved in some way with some of these external ratings.

KSI	Stage 1	Stage 2	Stage 3	Stage 4
Sustainability Ratings and Rankings	Limited or no engagement with external raters	Actively respond; gain external recognition for ESG strengths	Engage with ESG raters to drive stronger performance	Recognized as a model ESG performer

Below are some examples of companies that have been rated highly on several of these external rankings.

- **Caesars:** The world's most geographically diversified gaming company has received over fifty awards and certifications for sustainability leadership.[xxi]
- **Cisco:** In addition to being on CDP Leadership Index (six years) and the Dow Jones Sustainability Index, was rated third on the Corporate Knights Global 100 most sustainable corporations in the world list in 2017.[xxii]
- **Ingersoll Rand:** The global industrial company was selected to Dow Jones Sustainability World Index in 2017 for the seventh consecutive year.[xxiii]
- **Novo Nordisk:** The Danish pharmaceutical company has often been rated highly on DJSI, CDP and the Global 100.
- **SAP:** The information technology giant was named the world's most sustainable software company by DJSI for the 11th consecutive year.[xxiv]
- **Westpac Banking:** The Australian bank was not only named top company on the Global 100 list, but is also rated highly in: DJSI, CDP, FTSE4Good, and World's Most Ethical Companies.

In each of these company examples, companies moved beyond simply seeking recognition to also using these ratings to drive performance improvement.

In an interesting newer development, Fast Company announced winners of its second annual World Changing Ideas Awards, which recognize twelve companies, initiatives, concepts, and projects that are "poised to help shift society to a more sustainable and more equitable future."[xxv] Among the 2018 winners were Dell (ocean-bound plastics packaging); HP Inc. (ink cartridges from recycled bottles); Mastercard (2Kuze); Microsoft (Digital Geneva Convention); and Siemens (electrified highway).

KSI 1.8: Ethics and Trust Ratings. Because the link between sustainability and core values is critical for many companies, we include in the Scorecard a review of ethics and trust ratings. Unlike the general sustainability ratings described above, there are few ethics and trust ratings. Two of the best known are Ethisphere's annual list of the World's Most Ethical Companies and the Reputation Institute's Global RepTrak 100, which measures the public's perception of corporations based on innovation, governance, citizenship, leadership, and the like.

Ethisphere's research found that the listed World's Most Ethical Companies outperformed the large cap sector over five years by 10.72 percent and over three years by 4.88 percent. Ethisphere refers to this as the *Ethics Premium*.[xxvi]

The Reputation Institute notes that 2018 represents a strategic inflection point, with an overall decline in reputation for the first time since the end of the Great Recession. They summarized the 2018 winners as companies that are better at navigating macroeconomic and societal headwinds.[xxvii]

KSI	Stage 1	Stage 2	Stage 3	Stage 4
Ethics and Trust Ratings	Limited or no engagement with external raters	Actively respond; gain external recognition for ESG strengths	Engage with ESG raters to drive stronger performance	Recognized as a model ESG performer

- **3M, Accenture, Cisco, Colgate Palmolive, Dell, Eastman, Ecolab, Eli Lilly, Ford, Marriott, Mastercard, Microsoft, NextEra Energy, Praxair, Starbucks, UPS, Waste Management, and Xerox** are among the top-rated companies by Ethisphere.[xxviii]
- **Rolex, The LEGO Group, Google, Canon, Walt Disney, Sony, Adidas, Robert Bosch, BMW and Microsoft** comprised the top ten in 2018.
- **Johnson Controls:** Integrity is at the core of business practices.[xxix]

In each of these examples, the company places a very high priority on being recognized externally for its ethics and values—and in most cases also links those values to its sustainability positioning.

How Do Companies Stack Up?

Starting in 2018, we are capturing data from a group of founding participants—invited to use the Scorecard for a company self-assessment and to provide feedback. As we

assess the data from the first 60 companies (all Fortune 500 or equivalent), three key messages stand out:
- Thirty-seven of sixty companies say their CEO's view places sustainability near the core of how the company sees its role in society.
- Thirty-two of sixty say sustainability is integral to the company's vision and mission, with bold sustainability statements requiring significant investment
- Only twenty-six of sixty see that their core businesses are fully aligned with sustainability principles—suggesting that portfolio changes to the business in the coming years will be necessary.

A bar chart depicting this final point is shown in Figure 11.1 below. As the figure illustrates, of the twenty-six companies that see their core businesses aligned with sustainability; seven rated their company Stage 3; 13 rated their company at Stage 3.5, and six rated their company Stage 4 (the highest possible rating).

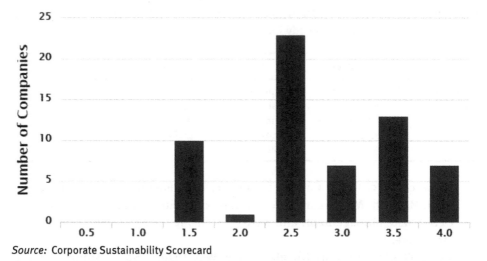

Source: Corporate Sustainability Scorecard

Figure 11.1: Scorecard Data from 60 on KSI 1.5: Managing the Long-Term Viability of Core Businesses

In summary, while many CEOs view sustainability as being integral to their company's role in society, the current degree of confidence in the long-term viability of the core businesses is markedly less positive.

i http://www.ashland.com/about/ashland-way

ii https://www.interface.com/US/en-US/about/mission/Our-Mission

iii https://www.patagonia.com/company-info.html

iv http://www.dupont.ca/en/corporate-functions/our-approach/sustainability/commitments.html

v http://www.zipcar.com/mission

vi https://www.jnj.com/about-jnj/jnj-credo

vii https://www.theguardian.com/business/2018/jan/21/lloyds-of-london-to-divest-from-coal-over-climate-change

viii https://www.ricoh.com/about/commitment/philosophy/

ix http://www.scjohnson.com/en/company/principles.aspx

x https://influencemap.org/site/data/000/308/Climate_Policy_Leaders_April_2018.pdf

xi http://www.marriott.com/corporate-social-responsibility/corporate-environmental-responsibility.mi

xii https://www.unglobalcompact.org/what-is-gc/participants/search?page=1&search%5Bkeywords%5D=&search%5Bper_page%5D=10&search%5Bsort_direction%5D=asc&search%5Bsort_field%5D=joined_on&utf8=%E2%9C%93

xiii https://www.unglobalcompact.org/what-is-gc/participants/search?page=1&search%5Bcountries%5D%5B%5D=209&search%5Bengagement_tiers%5D%5B%5D=1&search%5Bkeywords%5D=&search%5Bper_page%5D=10&search%5Bsort_direction%5D=asc&search%5Bsort_field%5D=type&utf8=%E2%9C%93

xiv https://www.unilever.com/sustainable-living/enhancing-livelihoods/fairness-in-the-workplace/advancing-human-rights-in-our-own-operations/

xv https://www.forbes.com/2010/05/03/david-steiner-waste-management-leadership-managing-reiss.html#183c2986754d

xvi http://novelis.com/about-us/

xvii https://www.nytimes.com/2017/12/19/business/energy-environment/australia-mining-company-climate-change.html

xviii https://www.nytimes.com/2002/03/23/your-money/tylenol-made-a-hero-of-johnson-johnson-the-recall-that-started.html

xix http://disneyatwork.com/disneys-four-keys-to-a-great-guest-experience/

xx https://www.ibm.com/ibm/values/us/

xxi https://sloanreview.mit.edu/case-study/how-caesars-entertainment-is-betting-on-sustainability/

xxii http://www.corporateknights.com/magazines/2017-global-100-issue/2017-global-100-results-14846083/

xxiii https://3blmedia.com/News/Ingersoll-Rand-Selected-2017-Dow-Jones-Sustainability-World-and-North-America-Indices-Seventh

xxiv https://news.sap.com/sap-named-worlds-most-sustainable-software-company-in-the-dow-jones-sustainability-indices-for-11th-consecutive-year/

xxv https://www.fastcompany.com/40532898/2018-world-changing-ideas-awards-winners

xxvi https://ethisphere.com/2018-worlds-most-ethical-companies/

xxvii https://blog.reputationinstitute.com/2018/03/15/what-it-takes-to-be-a-top-10-most-reputable-company-worldwide-in-2018/

xxviii http://www.worldsmostethicalcompanies.com/past-honorees/

xxix https://valuesfirst.johnsoncontrols.com/

Chapter 12
CEO Leadership

Any significant change initiative or major strategic thrust of a company starts at the top. Thus, CEO leadership is the second element of the Scorecard, after the company's vision, mission, and values.

Shortly after being named CEO of Waste Management, Inc., in 2004, David Steiner and his management team faced what could be considered a nightmare. Increasingly, their customers were embracing the concept of "zero waste." That was good news for the environment, but not for the biggest trash hauler in the United States. Consequently, Steiner looked for ways to extract value from the waste stream. The company introduced a new service: counseling large customers on how to reduce their waste. By 2017, "green services" accounted for half of Waste Management's revenue.

Current Waste Management CEO Jim Fish has taken the company's sustainability platform even further, identifying the environment as Waste Management's fifth and only silent constituent, joining employees, customers, shareholders and communities. Fish explains it this way, "As an environmental services company, we see our role as taking care of the environment and being a voice for this voiceless constituent. It's our business, our livelihood and our mission. *It's what we do.*"

Waste Management illustrates the key question every company should ask when candidly (and confidentially) assessing its sustainability position.

Key Question: How deeply engaged is our CEO and C-suite in spreading the "S"/ESG message; stimulating robust board discussions; and building accountability and leadership for sustainability?

To help answer this key question, the Scorecard analyzes how companies manage and perform in three areas:
- CEO engagement with sustainability—specifically how CEOs manages their time and resources to drive sustainability throughout the company
- Managing agendas of the board of directors (or equivalent if a private company) to ensure proper time and discussion of key environmental, social, and governance (ESG) issues
- Structuring the sustainability organization and initiatives within the company

Within each of these areas, executives evaluate their company performance on several key sustainability indicators (KSI).

DOI 10.1515/9781547400423-012

CEO Engagement with Sustainability

The level of interest CEOs have demonstrated in ESG issues has consistently risen over the past decade. In 2015, sustainability became a top five issue on The Conference Board's annual survey—then titled CEO Challenge Survey. Prior to that, sustainability had rated between six and nine on the top ten; since then it has remained in the top five.

At a meeting in early 2018 a group chief sustainability officers from sixty-three large, mostly U.S. companies said that over the past year, the level of interest by my CEO in sustainability/ESG has stayed about the same (38 percent); increased somewhat (37 percent) and increased significantly (24 percent). Only 2 percent said it had declined somewhat.

Transforming a company to be positioned for value creation in the sustainability era is incredibly challenging. It can be messy. While some CEOs appear to be successful in navigating this transformation, other CEOs have lost their jobs, arguably by moving too quickly. David Crane, the charismatic former CEO of power company NRG, is widely regarded as a sustainability visionary. He led NRG through a major transformation before finding that he and his board could not agree on executing some of the key fundamentals of the business.

The Scorecard addresses CEO engagement with sustainability with five KSIs: external speeches by the CEO; meetings and engagement with investors, customers, and employees; and the key sources of how the CEO learns about ESG issues and trends.

KSI 2.1: Speeches on Sustainability by CEO and C-Suite Executives. Looking back over the past several decades, some of the most powerful launches of major company sustainability thrusts have been with public speeches by the CEO. Companies today— large and small, public and private—can learn from this.

The range of current industry activity regarding CEO speeches on sustainability is as follows.

KSI	Stage 1	Stage 2	Stage 3	Stage 4
Speeches on Sustainability by CEO and C-Suite Executives	Little mention of "S" or major negative environmental or social impacts of company/ sector	Mentions "S" regarding risk/**footprint** reduction—also part of growth strategy	CEO is a "S" leader in sector; bold "S" goals and policy stance	Material ESG risks/ opportunities are core to many CEO speeches

Some examples of powerful CEO speeches on sustainability:

- **General Mills:** CEO Ken Powell told the Associated Press in 2015, "We think that human-caused greenhouse gas causes climate change and climate volatility, and that's going to stress the agricultural supply chain."[i]
- **IBM:** Sam Palmisano launched *Smarter Planet* with a keynote speech at the Council on Foreign Relations in 2008.[ii]
- **Unilever:** CEO Paul Polman launched the *Sustainable Living Plan* in November 2010—simultaneously in London, Rotterdam, New Delhi, and New York. Polman explained: "We have ambitious plans to grow the company. But growth at any price is not viable. We have to develop new ways of doing business which will ensure that our growth does not come at the expense of the world's diminishing natural resources." [iii]
- **Walmart:** In an October 2005 speech broadcast to all 1.6 million employees in all 6,000-plus stores (and shared with some 60,000 suppliers worldwide), CEO H. Lee Scott Jr. announced a commitment to three ambitious goals: "To be supplied 100 percent by renewable energy; to create zero waste; and to sell products that sustain our resources and the environment."[iv]

In each of these above examples, the CEO used a public speech to not only deliver a key message externally—but to also instruct and align employees behind the (often) new direction.

KSI 2.2: CEO Messages Regarding Sustainability to Shareholders. As noted previously in Chapter 2: Why Bother? on January 2018, Larry Fink, CEO of BlackRock—the largest investor in the world—wrote a letter to CEOs. In it he did not use "the S word" (which I applaud); but he did say: "To prosper over time, every company must not only deliver financial performance, but also show how it makes a positive contribution to society." Thus, a CEO's messages to shareholders is more important than ever.

KSI	Stage 1	Stage 2	Stage 3	Stage 4
CEO Messages Regarding Sustainability to Shareholders	Little proactive sharing of "S"/ ESG risks or opportunities	Mentions "S"/ ESG risks, but not core to analyst meetings	Proactively discusses "S"/ ESG risks and opportunities with investors	CEO sees role in part as teaching value of "S"/ ESG to investors

Perhaps the best example of a CEO's messages on sustainability to shareholders comes from **Unilever.** On his first day in office in January 2009, CEO Paul Polman put investors on notice—that Unilever is taking a longer view and is not interested in investors who demand results quarterly.[v]

DTE Energy CEO Gerry Anderson won the Individual Leadership Award at the 2018 Climate Leadership Conference (supported by Bloomberg Philanthropies). The award recognized individuals demonstrating extraordinary leadership both in addressing climate change and engaging their organization, peers, and partners.[vi]

KSI 2.3: CEO/C-Suite Meetings with Customers Regarding Sustainability. Many years ago, I sat with the vice president of environment and sustainability at a six billion dollar chemical company and he reviewed his sustainability pitch he would be making to his board of directors. The entire reason sustainability was on the C-suite and board agenda was because a key customer based in Scandinavia was asking about the company's work in this space.

The range of industry activity regarding C-suite meetings with customers on ESG issues follows.

KSI	Stage 1	Stage 2	Stage 3	Stage 4
CEO and C-Suite Meetings with Customers Regarding Sustainability	Respond to customer requests regarding sustainability	Understand customers' "S" goals; share "S" strategy and invite dialogue	Partner with customers for "S" innovation and growth	Major customers and market segments for "S" offerings are key to growth

Waste Management: A 2010 Forbes article titled "Saving the Planet while Generating a Profit" discussed how (then) Waste Management CEO David Steiner transformed the company from a disposal company wanting customers to *increase* waste to a services company helping its customers *reduce* waste.[vii] Since that time, the company has deepened its investment in working with customers to provide a wide range of waste solutions.

KSI 2.4: CEO Messages to Employees Regarding Sustainability. When CEOs hold "all employee" or "all hands" meetings, these provide an excellent forum for rolling out new initiatives and for reinforcing how sustainability is "just part of the way we do things around here."

KSI	Stage 1	Stage 2	Stage 3	Stage 4
CEO Messages to Employees Regarding Sustainability	CEO and C-suite encourage basic EHS and citizenship efforts	CEO and C-suite launch "S" teams to drive initiatives	CEO and C-suite personally lead key initiatives and promote others	CEO and C-suite actively promote "S" team efforts; reward accomplishments

The level of interest in sustainability by the general employee population is growing. In the same Conference Board poll mentioned earlier of sixty-three large companies in early 2018, 65 percent of companies said the level of interest by employees in ESG had increased over the previous 12 months; 15 percent said it had increased significantly.

Hang Seng Bank (Hong Kong): Referring to employees as ambassadors, relationship builders, and the public face of our business, the company in 2013 placed a high priority on attracting, developing and engaging staff with open, candid, two-way internal communication through many sustainability initiatives.[viii]

KSI 2.5: CEO's Sources of Sustainability Learning. There are many ways CEOs learn about sustainability and ESG issues. While the range of activities is depicted below, CEOs often learn through discussions with other CEOs, meetings with customers, competitive benchmarking, reading business books and articles, and increasingly preparation for investor discussions.

KSI	Stage 1	Stage 2	Stage 3	Stage 4
CEO's Sources of Sustainability Learning	Industry associations and "safe" NGOs	NGO partners; CEOs of most advanced "S: companies	**External Sustainability Advisory Board** (or equivalent)	Global NGO leaders, including those from more challenging NGOs

Most CEOs at companies rated highly on the Scorecard say that a key part of their learning is bringing the outside world in—namely from discussions with external stakeholders. Paul Tebo, longtime chief sustainability officer of DuPont, said that he learned from the "radical fringe" NGOs. Here are two other examples:

- **Dow Chemical:** Since its formation in 1992, the company's External Sustainability Advisory Council (SEAC) had a major influence on Dow's approach to environment, health and safety, and sustainability issues, and played a critical role in developing Dow's 2015 Sustainability Goals.[ix]
- **Walmart:** In 2005, (then) CEO Lee Scott launched the company on a bold environmental initiative—aiming for zero waste to landfill and dramatic greenhouse gas reductions. In 2007, he teamed with Environmental Defense Fund (EDF) CEO Fred Krupp. EDF opened an office in Bentonville, Arkansas in 2007 so it could have direct access to Walmart. It does not accept contributions from Walmart or other corporations it works with.[x]

In both examples, the company reached outside to highly-respected experts to help challenge and shape the company's sustainability positioning and future direction.

Managing Board Agendas

CEOs play a key role in deciding what the agendas will be—and especially the content that will be presented at board meetings—those of various standing board committees and of the full board.

KSI 2.6: Board Agendas Regarding Sustainability. One of the key roles a CEO normally has is overseeing and having a heavy hand in shaping how the time is spent in board meetings. The Scorecard now incorporates both board committee meetings and full board meetings under KSI. (Initially, we had these as separate KSIs, but we combined them based on feedback from Scorecard users. The important factors in board ESG reporting are the amount of time spent, the topics covered, and the degree of deep engagement. Whether the board interaction is at a committee level or the full board is less important.)

The range of activity regarding ESG topics on board agendas follows.

KSI	Stage 1	Stage 2	Stage 3	Stage 4
Board Agendas Regarding Sustainability	Main topics covered are EHS; "S" trends and emerging issues; philanthropy; competitive analysis of peer company "S" actions	Material ESG risks and opportunities are a main agenda item at least 2x/ year; includes benchmark data and trends	Planned "S" learning is part of meetings; Board members are actively engaged in "S" discussions between meetings	"S" is core to all key meetings, discussions and business decisions; Board meetings held in conjunction with "S" learning (site visit)

Information about the content of board agendas is highly confidential—and typically not publicly available. Based on the author's experience participating in over sixty board meetings of major (all Fortune 500 or equivalent) companies over many years, the following key items characterize best practices (Stage 3 or higher):
- Sustainability is the dominant or sole topic for a total of at least 90 minutes of discussion, two times a year.
- The time spent in board meetings is no more than 50 percent presentation and includes a robust discussion of: emerging issues and trends, best practices and benchmarking, link to company strategy and key business decisions; actions to take before the next board meeting.

Structuring the Sustainability Organization

Every CEO structures the sustainability activities differently. Based on detailed discussions at meetings of The Conference Board's executive councils that I have run (consisting of ~100 executives), there is no right way to organize. What matters is that there is enough high-level oversight and structure.

The most powerful structure to drive focus and accountability throughout the organization—from the boardroom to the shop floor—is where there are:
- Clear goals and metrics, starting with the C-suite.
- Interlocking committees—the idea is that looking at an organization chart, there might be three-four levels of sustainability-related councils or committees. They become "interlocking" when members of the highest level (call it Level A) are the ones who chair the next level down (Level B); then members of Level B chair the Level C committees—and so forth.
- Aligned incentives, annual goals and targets, etc.

The Scorecard addresses how the CEO structures the sustainability organization inside the company with two KSIs: "A-level" C-suite ownership of the subject and a "B-level" executive council to set policy and oversee activities.

KSI 2.7: C-Suite Ownership of Sustainability. Let's call the C-suite (CEO and direct reports) the "A-level" executives. In every company that is serious about sustainability, one or more members of the CEO's leadership has personal ownership of the most relevant and material issues. The range of ownership varies:

KSI	Stage 1	Stage 2	Stage 3	Stage 4
C-Suite Roles Regarding Sustainability	An existing officer (e.g., VP EHS) assumes role of sustainability leader	The full-time "S" leader reports to C-suite executive	A C-suite executive owns "S"—integral to corporate strategy & communications	The CEO personally drives an ambitious "S"/ ESG agenda

Below are some examples of Stage 3 (or higher) approaches:
- **Coca-Cola:** CEO Muhtar Kent said he personally was the company's chief sustainability officer; then in 2011, he appointed Beatriz Perez as the company's first CSO.[xi]
- **Nike:** Hannah Jones was the VP of Sustainable Business and Innovation for nearly nine years and in April 2014 was promoted to Chief Sustainability Officer.[xii]
- **Unilever:** CSO Jeff Seabright often says to his colleagues and friends that CEO Paul Polman is really the CSO.

In each case, the CEO takes a hands-on approach to managing sustainability.

KSI 2.8: Executive Sustainability Council. Let's call executives one level down from the C-suite the "B-level" executives. One of the most common weaknesses in sustainability governance at companies is the failure to have execution on key goals, with aligned incentives, hard-wired from the boardroom to the shop floor. As mentioned above, a key way to avoid this misstep is through "interlocking committees."

What is common is to develop a high-level sustainability council—perhaps one level down from the executive committee (we call this B-level)—and let things run their course from there. Here is the range of activity:

KSI	Stage 1	Stage 2	Stage 3	Stage 4
Executive Sustainability Council	Cross-functional sustainability team	Formal council led by C-suite executive; meets at least 2x/year	Robust Council—linked to operations council; led by COO or equivalent; meets quarterly	Executive Committee replaces the need for an Executive "S" Council; meets 6-12x/year

Below are a few of the many excellent examples of executive sustainability councils.
- **Hyatt:** CFO Gebhard Rainer has a leading role in sustainability efforts in the company.[xiii]
- **Unilever** (Netherlands)**:** Sustainability governance is fully integrated into the company's management structures. Guided by board level governance and oversight, Unilever Leadership Executive (led by CEO Paul Polman) oversees implementation of the Unilever Sustainable Living Plan (USLP). Divisional and functional leadership is aligned through the USLP Steering Team.[xiv]
- **UPS:** Former CFO Kurt Kuehn spoke widely regarding the value of sustainability, including at investor forums and published articles.[xv]

How Do Companies Stack Up?

Starting in 2018, we are capturing data from a group of founding participants—invited to use the Scorecard for a company self-assessment and to provide feedback. As we assess the data from the first sixty companies (all Fortune 500 or equivalent), two key messages stand out:

C-suite ownership of sustainability is mixed:

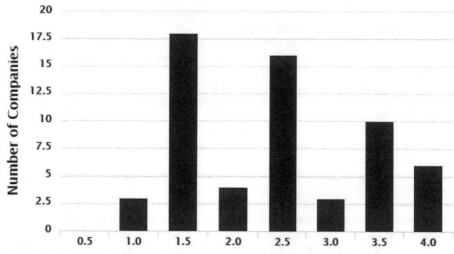

Source: Corporate Sustainability Scorecard

Figure 12.1: Scorecard Data from Sixty Companies on KSI 2.9: C-Suite Ownership of Sustainability

- As Figure 12.1 shows, there is a wide range of performance on C-suite ownership of sustainability—even among those large companies that are serious about sustainability.
- Only one in six companies (17 percent) say they are Stage 3 or higher in enabling CEO learning about ESG issues.

Not surprisingly, there currently exists a wide range of CEO engagement with ESG issues. That is changing at a fast pace. In a survey of sixty-three large (many leading) companies across almost all industry sectors at a February 2018 Conference Board meeting the author ran, we asked this question; over the past year, the level of interest by my CEO in sustainability/ESG has: declined (2 percent); stayed about the same (38 percent); increased somewhat (37 percent); and increased significantly (24 percent).

i https://www.huffingtonpost.com/entry/general-mills-warns-climate-change-will-lead-to-global-food-shortages_us_55e45e5ce4b0c818f6186305

ii https://www.cfr.org/event/smarter-planet-next-leadership-agenda

iii https://www.unileverusa.com/news/press-releases/2010/unilever-unveils-plan-to-decouple-business-growth-from-environmental-impact.html

iv https://ssir.org/articles/entry/the_greening_of_wal_mart

v https://www.forbes.com/sites/andyboynton/2015/07/20/unilevers-paul-polman-ceos-cant-be-slaves-to-shareholders/#4e7a08f1561e

vi https://www.climateleadershipconference.org/awards-3/

vii https://www.forbes.com/2010/05/03/david-steiner-waste-management-leadership-managing-reiss.html#1cb04dd754d2

viii http://www.hangseng.com/cms/ccd/csr/2013/eng/staff.html

ix https://www.dow.com/en-us/science-and-sustainability/collaborations/sustainability-external-advisory-council

x https://www.nytimes.com/2012/04/14/business/wal-mart-and-environmental-fund-team-up-to-cut-waste.html?_r=0

xi https://www.reuters.com/article/idUS399957228020110524

xii https://www.bloomberg.com/research/stocks/people/person.asp?personId=12296311&privcapId=291981

xiii https://blogs.wsj.com/cfo/2014/07/18/hyatt-cfo-bringing-sustainability-into-corporate-culture/

xiv https://www.unilever.com/sustainable-living/our-strategy/our-sustainability-governance/

xv https://hbr.org/2014/04/sustainability-a-cfo-can-love

Chapter 13
Board of Directors Leadership

The third element of the Governance and Leadership section of the Scorecard is leadership from the board of directors. The term **"board"** can actually be confusing.[1] In this book and the Scorecard, the term "board" refers only to the board of directors—charged with fiduciary oversight responsibilities. For privately held companies, this would be the equivalent of individuals representing the owners. In some cases, those are the owners.

One of the most powerful examples of board leadership comes from Sims Metal Management—the world's largest metal recycling company. Headquartered in New York City—but traded on both the Australian and U.S. exchanges, Sims has a truly engaged board. In 2015, the chairman of the board's Safety, Health, Environment, Community, and Sustainability (SHECS) Committee asked Ken Tierney, group vice president of SHECS to prepare a draft board sustainability commitment. The full board of directors later signed that commitment—putting their personal stamp on the company's commitment to sustainability and the circular economy. The Sims Metal Management example highlights the key question every company should ask:

Key Question: What oversight structure, processes, and systems support our board of directors' commitment and engagement with ESG?

To help answer this key question, the Scorecard analyzes how companies manage and perform in three areas:
- The structure and resources of the board (full board or board committee) to provide oversight of sustainability
- The assurance processes in place to report to the board key risks and opportunities
- The board of directors' commitment of time to learning about sustainability issues, best practices, and trends

Within each of these areas, executives evaluate their company performance on several key sustainability indicators (KSIs).

---

1 In Europe, it is common for business executives to refer to the board as the "management board"—meaning CEOs and their direct reports. In the United States, companies typically refer to that group as the executive leadership team or some equivalent term.

DOI 10.1515/9781547400423-013

Board of Directors Sustainability Structure and Resources

The Scorecard addresses board structure and resources with four KSIs that address the board's oversight role, its stated commitment to sustainability, its sustainability expertise, and its use of external advisors.

KSI 3.1: Board Responsibility for Oversight of Sustainability. In the United States, the National Association of Corporate Directors (NACD) conducts an annual survey of board members to gauge the importance of environmental, social, and governance (ESG) and the key trends, issues, concerns, etc. The 2017–2018 NACD Public Company Governance Survey reinforces the need for board action:
-   A strong majority of respondents in every industry sector ascribed importance to improving ESG strategy over the next twelve months, only a small minority saying that improving ESG was "not at all important."
-   Responses varied by industry; improving board oversight of ESG is viewed as being most important in materials, utilities, energy, and healthcare—and least critical in information technology.

A recent report titled "Systems Rule: How Board Governance Can Drive Sustainability Performance" examined 475 publicly held companies listed on the Forbes Global 2000 to determine the impact board governance systems have on sustainability performance. The study found that while most large companies state that they oversee sustainability at the board level, only a minority of companies evaluated had formal mandates and demonstrate board-management engagement on sustainability.[i]

The range of activity on board oversight of sustainability is as follows.

KSI	Stage 1	Stage 2	Stage 3	Stage 4
Board Responsibility for Oversight of Sustainability	ESG oversight not extensive; folded under a traditional committee (e.g., Audit, Governance, etc.)	ESG oversight is strong and growing each year	Significant oversight in terms of time spent and effectiveness (e.g., Sustainability Committee (or equivalent)	Full board actively involved in discussing ESG issues, risks, and opportunities

Several examples of leading practices in the area of board oversight of sustainability follow:
-   **Sims Metal Management:** As the world's largest metal recycling company, Sims is a global leader when it comes to board of directors' sustainability oversight. A board of directors—SHECS Committee has been in place since 1991. The SHECS

Committee charter was revised and updated in 2015 to reflect an even greater focus on sustainability. The SHECS Committee meets at least four times each year; the meetings are often multiday events including plant operations tours and safety reviews.[ii]

– **Iberdrola:** An international energy leader, the company stands out for its commitment to help decarbonize the economy. It is the leading renewable energy company. The actively engaged board reviews policies and external reports, evaluates stakeholder relations and oversees the company's activity with international sustainability rating indices.[iii]

– **Nike:** The Corporate Responsibility and Sustainability Committee of Nike's board of directors is mandated to work with management on integrating sustainability into Nike's businesses.[iv]

– **Unilever** (Netherlands): The company has two board committees providing independent oversight: Board Corporate Responsibility Committee to oversee Unilever's conduct as a responsible business and the Board Audit Committee reviews the company's overall approach to risk management.[v]

KSI 3.2: Board's Sustainability Commitment. Earlier in this chapter we provided the example of the commitment to ESG made by the board of directors of Sims Metal Management. Sims would be Stage 4 on the scale below.

KSI	Stage 1	Stage 2	Stage 3	Stage 4
Board's Sustainability Commitment	Board charter focuses on conventional EHS, public policy issues	Board charter explicitly discusses sustainability oversight	Board commitment specifically embraces sustainability	Full board of directors signs a personal commitment to sustainability

Other examples of how companies have addressed board commitment to sustainability are:

– **Ford Motor Company:** The company's sustainability committee needs to "assist management in the formulation and implementation of policies, principles and practices to permit the company to respond to evolving public sentiment and government regulation in the area of motor vehicle and stationary source emissions, especially in the area of greenhouse gas emissions and fuel economy and CO_2 regulation."[vi]

– **Intel:** The company agreed with a shareholder resolution in 2010 and created a board-level sustainability committee.[vii]

– **Sims Metal Management:** During 2015, the company's board of directors took the unique and powerful step to codify in writing their personal commitment to SHECS excellence.[viii]

KSI 3.3: Board's Sustainability Expertise. It is difficult to define or capture board sustainability expertise, and for this reason, the Scorecard criteria in the table below are deliberately a bit vague. One commonly used metric related to board composition is gender diversity. This metric is not a proxy for sustainability expertise; however, more diverse boards in general are more likely to have a balanced view of global ESG issues.

In the United States, boardrooms are showing a gradual increase in the share of women on the board. During the first five months of 2018, 31 percent of new board directors at the country's 3,000 largest publicly traded companies were women, according to an analysis by ISS Analytics, the data arm of Institutional Shareholder Services. This puts 2018 on track to be a record year for new female board members.[ix]

KSI	Stage 1	Stage 2	Stage 3	Stage 4
Board's Sustainability Expertise	Little to moderate	Moderate and growing	Strong and explicitly growing	Very strong and growing

In some cases, board expertise is very clear. An example is where a company invites a leading environmental or socially responsible voice to be on its board. Several examples follow:

- **Ashland:** The chemical and materials company had a leading environmentalist on its board starting in 1991; Patrick Noonan served from 1991–2007 and John Turner served from 2007 to 2015.[x]
- **DuPont:** Bill Reilly, former administrator of the U.S. Environmental Protection Agency, was on its board starting in 1993. Following Reilly's tenure, another EPA Administrator, Lee Thomas, served on the board.[xi]
- **International Paper:** Patrick Noonan, renowned NGO leader, served on the board from 1993–2004.[xii]
- **Nike:** Jill Ker Conway served on the board from 1987–2011.[xiii]

KSI 3.4: Board's External Sustainability Advisors. It is common for board members to either request their own external advisors or to suggest to management that it might be a good idea to hear from someone outside the company. Normally, the former situation (engaging directly with board advisors) comes when the board is concerned about something. The latter situation is more common when the directors just want to learn more.

KSI	Stage 1	Stage 2	Stage 3	Stage 4
Board's External Sustainability Advisors	Rely mostly on internal "S" experts and industry associations	Board gets periodic updates from outside sustainability experts	Formal, active **External Sustainability Advisory Board** or equivalent	Input from other CEOs, board members and global "S'" thought leaders

In my personal experience, I have had the privilege of meeting with outside board members as their external sustainability advisor on over 60 occasions. Roughly one third of the time, I met with the full board of directors; the other two thirds were meetings with the board committee overseeing ESG issues. Outside directors always want to know how their company compares with competitors and peers; what issues are on the horizon; and whether goals, systems and performance are top quartile.

Outside directors also want to know how the CEO and management team is doing. Often, the last question from the directors was "Is there anything else we need to know that has not come up during the meeting?"

Some examples of ways boards have enhanced their knowledge and expertise in ESG issues:

- **Dow Chemical:** The company's Sustainability External Advisory Council (SEAC), founded in 1992, is composed of thought-leaders from around the world and is chaired by a Dow SVP.[xiv]
- **Ingersoll-Rand:** As a world leader creating safe, comfortable, and efficient environments in commercial, residential, and industrial markets, the company created an external Advisory Council on Sustainability in 2010.[xv]
- **Kimberly Clark:** The company's Sustainability Advisory Board (SAB) was formed in 2007 to provide insight on sustainability issues and best practices to our Global Strategic Leadership Team.[xvi]

Board of Directors' Assurance Processes

Boards rely on independent audit and assurance processes to a significant degree. The independent role of the external financial auditor is well-established. In addition, many boards ask for and receive independent advisors on enterprise risk management and other key business matters.

When it comes to sustainability (and specifically the subset of sustainability related to core environment, health and safety function), audit results have been reported to boards for over three decades. In fact, many of the author's early meetings with boards of directors of Fortune 500 companies were when functioning as the "partner in charge" of the consulting engagement providing independent environmental, health, and safety (EHS) auditing oversight.

The Scorecard addresses board of directors' assurance processes with three KSIs: board review of **key business decisions**, reporting to the board of the most material ESG issues; and an **assurance letter process** or equivalent.

KSI 3.5: Board's ESG Review of Key Business Decisions (KBDs). In Chapter 10 we introduced the concept of key business decisions as an indicator of the extent to which a company ties major investment decisions to core values around sustainability. In that chapter (KSI 1.6), we defined *key business decisions* as the handful of major decisions the CEO and board make each year—typically involving mergers and acquisitions (M&A) or divestitures; large capital expenditures; new product launches; major research and development expenditures, etc.

In this KSI, we specifically examine the board of directors' role in factoring ESG considerations into those key business decisions.

KSI	Stage 1	Stage 2	Stage 3	Stage 4
Board ESG Review of Key Business Decisions (KBDs)	Traditional (e.g., EHS due diligence); informal "S" audit	"S"/ESG are key factors in M&A; otherwise situational	Formal "S" screen applied to all key business decisions	"S" is a critical factor in all key business decisions

Some examples of companies that have publicly discussed their board's review of key business decisions:

- **Ikea:** The company's board approved $1 billion for sustainable materials investments and pledged to invest €1bn (£850m) in recycling companies and forests.xvii
- **AkzoNobel:** The Dutch coatings company factors sustainability into financial decision-making: "Capital budget requests that exceed $5 million must now be routed through both the Controller and the CSO."[xviii]
- **KKR and TXU:** Together with Environmental Defense Fund, the two companies decided to cut investment in new coal power plants from eleven to three. The Texas utility agreed to deal valued at record $45 billion with debt; agrees to scrap permits for eight planned coal power plants.[xix]
- **Ingersoll Rand:** The industrial company committed $500M for R&D to reduce long-term GHG emissions.[xx]

KSI 3.6: Reporting to Board of Most Material ESG Issues. The process and content of how companies report the most significant risks, issues, and concerns to its board of directors is obviously highly confidential. The typical range of approaches companies take is:

KSI	Stage 1	Stage 2	Stage 3	Stage 4
Reporting to Board of Most Material ESG Issues	Report "S" risks in own operations and those of key suppliers	Report full supply chain "S" risks and performance vs. robust ESG goals and metrics for own operations	Report full supply chain "S" risks and performance vs. robust ESG goals and metrics across supply chain	Report full supply chain "S" risks and performance vs. robust goals and metrics are independently assured

Best practices include having enough time on board agendas for review of this and a robust process (or processes) in place to assemble and report that information. The assurance letter process described below is a key one.

KSI 3.7: Assurance Letter/Annual Risk Review Signed by Business Leaders. In my experience, the **"assurance letter** process" is one of the most powerful, least expensive, and least practiced assurance tools available to companies. We define an "assurance letter process" as an annual signed statement from business executives (normally business presidents) to the CEO stating that operations comply; risks and significant issues are identified and being managed; and processes are in place to ensure consistent implementation of company policies and values.

KSI	Stage 1	Stage 2	Stage 3	Stage 4
Assurance Letter or Annual Risk Review signed by Business Leaders	May or may not exist; if so, compliance and risk-focused	Comprehensive annual summary of "S" risks across full supply chain	Assurance letter seen as a critical and highly valued process by board, CEO, C-suite	Comprehensive annual summary of "S" risks and opportunities across full supply chain

Ashland has had an environment, health, safety, security, and sustainability "assurance letter process" in place since the late 1990s. At the time the process was initiated, Ashland was quite a different company (see Chapter 6: Strategy and Execution). Ashland's assurance letter process was initiated at the suggestion of the board of directors, the process provides an attestation letter, signed by company presidents and the VP EHS, built on a "bottom-up" view of risks.

Board of Directors' Commitment of Time to Sustainability

Perhaps the most precious allocation of time each year for any company is that allocated on the agendas of board meetings (or equivalent for private companies).

The Scorecard addresses the board's time commitment to sustainability in two ways: the actual time spent in board (full board or board committee) meetings and the time spent on learning about the subject outside of board meetings.

KSI 3.8: Time Spent on Sustainability in Board Meetings. This KSI addresses time spent either in one of the various board committees—or the full board. The range of hours in the table below are based on the author's personal knowledge from working with many companies and participating in many board meetings. The rating criteria are reinforced by surveys taken at meetings of chief sustainability officers (or equivalent) that I run for The Conference Board.

KSI	Stage 1	Stage 2	Stage 3	Stage 4
Time Spent on Sustainability in Board Meetings	Typically < 4 hours/year; major agenda item at 1 or more meetings	Same or more than average among sector peers; typically 4–8 hours/year	Significant—and likely growing; typically 8–12 hours/year	Very significant—and likely growing; typically > 12 hours/year

In a survey of fifty-nine public companies at a Conference Board meeting the author ran in February 2018, we asked the question: "How many times each year do the Sustainability/EHS functions meet with/present to the board of directors (committee or full board)?" The answers were: never (22 percent); once a year (36 percent; twice a year (12 percent); three time a year (5 percent); more than three times each year (25 percent). Note the bimodal distribution!

KSI 3.9: Board of Directors' Sources of Sustainability Learning. Here is one of the ironies related to board learning:
- "We want more." Board members tell me they want to have background reading and information on subjects—especially concise, thought-provoking, fact-based, business articles. They love a several-page McKinsey piece or similar thought pieces authored by respectable sources such as The Conference Board or NACD.
- "Don't send anything." The "rule of thumb" in most companies—often driven by the general counsel and corporate secretary is: only send board members copies of the slides you will present and nothing more.

KSI	Stage 1	Stage 2	Stage 3	Stage 4
Board of Directors' Sources of Sustainability Learning	Mostly limited to presentations at board meetings; little "S" thought leadership prereading	Board members are provided key "S" articles/books; spend 1+ days/year; formal, continuous sharing of best 'S' learning	Board members receive thought-provoking ESG pre-reads; spend several days/year, including off-site meeting to explore material ESG issue(s)	Ongoing, structured learning between board meetings involves ~3–5 days/year

Board members read extensively and do attend periodic training courses. The NACD, a leading organization of board directors, offers many short training courses for directors, including ones on ESG. The organizations' journal, *NACD Directorship*, often includes articles on ESG.

One of the ways boards of directors learn about sustainability is through shareholder resolutions. When the company they oversee or any peer company is subject to a shareholder resolution on ESG matters, they pay attention.

As mentioned in Chapter 9 (The New ESG Regulators), in 2018, more than 400 shareholder resolutions were filed on ESG issues. Resolutions demanding that companies address climate risk rated highest (tied with political activity spending) with eighty resolutions; there were seventy resolutions about equal treatment for women.[xxi]

The mainstream business press is full of articles about ESG, and this has been growing steadily over the past decade. The clear majority of these articles are about companies taking ESG seriously, investing in clean technology, renewable energy, investors paying more attention to ESG issues.

Several short books or articles aimed at the boardroom include:
- *Sustainability: A Guide for Boards and C-Suites* (book)
- "Seven Pillars of Sustainability Leadership"—a 2014 Conference Board publication.
- "Navigating the Sustainability Transformation"—a 2015 Conference Board publication.

How Do Companies Stack Up?

Assessing data from the first sixty companies completing the Scorecard, the data suggest some big gaps.

A good indicator of board involvement on ESG issues is with KSI 3.5: Board ESG Review of Key Business Decisions. The data from the first sixty companies completing the Scorecard is about what the author expected; however, the involvement of the board is notably low, as depicted in Figure 13.1.

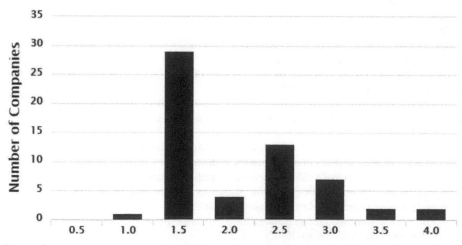

Source: Corporate Sustainability Scorecard

Figure 13.1: Scorecard Data from Sixty Companies on KSI 3.5: Board Review of Key Business Decisions

Several other data points from these Scorecard results:
- Only 11 percent of companies say their board is actively engaged on ESG issues between board meetings
- Only 10 percent say they have planned ESG learning as part of board meetings

Suffice it to say, the Scorecard data soundly reinforces what board members themselves said in the NACD 2017–2018 survey mentioned earlier in this chapter. In that survey, a strong majority of respondents in every industry sector ascribed importance to improving ESG strategy over the next twelve months.

———

i https://www.ceres.org/news-center/press-releases/ceres-new-analysis-large-global-companies-links-sustainability

ii https://simsmetalmanagementlimited.gcs-web.com/static-files/94983c52-add1-483f-a503-11028895c60b

iii https://www.ceres.org/systemsrule

iv https://www.ceres.org/systemsrule

v https://www.unilever.com/investor-relations/agm-and-corporate-governance/board-and-management-committees/

vi https://irrcinstitute.org/wp-content/uploads/2015/09/final_2014_si2_irrci_report_on_board_oversight_of_sustainability_issues_public1.pdf

vii http://www.socialfunds.com/news/article.cgi/2921.html

viii https://s3.amazonaws.com/sims-us-media/SMM+Corporate+2015/Sims-Sustainability-Report-2015-Final_.pdf

ix https://www.wsj.com/articles/women-on-track-to-gain-record-number-of-board-seats-1529573401

x https://www.bloomberg.com/research/stocks/people/person.asp?personId=23033355&privcapId=252339

xi http://www.nndb.com/people/955/000128571/

xii http://www.nndb.com/people/586/000053427/

xiii https://hbr.org/2014/07/sustainability-in-the-boardroom

xiv https://www.dow.com/en-us/search#q=SEAC&t=All

xv https://s21.q4cdn.com/515635695/files/doc_news/archive/IR_News_2010_11_8_General.pdf

xvi https://www.greenbiz.com/blog/2012/06/11/external-advisors-crucial-kimberly-clark-sustainability-goals

xvii https://www.theguardian.com/business/2016/dec/07/ikea-plans-investment-recycling-companies-forests-sale-product-development-supply-chain

xviii http://www.wri.org/blog/2013/03/factoring-sustainability-financial-decision-making

xix http://money.cnn.com/2007/02/26/news/companies/txu/?postversion=2007022608

xx https://company.ingersollrand.com/strengths/sustainability/our-climate-commitment.html

xxi https://www.asyousow.org/press-releases/2018/3/8/climate-politics-and-women-top-shareholder-issues-for-proxy-season-2018

Chapter 14
Goals and Metrics

We all know that "what gets measured gets managed"—and for sustainability-related initiatives it is no different. Thus, the fourth element of the Corporate Sustainability Scorecard—in the Governance section—is goals and metrics.

The overarching strategic question that senior executives and board members should be asking is:

Key Question: How does our company set goals that drive footprint reduction and long-term value creation for the most material issues across our value chain?

Unilever (#150 on the 2017 Fortune 500 list) is well into its multiyear Sustainable Living Plan, which was launched in 2010 to "decouple" revenue growth and value creation from environmental and social impacts. This decoupling is driven by the company's 2030 goal: *to cut in half the environmental impacts/footprint associated with making and using its products as the company continues to grow its business.* In 2012, Unilever CEO Paul Polman further drove the focus on long-term value creation when he stated at the World Economic Forum in Davos, "We don't do three-month (financial) reporting anymore."[i] Unilever has inspired many "smart follower" companies to grow their revenue while cutting their impacts and footprint.

To help answer this key question, the Scorecard analyzes a company's approach to establishing and tracking performance of sustainability goals, including:
- The goal-setting process
- The time horizon for framing the sustainability goals and metrics
- The content and impact of the individual targets that are set, measured, and reported on

Within each of these buckets, executives evaluate their company performance on several KSIs. For each KSI, they rate their company performance on the scale of Stage 1 through Stage 4.

Goal-Setting Process

For many companies, the goal-setting process, as it relates to environmentally and socially related topics, is evolutionary rather than revolutionary. By that we mean today's goals are likely grounded in a history that dates to early goals—especially around occupational safety and environmental, health, and safety (EHS) compliance.

DOI 10.1515/9781547400423-014

The Scorecard addresses the goal-setting process with three key sustainability indicators (KSIs): the critical starting point (materiality assessment of key ESG impacts and risks; the general company philosophy about sustainability goals; and the extent of external stakeholder input into the goal-setting process.

KSI 4.1: Materiality Assessment of Sustainability Impacts/Risks. The "right" starting point for any set of sustainability goals is what is commonly referred to as a **materiality assessment**.

The term *materiality* is a convention within the financial community relating to the importance or significance of something relative to the corporation. In financial terms, information is material if its omission or misstatement could influence the economic decision of users based on the company's financial statements.

In the sustainability world, a materiality assessment is a comprehensive review of the key (negative) environmental and social impacts and issues associated with the company and its industry sector. Of course companies have many positive impacts, especially on the "social" side—such as offering employment, benefits, community outreach, etc. But a materiality assessment identifies major negative impacts a company has—including, for example:

- *Environmental Impacts:* Greenhouse gas (GHS) emissions, other air emissions, water use; water contamination; waste disposal; etc.
- *Social Impacts:* Lack of diversity and inclusion; adverse impacts on health and wellness; labor issues; human rights abuses in the organization and the supply chain; etc.
- *Governance Impacts:* Lack of active board involvement in sustainability; lack of diversity on the board of directors; etc.

As companies move from Stage 1 to Stage 2, their materiality assessment becomes more formal, addressing impacts not only in the company's own operations but also throughout its value chain.

KSI	Stage 1	Stage 2	Stage 3	Stage 4
Materiality Assessment of Sustainability Impacts and Risks	Issues analysis process includes "S" issues; basic materiality evaluation	Formal "S" materiality assessment (full value chain) that incorporates NGO input	Strong partnerships with leading NGOs on most material ESG issues in sector	C-suite executives own key "S" issues; making progress toward becoming **net-neutral**

As companies advance to Stage 3 and beyond, they reach out to various key stakeholder groups to solicit input on identifying material issues—and then ultimately address those issues. Key stakeholders with a strong interest in these issues certainly include not for profit environmental groups or socially related groups—typically referred to as nongovernmental organizations (NGOs). Several examples of companies in Stage 3 or beyond include:

- **Chipotle Mexican Grill:** Conducted a formal materiality assessment in 2015–2016; a major issue for the restaurants was waste management. The company set a goal to divert 50 percent of its restaurant waste from landfills by 2020, and achieved a 40 percent diversion rate in 2017.
- **Nestlé Waters:** The North American company committed to certifying 100 percent of its sites to the Alliance for Water Stewardship Standard by 2025.[ii]
- **Skandinaviska Enskilda Banken:** The Swedish company works with stakeholders as they plan to create and sustain value on a three to five-year basis.[iii]

In each of these examples, the company set a major long-term goal directly aligned with one of its most material ESG issues.

KSI 4.2: Philosophy Regarding Sustainability Goals. For most companies, publicly stated goals tend to receive considerable external scrutiny. As a result, two things typically happen. First, the draft goals and metrics undergo extensive internal review before they are made public. Second, partly because of that internal review, the public goals are often conservative. CEOs and senior executives like to meet their goals; thus, it is only reasonable that—at least early in their sustainability journey—the goals have a high likelihood of being achieved. That situation defines Stage 1 goals.

As companies move beyond Stage 1, the most important factor is ensuring that their primary public sustainability goals address the company's most material environmental, social, and governance (ESG) impacts. For a further discussion of materiality, see Chapter 7—Environmental Stewardship: The "E" in ESG.

KSI	Stage 1	Stage 2	Stage 3	Stage 4
Philosophy Regarding Sustainability Goals	Goals may be a stretch, but are achievable; compliance mindset; stay in comfort zone	Goals are a stretch to achieve, aligned to most material ESG impacts	Pursuing a dual track: driving to zero footprint as well as "S" innovation and growth	Best-in-class across all industry sectors

Companies that move to the leadership level (Stage 3 and beyond) have goals that are very aggressive in reducing their most material risks and impacts throughout the value chain. They also have goals that focus on growth—namely goals that embed sustainable thinking into research and development, and that drive sales of more sustainable products, services, and solutions. A few examples:

- **Anheuser-Busch InBev:** The global beverage company launched 2025 goals tied to its most material issues: reducing CO_2 emissions by 25 percent; sourcing 100 percent of electricity from renewables; using circular packaging for all products;

improving water availability and quality in all communities in high stress areas and improving the livelihoods of its direct farmers.[iv]
- **Walmart:** Project Gigaton was launched to cut GHG emissions across the company's global supply chain by one gigaton (one billion tons) from 2015 levels by 2030.[v]
- **Xerox:** An early leader, the company's focus since the 1990s has been to produce "waste-free products from waste-free factories."[vi]

In each of these examples, the company took a bold step that garnered the support of NGOs. In the case of Vodafone, the effort was done in direct collaboration with NGOs.

KSI 4.3: Stakeholder Input to Sustainability Goals. Let's face it: the process of setting goals at companies is inherently internally focused. Sure, the starting point is to benchmark competitors and peer companies—to make sure your company goals are aligned or stronger. But the nuts and bolts of setting goals is internal.

KSI	Stage 1	Stage 2	Stage 3	Stage 4
Stakeholder Input to Sustainability Goals	Limited input; mostly from customers, suppliers and "safe hands" NGOs	Understand and align with customer "S" goals; engage with business-friendly NGO(s)	Actively engage, listen, and learn; including full range of NGOs (not just friendly ones)	Process is institutionalized—not done as a one-off activity

In setting sustainability goals, leading companies have reached outside their companies to solicit input from external stakeholders, thought leaders and advisors in various ways.
- **Dell:** The company worked with NGOs to set carbon reduction goals; committed to reduce GHG emissions 20% by 2020.[vii]
- **Vodafone:** The company committed to sourcing 100 percent renewable electricity across its operations by 2025, as part of The Climate Group and CDP-led RE100 initiative.[viii] Twenty-five of the RE100 member companies had reached 100 percent renewable electricity by the end of 2016.

In each of these examples, companies clearly viewed the benefits of NGO input to their goals outweighing the risks of perhaps inviting unrealistic or very difficult to achieve goals.

Time Horizon of Sustainability Goals

Most environmental and social issues are complex, diffuse, and more regional, national, or global in nature than they are short-term and local. As a result, the time horizon for sustainability goals typically involves looking out at least three to five years. For larger companies with global operations and for any company with a global supply chain and global customer base, the time frame can be even longer.

The nature of your industry sector certainly has an impact on the time horizon as well. For service providers and information technology companies, two to three years is a very long horizon. At the other extreme, electric utilities, oil and gas companies, chemical companies often make capital investments that are on the books for thirty to fifty years or longer.

The Scorecard addresses time horizon of goals with two key sustainability indicators: one dealing with the typical horizon for long-term goals for most companies; and a second that looks at what a growing number of companies state in terms of what we call "ultimate" sustainability goals.

KSI 4.4: Long-Term (5–15 Year) Sustainability Goals. The clear majority of public companies today—especially large ones—have a set of sustainability-related goals. In many cases, these current goals have their roots in earlier environment, health, and safety goals that may have existed for decades. Common EHS goals deal with safety, compliance, etc.

Today, the range of company activity on long-term sustainability goals is given below.

KSI	Stage 1	Stage 2	Stage 3	Stage 4
Long-term (typically 5–15 year) Sustainability Goals	They may exist; focus on your own operations and your suppliers	They exist; focus on your own operations, suppliers, and products; align to **SDGs**	Top quartile goals in most material KPIs across full value chain	Following a roadmap toward zero net impact; or **net positive** impact

Some examples of robust sustainability goals follow:
- **AT&T:** The telecommunications leader set a goal to enable carbon savings 10x the footprint of its operations by 2025.[ix]
- **Campbell Soup:** The iconic company announced its 2020 Destination Goals for CSR and Sustainability in 2011. The goals include efforts to improve the health of young people and reduce the environmental footprint of its products.[x]
- **Ingersoll Rand:** Committed to a 35% reduction in GHS footprint by 2020.[xi]
- **Marks & Spencer:** The UK retailer launched Plan A in 2007 as the company's way to help build a sustainable future, enabling its customers to have a positive

impact on wellbeing, communities and the planet. The first phase of Plan A had 100 new social and environmental commitments. The second phase launched in 2010 had 80 new commitments and a goal to become the world's most sustainable major retailer. The company is now in the third phase, called Plan A 2020. [xii]

- **Nestlé:** The Swiss-based multinational announced target year 2020 commitments in support of UN SDGs in March 2017[xiii] and plans for all its 150 European factories to be zero waste by 2020.[xiv]
- **Sainsbury:** The UK retailer launched its "20 by 20 Sustainability Plan" in 2011, setting out twenty sustainability targets to be achieved by 2020.[xv]

In each of these examples, the goals are public commitments—often quite bold ones— that drive the company to make significant performance improvements.

KSI 4.5: Ultimate (e.g., 2050) Sustainability Goals. Over the past decade or so, a small but growing number of companies have made bold statements about the sustainability ambition they ultimately aimed to achieve—without naming a specific target year. One example is noted just above: Marks & Spencer's goal to become the world's most sustainable major retailer.

Today, the range of company activity related to these ultimate sustainability goals is given below.

KSI	Stage 1	Stage 2	Stage 3	Stage 4
Ultimate (e.g., 2050) Sustainability Goals	Not on CEO's radar—as noted in public speeches	General references to being around long-term	Company has a **net positive** impact goal— across its full supply chain; could be a single issue: for example, goal to be **carbon neutral**	Company has goals and metrics driving to net positive impact across its full supply chain; aligned with **SDGs**; includes **closed-loop; circular economy**

Below are some of the impressive sets of goals around essentially zero negative impacts—either in total or in a key material issue such as carbon or water.

- **AkzoNobel:** The Dutch coatings company committed to accelerating its sustainability agenda by announcing in 2017 a new ambition to use 100% renewable energy and become carbon neutral by 2050.[xvi]
- **Coca-Cola:** The company met its 2020 water replenishment goal by the end of 2015. The 2020 goal involved safely returning to communities and nature an amount of water equal to what the company uses in its finished beverages.[xvii]

- **DHL:** The German package delivery company committed to zero emissions logistics (meaning zero net GHG emissions in its own operations and its transportation contractors) by 2050. This goal was DHL's contribution to achieving the goal of limiting global warming to well below 2° Celsius established at the 2015 Paris climate conference (COP 21).[xviii]
- **Interface:** The carpet manufacturer embarked on what the company called a "mid-course correction" in 1994 and later launched Mission Zero with a goal to eliminate any negative environmental impact by 2020.[xix]
- **Kingfisher:** The international home improvement company based in the UK set a clear direction: "Net positive is our sustainability ambition. It means innovating in our products and services to enable our customers to have more sustainable homes; transforming our business to have a restorative impact on the environment; and making a positive contribution to society and the communities in which we operate."[xx]
- **Nestlé:** stated its overall ambition to strive for zero environmental impact in our operations. "We have set clear commitments and objectives to use sustainably managed and renewable resources, operate more efficiently, achieve zero waste for disposal and improve water management. We also continue to actively participate in initiatives that reduce food loss and waste, and that preserve our forests, oceans and biodiversity."[xxi]
- **Sony** (Japan): Has a goal of "zero impact" by 2050; its plan is outlined in its "Road to Zero" Initiative.[xxii]
- **Walmart:** The CEO set three long-term, aspirational goals in 2005: to operate with 100 percent renewable energy; to create zero waste; and to sell products that sustain resources and the environment.[xxiii] While these aspirational goals did not have a specific deadline, Walmart subsequently set more specific goals and metrics, including a set of 2025 goals.

In each of these examples, these leading companies go beyond setting the more typical five- to ten-year "long-term" sustainability goals (discussed above in KSI 4.4) and also set a "net positive" or similar ambition.

Content and Impact of Sustainability Goals

The first two sub-elements of goals and metrics that we discussed assess a company's status on the goal-setting process and the time horizon of sustainability goals. This third (sub-element) focuses on results.

The results of sustainability goals normally fall into one of two buckets:

- *Reducing Cost and Risk*—All the actions and initiatives companies take to minimize their impacts in their own operations and throughout their supply chain to reduce cost and/or risk.
- *Growing Revenue, Options for Future Growth and Brand*—The investments in research, product development, and customer relationships that result in a suite of company offerings (products, services, solutions) that collectively have a lighter footprint and help the customer achieve its sustainability goals.

The two KSIs in this section address those two sides of the coin and assess the extent to which the company's accounting systems are set up for tracking them.

KSI 4.6: Magnitude of Reduction in Company Footprint or Impact. In characterizing a company's sustainability goals, it is important to consider not only the content and degree of "stretch" in the individual goals—but also the track record of accomplishment. Over time, incremental improvements in footprint reductions are tougher to achieve, like improvements in a company's safety performance.

The rating criteria in the Scorecard are shown in the table below.

KSI	Stage 1	Stage 2	Stage 3	Stage 4
Magnitude of Reduction in Company's Footprint or Impact	Ongoing, even significant cuts (e.g., < 20%) from baseline year (or when major footprint reduction efforts began)	Very impressive cuts (e.g., ~20–30%) from baseline year (or when major footprint reduction efforts began)	Dramatic cuts (e.g., ~30–60%) from baseline year (or when major footprint reduction efforts began)	Transformational cuts (e.g., > 60%) from baseline year (or when major footprint reduction efforts began)

- **3M:** The company's Pollution Prevention Pays (3P) program celebrated its fortieth anniversary in 2015. The program has prevented more than 2.0 million tons of pollutants and saved nearly $1.9 billion.[xxiv]
- **Hasbro:** The toy company achieved 100 percent renewable energy and carbon neutrality across its owned and operated U.S. operations in 2015 and 2016 (the most recent years reported).[xxv]
- **Nike:** In a bold move, the company committed to eliminate hazardous chemical discharge from its supply chain by 2020.[xxvi]

In each of these examples, the company has made, and continues to make, very significant reductions in its footprint, while supporting positive contribution to the company operations and financial performance.

KSI 4.7: Tracking Revenue from Sustainable Products, Services, and Solutions.
The Conference Board has done an excellent job of conducting research on companies that are pursuing revenue growth from "green" or "healthy" or "sustainability" products, services, and solutions.

KSI	Stage 1	Stage 2	Stage 3	Stage 4
Tracking Revenue from Sustainable **Products, Services, and Solutions (PSS)**	Pursuing "S" products, services, & solutions (PSS) is not a major priority	Establishing criteria for "S" PSS—either as a defined portfolio or an alternative defined by the company	Explicitly defined "S" product attributes; track revenue from "S" portfolio (or equivalent)	Goals for > 50% of revenue from "S" products, services or solutions (or equivalent if you do not have a separate "S" portfolio)

The following examples are all from publicly reported data by the individual companies:

- **BASF:** Accelerator Solutions (the company's green portfolio) accounted for 27 percent of BASF's relevant sales in 2017, or about €15.5 billion.
- **DSM:** The company's ECO+ solutions accounted for 57 percent of the company's total sales in 2015. ECO+ sales have an average annual growth rate of about 10 percent, and across several of DSM's businesses, ECO+ sales have higher margins than do non-ECO+ sales. Today, ECO+ and People+ are combined into the "Brighter Living Solutions" portfolio, which in 2017 accounted for 62 percent of total sales.
- **Johnson & Johnson:** The company's Earthwards® portfolio of sustainable products grew from nine products in 2009 to one hundred products in 2017. This portfolio represented over $11 billion in revenue and about 15 percent of the company's 2017 revenue.
- **Kimberly-Clark:** The company's ecoLOGICAL portfolio accounted for 52 percent of the company's revenue in 2014 (up from 10 percent in 2010), or more than $10 billion.
- **Philips:** The company's "green products" accounted for 64 percent of the company's overall revenue in 2016.
- **Siemens:** The German company's Environmental Portfolio grew to €39 billion, 47% of 2017 revenue.
- **Toshiba:** Sales of "Excellent Environmentally Conscious Products" rose from $3.6 billion in 2011 to $24 billion in 2015 (accounting for 42 percent of 2015 revenue).

The examples above are impressive; however, I do not want to leave the impression that this is always the case. As mentioned in Chapter 9 (The New Regulators), the picture for green investments is not all rosy. Over the years there have been many bankruptcies in the solar and renewable energy sectors.

In each of these examples, the companies decided that it was useful to define a specific portfolio of its products and services as being especially "green" or "healthy" or "sustainable." And, in tracking revenue growth of these portfolios, the companies find that it pays to go down this path.

***KSI 4.8: Accounting for Most Material Externalities (e.g., Cost of Carbon).* Externalities** are defined as the cost or benefit that affects a party that did not choose to incur that cost or benefit. For example, manufacturing activities that cause air pollution or carbon emissions may impose health, cleanup, or other costs on society.

This KSI aims to assess the bridge between impact reduction initiatives many companies take (e.g., waste reduction; energy conservation; reducing risk of major incidents; etc.)—and the accounting systems that run the company's financial metrics.

Financial systems for pricing raw materials such as water or placing a cost on discharges such as GHG—are not aligned with resource availability. Here are some key examples:

- Cape Town, South Africa residents are awaiting "Day Zero"—the day when the city will shut off its taps and faucets will stay off until it rains.
- Cape Town is not the only city facing water shortages; Bangalore, Beijing, Cairo, Jakarta, Moscow, Istanbul, Los Angeles, London, Mexico City, Miami, São Paulo and Tokyo all face water shortages.[xxvii]
- In the United States, residents pay ten times more for water in in Flint, Michigan (located 40 miles from the Great Lakes than they do in arid Phoenix, Arizona.[xxviii]

The pricing of water is highly inconsistent across regions, and the same is certainly true of carbon. However, in the case of carbon, companies have been taking a leading role in assigning a cost associated with it for many years.

Over the past several years, a number of leading companies globally have been working to measure the total (financial, environmental and societal) impacts of the company. In a 2018 research report, Thomas Singer of The Conference Board provides an overview of current practices in this emerging area of total impact valuation.[xxix]

The range of ways companies measure their total impacts and account for carbon, water, and other material externalities is as follows:

KSI	Stage 1	Stage 2	Stage 3	Stage 4
Accounting for Most Material Externalities (e.g., Cost of Carbon)	Only in countries that require or encourage it	Factored into **key business decisions**	Assign cost of carbon and, as appropriate, other factors	Approaching **carbon neutral;** Factored into key business decisions for > 5 years

The following examples are from The Conference Board's report titled "Total Impact Valuation" referenced above:

– **AkzoNobel:** In its 3D P&L, the company shows its calculated economic, environmental, and social impacts across its full value chain.

– **BASF:** The company's Value-to-Society model shows its economic, environmental, and social impacts for the external supply chain (direct and indirect suppliers), own operations, and customer industries.

– **LafargeHolcim:** The company's 2016 Integrated Profit & Loss (IP&L) statement shows the results of its total impact calculation. The IP&L is divided into financial, socio-economic, and environmental categories.

In 2017, almost 1,400 companies were factoring an internal carbon price into their business plans, representing an eight-fold leap over four years. Despite this impressive increase, the number of companies using carbon pricing remains a very small fraction of all companies globally.

By making this commitment, companies are agreeing to align with the UN Global Compact's Business Leadership Criteria on Carbon Pricing:

– Set an internal carbon price high enough to materially affect investment decisions to drive down GHG emissions

– Publicly advocate the importance of carbon pricing through policy mechanisms that consider country specific economies and policy contexts

– Communicate on progress over time on the two criteria above in public corporate reports

As of 2017, 607 companies had set an internal price on carbon, principally as a risk management tool. Of that number, 255 were companies based in Europe; 136 were based in the United States.[xxx]

How Do Companies Stack Up?

Starting in 2018, we are capturing data from a group of founding participants—invited to use the Scorecard for a company self-assessment and to provide feedback. As we assess the data from the first 60 companies (all Fortune 500 or equivalent), several key messages stand out:

- A significant majority of companies base their sustainability goals on a detailed materiality assessment of key ESG impacts.
- Most companies do, in fact, have long-term sustainability goals (typically looking out five to ten years or a bit longer).
- Fewer than a third (30 percent) of companies have goals around growing revenue from sustainable products (however defined).
- Only 16 percent of the companies claim they are accounting for their most material externalities—such as carbon emissions, pollution, etc. The most common example of accounting for externalities is assigning a cost to carbon, as a growing number of companies currently do (see Figure 14.1).

Thus, like with the past several elements of governance, we see that this is a good news–bad news story. The positive story is that many companies have robust long-term goals based at least in part on a materiality assessment. The bad news is that there is a very long way to go—and companies may not be focused on the most impactful ESG issues.

For example, look at the data from sixty companies on the extent to which companies account for their most material externalities.

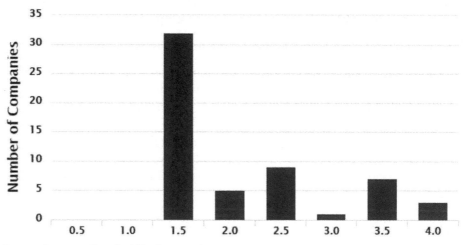

Source: Corporate Sustainability Scorecard

Figure 14.1: Scorecard Data from Sixty Companies on KSI 4.8: Accounting for Most Material Externalities

As we approach the year 2020, many companies are in the midst of setting the next range of sustainability goals and metrics. This is because the most common time frame for these goals has been five years—and many companies have been working toward their 2020 goals, which were set earlier around 2015.

i "Corporate sustainability: Unilever CEO Paul Polman on ending the 'three month rat race,'" Reuters, October 2012.

ii https://www.nestle.com/media/news/nestle-waters-sites-certification-alliance-for-water-stewardship-by-2025

iii https://sebgroup.com/about-seb/sustainability/our-approach-and-ambitions/our-material-issues

iv http://www.ab-inbev.com/content/dam/universaltemplate/ab-inbev/News/press-releases/public/2018/03/20180321_EN.pdf

v https://news.walmart.com/2018/03/29/walmart-commits-to-reduce-emissions-by-50-million-metric-tons-in-china

vi https://www.xerox.com/corporate-citizenship/2011/sustainability/waste-prevention.html

vii http://www.dell.com/learn/us/en/uscorp1/corp-comm/cr-earth-emissions?c=us&l=en&s=corp&cs=uscorp1

viii https://www.theclimategroup.org/news/vodafone-becomes-latest-business-join-re100

ix http://about.att.com/content/csr/home/blog/2015/11/at_t_commits_to_goal.html

x https://www.campbellsoupcompany.com/newsroom/press-releases/campbell-reports-progress-on-2020-sustainability-and-citizenship-goals/

xi https://company.ingersollrand.com/strengths/sustainability/our-climate-commitment.html

xii https://corporate.marksandspencer.com/blog/plan-a-2020

xiii https://www.nestle.com/media/news/nestle-csv-creating-shared-value-summary-report-2016

xiv https://www.environmentalleader.com/2013/10/nestle-makes-zero-waste-pledge-for-all-europe-factories/

xv https://www.2degreesnetwork.com/groups/2degrees-community/resources/sainsburys-20-by-20-sustainability-plan_2/

xvi https://www.akzonobel.com/for-media/media-releases-and-features/akzonobel-be-carbon-neutral-and-use-100-renewable-energy-2050

xvii http://www.coca-colacompany.com/press-center/press-releases/coca-cola-on-track-to-meet-100-water-replenishment-goal

xviii http://www.dhl.com/en/press/releases/releases_2017/all/dpdhl_commits_to_zero_emissions_logistics_by_2050.html

xix http://www.interface.com/US/en-US/about/mission/Our-Mission

xx https://www.kingfisher.com/sustainability/index.asp?pageid=173

xxi https://www.nestle.com/csv/impact

xxii https://www.greenbiz.com/news/2010/04/08/Sony-Targets-Zero-Environmental-Footprint-2050

xxiii https://ssir.org/articles/entry/the_greening_of_wal_mart

xxiv https://www.3m.com/3M/en_US/sustainability-us/goals-progress/

xxv http://files.shareholder.com/downloads/HAS/5793441862x0x966251/5A6E4060-BF62-4B21-80CB-B2008E43C01C/Hasbro_Celebrates_5th_Anniversary_of_Global_CSR_Practice_with_Release_of_CSR_Report_Playing_with_Purpose.pdf

xxvi https://www.bizjournals.com/portland/blog/sbo/2011/08/nike-to-eliminate-hazardous-chemical.html?page=all

xxvii https://www.bbc.com/news/world-42982959

xxviii https://www.citylab.com/equity/2016/02/why-water-costs-100-times-more-in-flint-than-in-phoenix-water-value-crisis/463152/

xxix Thomas Singer, "Total Impact Valuation: Overview of Current Practices," The Conference Board, 2018.

xxx http://b8f65cb373b1b7b15feb-c70d8ead6ced550b4d987d7c03fcdd1d.r81.cf3.rackcdn.com/cms/reports/documents/000/002/738/original/Putting-a-price-on-carbon-CDP-Report-2017.pdf?1508947761

Chapter 15
Culture and Organization

The fifth element in the Governance and Leadership section of the Scorecard addresses company culture and organization. This element illustrates how the Scorecard attempts to measure the "softer" aspects of how employee behavior is aligned to drive (or not drive) sustainability-related activities.

In 2014, Ingersoll Rand, a diversified industrial company, decided that one way to get serious about reducing carbon emissions was for CEO Michael Lamach to commit to a carbon reduction goal. Launched at the Clinton Global Initiative Annual Meeting and the UN Climate Summit, the commitment was to reduce the company's carbon footprint related to its operations by 35 percent by 2020 and the carbon footprint of its products by 50 million metric tons by 2030. The company is ahead of schedule on the operations side and on track to meet the aggressive product-related target.

When the CEO has a personal goal about most anything, that sends a powerful message throughout the organization—and defines the culture around that issue. Organization is important—but it is much more than boxes on a chart, titles, or reporting levels.

This element of the Scorecard addresses the overarching strategic question that senior executives and board members should be asking with respect to culture and organization:

Key Question: How does our company's culture and organization promote robust integration of ESG into the core of our company's actions and performance—from the C-suite to the shop floor?

To help answer this key question, the Scorecard analyzes how companies manage and perform in three areas:
- The management attention and accountability directed to sustainability by the CEO and executive team
- The key culture indicators related to environmental stewardship and social responsibility in place that define the actual culture (including the unwritten rules of the game)
- The people and structure that comprise the sustainability organization.

Within each of these areas, executives evaluate their company performance on several key sustainability indicators (KSIs).

DOI 10.1515/9781547400423-015

Management Accountability for and Attention to Sustainability

The Scorecard addresses management focus on environmental, social, and governance (ESG) with three KSIs: the **executive committee** role, the extent to which ESG is factored into executive compensation, and sustainability communications with employees.

KSI 5.1: Executive Committee Role Regarding Sustainability. Unless the CEO's executive team is engaged in some serious way with sustainability issues, chances are very good that the company is destined for no higher than Stage 2 on the Corporate Sustainability Scorecard. There may be a few areas where the company exceeds Stage 2; however, more deliberate ESG leadership from the C-suite drives higher level performance. The typical range of maturity follows:

KSI	Stage 1	Stage 2	Stage 3	Stage 4
Executive Committee Role Regarding Sustainability	Address specific sustainability risks during crises and as part of formal risk reviews	Dedicated "S" meeting ~2x/ year for 2–3 hours / meeting	"S" is a core part of key planning and operations meetings	"S" is central to plans and all Executive Committee meetings

Several examples of Stage 3 executive committee role are listed below:
- **Danone** (France): The sustainability function reports directly to top executives, with environmental directors in every division.[i]
- **Seardel Investment Corporation:** The South African clothing and textile manufacturer put a governance structure in place that aligns with the King Report on Corporate Governance.[ii]

KSI 5.2: Sustainability Factored into Executive Compensation. As part of its ongoing sustainability research, The Conference Board identifies leading practices related to executive incentives for environment, health, and safety (EHS) performance. The range of practices is as follows:

KSI	Stage 1	Stage 2	Stage 3	Stage 4
Sustainability Factored into Executive Compensation	Safety / EHS may be part of executive incentive compensation	"S" is a very small part of incentive compensation, if any	"S" = 10–15 percent of incentive compensation	"S" >15 percent of incentive compensation

Two separate 2018 reports tell the story as it exists today:

- A 2018 report from Ceres reviewed board ESG governance from 475 publicly held companies examined (from the Forbes Global 2000). The study found that a third of companies analyzed state that they link executive compensation to sustainability.[iii]
- However, a separate 2018 report from CDP (examining 1,681 global companies) found that only one in ten companies currently provide incentives for boards and executive teams linked to ESG.[iv]

Examples of leading practices were initially provided in a Conference Board report authored by Thomas Singer titled "The Seven Pillars of Sustainability Leadership." Updated data includes:

- **Alcoa** has long had sustainability performance as part of its executive bonus plans. The company's 2017 proxy statement noted that the company uses safety metrics, CO_2 emissions and diversity together account for 20 percent of annual incentive compensation.[v]
- **AEP:** Ten percent of annual incentive compensation is based on safety metrics, culture, and employee engagement metrics and a small portion on renewable energy projects.[vi]
- **Akzo Nobel** (NL): As part of its long-term incentive program for the top 600 executives, 30 percent of the conditional grant of shares is dependent on AkzoNobel's relative sustainability performance.
- **XCEL Energy:** The power company bases 30 percent of long-term incentive compensation on achieving specified CO_2 emission reductions.[vii]

In each of these cases, companies use the powerful, proven tool of executive incentive compensation to attempt to instill a culture that values ESG.

KSI 5.3: Sustainability Communication to Employees. Many company executives use town hall meetings to speak directly to employees. This is one of many ways to drive home the importance (or lack thereof—by not mentioning it) of ESG and sustainability. The range of approaches companies use to communicate the importance of ESG to employees is:

KSI	Stage 1	Stage 2	Stage 3	Stage 4
Sustainability Communication to Employees	Regularly update employees on "S" goals, plans, progress	Survey employees re "S"; candid; genuine; top-down; establish "S" **communities of practice**	CEO-sponsored "S" initiatives and teams; growing strategy and market discussions	Robust strategy, market and investment discussions

- **Campbell Soup:** As soon as you walk into Campbell Soup's world headquarters you see sustainability messaging in the waiting area, in the company cafeteria and yes, in the washrooms with reminders to limit use of water, conserve energy and minimize waste.[viii]
- **Intel:** Starting back in 2008, the company took an unusual step to encourage employees to help: it linked environmental performance to every employee's compensation, effectively making its sustainability goals everyone's job.[ix]

Key Culture Indicators Related to Sustainability

Companies motivate behavior in various ways: rewards, incentives, compensation, benefits, and challenging jobs. The Scorecard addresses internal mechanisms to embed ESG into company culture with two KSIs.

KSI 5.4: Internal Reward and Recognition Regarding Sustainability. There are many kinds of successful reward and recognition programs across the industry—suited to the culture, style, and preferences of the company executives. What differentiates leaders from others is the degree of recognition by the CEO and board. The range of approaches is as follows:

KSI	Stage 1	Stage 2	Stage 3	Stage 4
Internal Reward and Recognition Regarding Sustainability	For traditional EHS excellence only	Informal across corporation	Formal corporate "S" programs recognized by CEO	Formal recognition annually by CEO and Board member(s)

Examples of ways companies link sustainability to internal reward and recognition schemes include:
- **DuPont:** Since 2005, the company has honored teams of employees who champion sustainable growth, creating shareholder, and societal value while reducing our environmental footprint in the value chains in which we operate. These awards have been called the company Sustainable Growth Excellence Awards.[x]
- **Smithfield:** The company issues annual Environmental Excellence Awards, supporting the company commitment to sustainability.[xi]
- **Medtronic:** The medical products company has an annual EHS Sustainability Award that recognizes sustainability accomplishments—in line with the company goals. Medtronic sites and offices must meet strict criteria to even be considered for an EHS Sustainability award — potential winners are assessed in terms of innovation, teamwork and the ability to create scalable solutions and campaigns around energy conservation, waste reduction and employee safety.[xii]

KSI 5.5: "Unwritten Rules of the Game" Regarding Sustainability. We define the **unwritten rules of the game** at any organization as the way a cross-section of employees would describe "the way things work around here." This KSI is getting at the well-known situation whereby the CEO and/or senior executives say "the right things" in one breath, yet the harsh reality is that employee behavior is driven by incentives and norms that may be counter to that message. Simply stated, the CEO might say, "sustainability is vital to our future" yet the common reality is that you get measured by just "making your numbers." With respect to ESG issues, the rating criteria are:

KSI	Stage 1	Stage 2	Stage 3	Stage 4
"Unwritten Rules of the Game" Regarding Sustainability	Healthy skepticism re "S"—"seems like just another initiative"	CEO is serious about "S"—but incentives are not fully aligned	CEO and few business leaders are driving; "better get on board"	*"Sustainability is core to our business; get out if you don't fit"*

In reviewing the data from the first sixty companies that completed a self-assessment on the scorecard, it was most interesting to look at the companies that rated themselves Stage 3.5 or Stage 4. The companies have had:
- Enduring CEO focus not only on the importance of sustainability but also the very strong linkage between ESG and corporate strategy—for over a decade. In many cases, this enduring focus is reinforced by CEO and C-suite goals that drive behavior throughout the organization—as illustrated by the Ingersoll Rand example at the beginning of this chapter.
- Visible CEO leadership on ESG—internally and externally. Companies including Walmart, Waste Management, Novelis, Monsanto, and DTE have had highly visible, strong, consistent, and repeated messages from the CEO for many years reinforcing the importance of ESG.

Sustainability Organization

Remember the quality movement, back in the 1980s when many companies appointed a "chief quality officer." What happened? Ten years later, almost no company still had this role; they had driven the responsibilities into other core business leadership functions. The same may well be happening with sustainability.

The Scorecard addresses the sustainability organization with three KSIs: the chief sustainability officer (CSO) role; the CSO reporting level; and the inclusion of ESG into performance goals and job descriptions.

KSI 5.6: CSO Role. In recent years, a growing number of companies globally have appointed an officer of the company (typically a corporate vice president or higher) with the title of chief sustainability officer. Many other companies do not use that title. They may add sustainability to the existing title of, for example, a vice president of EHS.

In the Scorecard, what characterizes leadership is not the title but rather the degree of CEO and C-suite oversight of ESG. The range of approaches is:

KSI	Stage 1	Stage 2	Stage 3	Stage 4
Chief Sustainability Officer (CSO) Role	Not formally designated; existing SVP or VP (e.g., VP EHS) is *de facto* CSO	Director or VP of Sustainability	"S" is owned by C-suite executive; CSO is discrete role at VP or SVP level	CSO reports directly to CEO and has remit broader than "S"

It is instructional to look back in time at how companies have evolved with the CSO role. A report about the state of the sustainability profession in 2016 noted that the number of companies with a designated CSO had increased from 29 to 36 between 2011 and 2014. However, this data is misleading; it does not include the many companies where the sustainability leadership role is tacked on to that of an existing corporate officer, often a vice president. As noted above, many vice presidents of EHS also "own" sustainability. They may not be officially called the CSO; their title might be VP, EHS and Sustainability (or equivalent).[xiii]

A few examples of companies that have chosen to be highly visible in their approach to the CSO role are:
- **Coca-Cola:** The CEO announced in early 2017 that Bea Perez, previously vice president and CSO, will retain this role with broader responsibilities overseeing public affairs and communications. In this new role, Perez will leverage the important external stakeholder work done in public affairs and communications, sustainability and partnerships in a more strategic, integrated and holistic way.[xiv]
- **Nike:** Hannah Jones remained CSO when she was named vice president, sustainable business and innovation in 2012.[xv]

What is important is not the title—but rather the stature of the position, the impact within the company, and the degree of direct and frequent access to the CEO and other C-suite executives.

KSI 5.7: CSO (or Equivalent) Reporting Level. When a C-suite member has personal ownership and accountability for sustainability, that defines Stage 3. The title is not important; the level and specific accountability is critical.

KSI	Stage 1	Stage 2	Stage 3	Stage 4
CSO (or equivalent) Reporting Level	Two or more levels below CEO	One level below CEO	Direct to CEO	NA

A 2016 report titled "State of the Profession" by GreenBiz commented specifically on the CSO reporting level. The report states:

"The results, while perhaps not statistically significant, support a finding from our recent State of the Profession research. We asked who vice presidents of sustainability reported to at organizations with revenues greater than $1 billion. Fifty seven percent report to another vice president or senior vice president while 43 percent report to either the C-suite or the board of directors. This is a significant increase from surveys in previous years."[xvi]

KSI 5.8: Inclusion of Sustainability in Performance Goals and Job Descriptions. What gets measured gets managed. When specific environmental, social or governance priority initiatives are included in a job description and annual goals, it tends to result in action. Here is the range of activity across industry today.

KSI	Stage 1	Stage 2	Stage 3	Stage 4
Inclusion of Sustainability in Performance Goals and Job Descriptions	Limited (e.g., safety; diversity, compliance) in C-suite KPIs	Performance on key, material "S" metrics are included in C-suite annual goals	"S" criteria in C-suite job descriptions, performance objectives; KPIs—tied to "top five" most material issues	"S" criteria in job descriptions of all relevant staff and contractors

Companies that do an excellent job here "hard-wire" the goals of the C-suite and supporting managers directly to the company's long-term sustainability goals. A great example of this is Ingersoll Rand—mentioned at the beginning of this chapter. Another good example is Danone (the French food company). In addition to the accountability measures mentioned earlier in this chapter, Danone created a community of 110 carbon masters across the world to push through reduction plans in every unit, and created a committee to review progress twice a month.[xvii]

How Do Companies Stack Up?

Starting in 2018, I have been capturing data from a group of founding participants—invited to use the Scorecard for a company self-assessment. As I assess the data from the first sixty companies (all Fortune 500 or equivalent), three key messages stand out with respect to culture and organization:

- The sixty companies (admittedly many by their nature tend to be leaders in their industry sectors) score quite well on the "unwritten rules of the game." What this means is that the alignment between the CEO messages and "the way things work around here" is reasonably strong; 75 percent rated their company 2.5 or higher.
- When it comes to inclusion of sustainability in performance goals and job descriptions of key individuals throughout the organization, companies have a long way to go. Only twelve of sixty (20 percent) rated 3.0 or higher; a full 50 percent rated themselves 2.0 or lower.
- Companies have a long way to go when it comes to factoring ESG strongly into executive compensation. Less than 15 percent of companies scored this three or higher (see Figure 15.1).

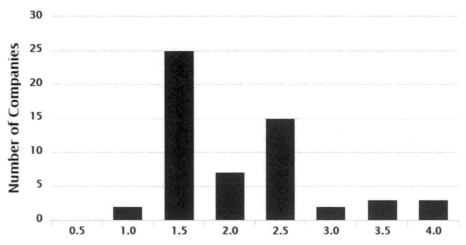

Source: Corporate Sustainability Scorecard

Figure 15.1: Scorecard Data from Sixty Companies on KSI 5.2: Sustainability Factored into Executive Compensation

In my experience working with companies, culture around sustainability is defined by the CEO's personal stance on the issue; the extent to which goals, metrics, and incentives are robust and widely communicated and reinforced; and the extent of communication both internally and externally.

i https://www.theguardian.com/sustainable-business/best-practice-exchange/danone-carbon-reduction-is-key

ii https://www.pdffiller.com/jsfiller-desk5/?projectId=183033956&expId=3350&expBranch=1#1a02940fd0d340f0af546ae6d51d8e90

iii https://www.ceres.org/news-center/press-releases/ceres-new-analysis-large-global-companies-links-sustainability

iv https://www.cdp.net/en//articles/media/new-research-shows-clear-gap-between-companies-awareness-of-climate-risks-and-actions-for-tackling-them

v Alcoa 2017 proxy statement, page 46.

vi AEP 2017 proxy statement, page 37.

vii XCEL Energy 2017 proxy statement, page 36.

viii https://www.greenbiz.com/blog/2011/10/12/10-communication-strategies-engage-employees-sustainability

ix https://www.theguardian.com/sustainable-business/2014/jun/26/green-executive-compensation-intel-alcoa-pay

x http://www.dupont.com/corporate-functions/sustainability/employee-engagement.html

xi https://www.smithfieldfoods.com/newsroom/press-releases-and-news/smithfield-foods-hands-out-2012-environmental-excellence-awards-to-company-facilities-and-employees

xii http://www.medtronic.com/us-en/about/news/ehs-award.html

xiii "State of the Profession 2016," GreenBiz and Weinreb Group.

xiv https://www.coca-colacompany.com/press-center/press-releases/the-coca-cola-company-announces-senior-leadership-appointments

xv https://www.theguardian.com/activate/hannah-jones

xvi "State of the Profession 2016," *op cit*.

xvii https://www.theguardian.com/sustainable-business/best-practice-exchange/danone-carbon-reduction-is-key

Chapter 16
Stakeholder Engagement

This chapter (the final element in the Governance and Leadership section of the Scorecard) addresses how companies engage with key stakeholders, especially non-governmental organizations (NGOs); investors, customers and suppliers.

For much of the twenty-first century to date, **HP** (today, two companies HP Inc. and Hewlett Packard Enterprise) has earned a strong reputation among various external stakeholders as a sustainability leader. The company has rated highly on many sustainability rankings. A key reason HP has won this recognition has been the company's long-standing engagement with external stakeholders as a source of insight into sustainability challenges.

Stakeholders broadly refer to individuals or groups of people who can be affected by an organization's business activities, outputs or outcomes.

- Internal stakeholders typically include the organization's governing body, management, employees and shareholders. (These relationships are addressed in other parts of the Scorecard.)
- External stakeholders (the principle focus of this chapter) typically include communities, government, environmental groups, as well as suppliers, customers and consumers.

The overarching strategic question that senior executives and board members should be asking with respect to stakeholder engagement is:

Key Question: How actively and deeply do we engage with key stakeholders to help our company reduce (full value chain) footprint, manage risks, and create opportunities—providing value to shareholders and to society?

To help answer this key question, the Scorecard analyzes the quality and impact of how companies engage with external stakeholders in four areas:
- Why do companies engage with external stakeholders?
- Who engages with stakeholders?
- What topics to engage on with stakeholders
- How and when to engage with stakeholders

Within each of these areas, executives evaluate their company performance on several key sustainability indicators (KSIs).

DOI 10.1515/9781547400423-016

Why Engage?

The Scorecard addresses the question of "why engage" with two KSIs: the overall approach to stakeholder engagement and the specific reasons for engaging.

KSI 6.1: Approach to Stakeholder Engagement. When Stage 1 companies think of stakeholders, they often think of Greenpeace or other environmental or human rights groups—the ones that accuse the company of doing bad things. As a result, the natural reaction is to be risk averse—and only engage where the audience and the settings are safe. The range of approaches companies take to stakeholder engagement follows.

KSI	Stage 1	Stage 2	Stage 3	Stage 4
Approach to Stakeholder Engagement	Ongoing talks with customers and suppliers; approach with NGOs and communities is to state our position and win approval ("declare; listen; defend")	Partner with customers re "S" solutions; approach with NGOs and communities is to learn, share, and compromise ("declare; learn; respond")	Building strategic partnerships re "S" solutions; with NGOs and communities engage deeply ("listen; learn; respond")	Engage and partner on very big initiatives ("listen; engage; learn; respond")

Stage 3 and Stage 4 companies, not surprisingly, see this completely differently. They view stakeholders as partners to learn from. Here are two examples:
- **Novo Nordisk** (Denmark)**:** The company has a very simple yet powerful approach to stakeholder engagement; they always focus on building trust, openness, and transparency. For decades, the company has systematically engaged with many stakeholders to impact trends, plans, strategies, and policies affecting people with diabetes, obesity, and related health issues the company is focused on.[i]
- **Johnson & Johnson:** The company engaged with key NGOs when deciding on its sustainability goals.[ii]

In these examples, the company takes a "listen, learn, respond" approach; they see strong business value in key strategic engagements.

KSI 6.2: Reasons for Stakeholder Engagement. The reasons for engaging with key external stakeholders are directly linked to the way the C-suite thinks about sustainability. If they see environmental and social issues as risks to be managed, their engagement with NGOs and others tends to be reactive. If they view environmental, social, and governance (ESG) issues as offering business opportunities—their external stakeholder outreach to customers, suppliers, and even NGOs is more proactive and growth-focused.

The table below depicts the various stages of evolution regarding how companies have evolved in their thinking about stakeholder engagement.

KSI	Stage 1	Stage 2	Stage 3	Stage 4
Reasons for Stakeholder Engagement	Respond to concerns; protect brand and reputation	Anticipate future expectations (e.g., carbon reporting); gain PR value (e.g., by participating in sustainability ratings - e.g., CDP, DJSI, etc.)	A key strategy driver is to address customers' "S" goals and ESG concerns	Drive strategic partnerships (e.g., regarding the circular economy)

Ecolab, the global provider of water, hygiene and energy technologies and services to the food, energy, healthcare, industrial, and hospitality markets, takes a Stage 4 approach to stakeholder engagement. Ecolab invests in building strategic ESG partnerships. The company partnered with Trucost and Microsoft to create the Water Risk Monetizer. This tool helps businesses understand water-related risks and quantify risks in financial terms to inform responsible decisions that enable growth. The tool is available to the public at no cost.[iii]

With Whom to Engage?

The Scorecard addresses the question "with whom to engage" with KSIs focused on the two largest audiences: one dealing with NGOs and a second focused on interaction with investors.

KSI 6.3: NGO Partnerships Regarding Sustainability. Over the past two decades, many of the mainstream NGOs—often referred to as "environmental groups" or various social responsibility entities like "human rights groups"—have become more business friendly. This does not mean NGOs have "sold out" to business; on the contrary, they have held fast to their missions. However, many have decided that the way to affect change is to work with companies—not to just sit on the outside throwing stones.

KSI	Stage 1	Stage 2	Stage 3	Stage 4
NGO *Partnerships re Sustainability*	Solid philanthropy; Local NGOs; national NGO on specific projects	Active engagement with NGOs for common "S" goals	Proactive with national NGO leaders; get input from more challenging NGOs	Active and deep engagement; major strategic partners with global NGOs

Several excellent examples include:

- **Coca-Cola:** Joining forces with USAID, the company was a founding member of the Global Water Challenge (GWC) in 2006. GWC accelerates the delivery of safe water and sanitation through partnerships that catalyze financial support and drive innovation for sustainable solutions.[iv]
- **Danone:** The company's Ecosystem Fund supports the transition toward sustainable farming practices. Created in 2009, the Danone Ecosystem Fund is an endowment fund of 100 million Euros aimed at co-creating inclusive business solutions with social and economic value for Danone and its Ecosystem partners, for example, small producers and farmers (milk and fruits), small distributors and street vendors, waste pickers, caregivers (midwives, nutritionists etc.), micro-entrepreneurs.[v]
- **Henkel:** The company partnered with NGO Waste Free Oceans to remove plastic waste from oceans and rivers and use it to produce around one million plastic bottles for its Lovables laundry brand.[vi]
- **Walmart:** The company launched a partnership with Environmental Defense Fund in 2005, shortly after Walmart announced (then) new long-term sustainability goals. Environmental Defense Fund brings expertise in science and economics and Walmart brings its size, influence, and openness to innovate.[vii]

In each of these examples, highly principled NGOs have found common ground with these organizations.

KSI 6.4: Interaction with Investors on Sustainability. In a February 2018 poll, more than fifty Fortune 500 companies responded to the question: "Over the past 12 months, the level of interest in ESG (expressed directly or indirectly through your company's investor relations team) has ... " as follows:[1]

- Stayed about the same = 28%
- Increased somewhat = 48%
- Increased significantly = 19%

---

1 I conducted this survey at a meeting of three sustainability executive councils of The Conference Board.

No respondents said the level of interest had decreased (or decreased significantly; 6 percent (likely privately held companies) said the question was not applicable.

In terms of how companies interact with investors on ESG issues, the range of approaches are as follows:

KSI	Stage 1	Stage 2	Stage 3	Stage 4
Interaction with Investors on Sustainability	Little "S" mention; CSO or equivalent answers questions	CEO and CFO discuss material sustainability risks; CSO sometimes pulled into analyst meetings	CEO, CFO and CSO periodically engage with mainstream investors re ESG issues	CEO, CFO and CSO frequently engage with mainstream investors on "S" issues and policy

Several examples of how leading company CEOs and CFOs proactively incorporate ESG into their outreach to mainstream investors include:
- **Shell:** The company has conducted annual investor briefings on social, environmental and governance issues since 2007, and maintains an impressive archive of presentations and materials on its website.[viii]
- **BASF:** The global chemical company explicitly touts environmental and social performance as a boon for investors. It notes that there is a growing awareness in the financial market that a company geared toward sustainable development can outperform peers over the long-term while minimizing risks.[ix]
- **Unilever:** CEO Paul Polman "famously stopped quarterly reporting" to investors.[x]
- **UPS:** Former CFO Kurt Kuhn was a leading voice for ESG with Wall Street and one of the early internal supporters of UPS's sustainability program, working on the very first sustainability report in 2002. He was an early member of the corporate sustainability steering committee.[xi]
- **Siemens:** Company executives consistently educate investors regarding growth of their Environmental Portfolio.[xii]

The landscape of ESG outreach to investors is changing rapidly. In a June 2018 survey, the Conference Board gathered information from about fifty large global companies (60 percent headquartered in the United States and 40 percent headquartered in Europe).[xiii] We found that while the approach to investor interaction and the frequency varies significantly, some key points emerged:
- 82 percent of companies proactively offer institutional investors the opportunity to engage on ESG matters. Of this large group, the actual frequency is roughly evenly split among: annually, biannually, quarterly, and other.

- 85 percent of the companies said institutional investors ask about ESG matters. Of these, around 75 percent were generic ESG information requests about the company's overall ESG approach and performance. The rest pertained to a specific ESG topics such as CEO compensation, climate risk strategy, board diversity, data privacy, etc.
- TCFD (Task-Force on Climate-Related Financial Disclosures) is having a growing impact. Only one quarter of the companies said TCFD is having no significant impact; they are proceeding as before. Most companies surveyed said that (as of June 2018) they are seriously assessing TCFD.

What to Engage On?

The Scorecard addresses the question, "what to engage on" with two KSIs: one dealing with content (focused on materiality); and a second addressing scale (the impact of the engagement.

KSI 6.5: Engaging on Most Material Issues Across Supply Chain. The Ecolab example noted earlier in this chapter is a great example of developing a tool in collaboration with business and NGO partners—focused on a highly material issue (in that case, clean water). The range of industry activity is depicted below.

KSI	Stage 1	Stage 2	Stage 3	Stage 4
Engaging on Most Material Issues Across Supply Chain	Engage on an issue in own operations to gain visible PR	Engage on most material issue(s) in own operations	Engage on most material issue(s) across full supply chain	Most material issue(s) fully supply chain—with focus on opportunity

A group of large companies in the plastics value chain, including Nestlé, Procter & Gamble, and Unilever, joined a collaborative called WRAP's UK Plastics Pact aimed at creating a circular economy for plastics. They set 2025 goals around reusable, recyclable and compostable plastic packaging and the elimination of single use packaging, among other things.[xiv]

This issue is rapidly spanning the globe. On June 25, 2018, the largest city in India, Mumbai, banned single-use plastics. Residents caught using plastic bags, cups, or bottles face penalties of up to 25,000 rupees ($364) and three months in jail. Penalties had already kicked in for businesses and several, reportedly including a McDonald's and Starbucks, have already been fined. Local consumers are starting to carry cloth bags and vendors have begun wrapping meat in newspaper rather than plastic sheets.[xv]

The article referenced in the example above notes that half of the world's plastic was created in the past thirteen years and about half of that is thought to be used once and then thrown away.

Some additional examples of what companies engage in with key stakeholders follow:
- **BT:** Formerly known as British Telecom, BT committed that by 2020 the company will help customers reduce their carbon emissions by three times the end-to-end carbon impact of BT's business.
- **Ingersoll Rand:** The industrial company provides an Energy Efficiency Leader Award to other companies implementing sustainability best practices. The award showcases and recognizes organizations that have shown significant achievements in energy efficiency and sustainability.[xvi]

In each of these examples, the company focuses on a critical (material) ESG issue and extends external outreach in a highly focused way to drive footprint reductions and business improvement.

KSI 6.6: Scale of Typical Stakeholder Engagement Regarding Sustainability. Bigger is not necessarily better. However, large multinational companies with a global reach and complex supply chains have the scale to tackle global problems. Unilever did this with depletion of global fisheries back in the 1990s; Coca-Cola has been doing this with fresh water supplies for over a decade.

The varying degrees of scale companies focus upon with key outreach are depicted below:

KSI	Stage 1	Stage 2	Stage 3	Stage 4
Scale of Typical Stakeholder Engagement Regarding Sustainability	Partnerships with NGOs, communities, suppliers, etc. tend to be small (often local)	Partnerships tend to be large (often with regional impact)	Large partnerships involving peer companies, often with national or impact	Partner on very large initiatives, often with global impact

One of the most powerful examples of using scale to address environmental and social issues comes from Walmart. As noted previously in this book, **Walmart**'s (then) CEO Lee Scott committed to three aspirational goals back in 2005: to be supplied 100 percent by renewable energy; to create zero waste; and to sell products that sustain our resources and environment. To meet those goals, Walmart set to transform its supply chain, in partnership with Environmental Defense Fund, a leading NGO.[xvii]

Two other examples of how companies address strategic partnerships follow:

- **Baxter:** The healthcare company engages stakeholders worldwide to share information and to collaborate.[xviii]
- **Ecolab:** The company was a founding partner of the International Water Stewardship Standard, launched in 2014.[xix]

How and When to Engage

The Scorecard has two KSIs addressing how and when to engage with stakeholders: one dealing with the link to business strategy and a second that looks at time spent by the C-suite with NGO stakeholders.

KSI 6.7: Link between Stakeholder Engagement and Business Strategy. This is tricky; formation and execution of business strategy is a tightly controlled process—with carefully scripted messages to investors. For the clear majority of companies (that fall into Stage 1 or Stage 2), there might be a few touted partnerships with customers or NGOs—but not much more. This changes notably for Stage 3 companies—where a CEO sponsored initiative garners considerable attention.

KSI	Stage 1	Stage 2	Stage 3	Stage 4
Link between Stakeholder Engagement and Business Strategy	Cautious approach to reduce risk and enhance brand	Visible partnerships on major regional initiatives	CSO and C-suite partner; leverage key advisors (e.g., External Sustainability Advisory Board)	CEO-led; most material issues among SDGs; a key growth driver

A great example of a Stage 3 approach is JPMorgan Chase's work with the city of Detroit. After doing business in Detroit for more than eighty years, the company decided to make a $100 million, five-year investment in the city's economic recovery. The company now expects to invest $150 million in Detroit by 2019. JPMorgan Chase believes that public–private partnerships are vital to the future, stabilizing neighborhoods, retraining the workforce for today's job market; bolstering local small businesses; and (yes) attracting new investors. The revitalization is about more than access to capital; it is about inclusive collaboration and public-private partnerships.[xx]

KSI 6.8: Time Spent by C-Suite with NGO Stakeholders. Does the CEO or other members of the C-suite personally spend time with key stakeholders? Of course the CEO and CFO spend time with investors, but how about environmental and socially related NGOs? The range of actions are depicted below.

KSI	Stage 1	Stage 2	Stage 3	Stage 4
Time Spent by C-Suite with NGO Stakeholders	< 5 hours / year	5–10 hours / year	10–20 hours / year	> 20 hours / year

In the Walmart example described above, CEO Lee Scott personally spent time with Environmental Defense Fund CEO Fred Krupp. Some additional examples of Stage 3 or higher:

- **Marks & Spencer** (UK): The CEO views Plan A (discussed in Chapter 14, KSI 4.4) as integral to the rebirth of M&S.[xxi]
- **Campbell Soup:** For the duration of her tenure as CEO, Denise Morrison reinforced her goal for the company to "become one of the most sustainable consumer products goods companies in the world."[xxii]

In each of these examples, The CEO and other C-suite executives are personally involved—not just for a single meeting or "ribbon cutting" event, but deeply throughout the engagement.

How Do Companies Stack Up?

Starting in 2018, we are capturing data from a group of founding participants—invited to use the Scorecard for a company self-assessment and to provide feedback. As we assess the data from the first sixty companies (all Fortune 500 or equivalent), three key messages stand out:

- Companies involved are doing a decent job of engaging on the most material issues across the supply chain, with three of four companies rating themselves 2.5 or higher.
- The linkage between stakeholder engagement and business strategy is generally weak. Only one in four companies rated themselves 3.0 or higher here.
- When it comes to engaging with mainstream investors on sustainability, as of February 2018, only one in four (27 percent) rated themselves 3.0 or higher (see Figure 16.1).

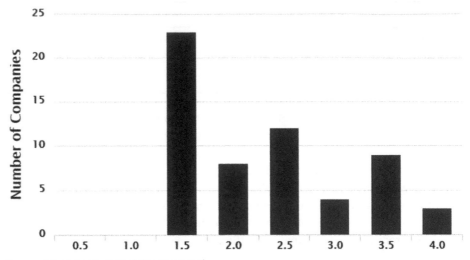

Source: Corporate Sustainability Scorecard

Figure 16.1: Scorecard Data from Sixty Companies on KSI 6.4: Interaction with Investors on Sustainability

Stakeholder engagement is, by definition, vast, complex, fraught with risk, and a potential time sink—sucking up lots of time with less than certain return on investment. Smart companies focus! They focus on their top one to three material ESG issues. They focus on a very few external partners that share a keen interest in that/those issue(s). They focus their investment, talent and resources to drive themselves toward clear, measurable results.

i https://www.novonordisk.com/about-novo-nordisk/novo-nordisk-in-brief/positions/public-affairs.html

ii https://www.jnj.com/caring/citizenship-sustainability

iii https://www.ecolab.com/sustainability/water-risk-monetizer

iv https://www.coca-colacompany.com/stories/our-partners-global-water-challenge

v http://ecosysteme.danone.com/

vi https://www.henkel.com/press-and-media/press-releases-and-kits/2018-03-22-henkel-partners-with-waste-free-oceans-to-fight-marine-plastic-litter/839218

vii https://www.edf.org/partnerships/walmart

viii https://www.shell.com/investors/environmental-social-and-governance/sri-news-presentations-and-annual-briefings.html

ix https://www.basf.com/en/company/sustainability/economy.html

x https://www.theguardian.com/sustainable-business/unilever-ceo-paul-polman-interview

xi https://www.cnbc.com/id/100491678

xii https://www.siemens.com/global/en/home/company/sustainability.html

xiii "Investor ESG Interaction," Survey by The Conference Board's Global Sustainability Centre; June 2018.

xiv http://www.wrap.org.uk/content/the-uk-plastics-pact

xv https://www.theguardian.com/world/2018/jun/25/mumbai-india-bans-plastic-bags-and-bottles

xvi https://company.ingersollrand.com/strengths/sustainability/energy-efficiency-leader-award.html

xvii https://www.gsb.stanford.edu/sites/gsb/files/publication-pdf/greening.pdf

xviii http://www.baxter.com/corporate-responsibility.page

xix https://www.ecolab.com/sustainability/water-stewardship

xx https://www.jpmorganchase.com/corporate/Corporate-Responsibility/detroit.htm

xxi https://www.theguardian.com/business/2013/jul/07/plan-a-integral-rebirth-marks-spencer

xxii "Create, Grow, Sustain: How Companies Are Doing Well by Doing Good," Business Roundtable 2013 Report.

Chapter 17
Disclosure, Reporting, and Transparency

The final element of the Scorecard section on Governance and Leadership addresses the broad subject of reporting, especially to key external audiences.

To truly grasp the complexities of sustainability reporting, it is best to look at complex situations where a highly visible CEO took a stance on sustainability. The Monsanto evolution since the late 1980s is a case in point.

In 1997, Monsanto's (then) CEO Robert Shapiro spun off the company's chemical operations into a separate company (Solutia). He focused the "new" Monsanto on biology and agriculture (combined with chemistry) under the banner of "Food, Health, Hope."

Following the Solutia spin-off, Monsanto issued its annual report, packaged together with its sustainability report. (The reports are no longer available on the company's website.) These reports, an early manifestation of and reinforcement for what today is called "integrated reporting," won plaudits from Ceres and other environmental groups. I was at a Ceres meeting of business executives and nongovernmental organizations (NGOs) in the late 1990s when the president of the Sierra Club stood up and applauded Monsanto's efforts and disclosure and transparency.

The overarching strategic question that senior executives and board members should be asking when it comes to reporting of environmental, social, and governance (ESG) issues is:

Key Question: To what extent is our disclosure and reporting of ESG risks and opportunities transparent, robust, and aligned with financial/business reporting?

To help answer this key question, the Scorecard analyzes how companies manage and perform in three areas:
- The information that is disclosed to stakeholders related to the company's own operations, suppliers, and the full supply chain ESG impacts
- The way sustainability data and information is reported—showing progress and performance
- The extent to which the company has earned a reputation for transparency

Within each of these areas, executives evaluate their company performance on several key sustainability indicators (KSIs).

DOI 10.1515/9781547400423-017

Disclosure of Sustainability Risks, Posture, Programs, and Plans

Companies have been issuing public reports on ESG matters for four decades. Back in the 1980s and especially the 1990s, many companies—especially those in "heavy footprint" industry sectors (e.g., chemicals, mining, oil and gas, heavy manufacturing, etc.) issued environment, health and safety—or broader corporate responsibility reports.

The early decades of reporting were characterized by "feel good" content and in some cases complaints of greenwashing—sharing the "feel good" stories without airing the dirty laundry.

Then came the Global Reporting Initiative in the last 1990s—and some semblance of structure for these reports. Unfortunately, many "GRI conforming" reports still came across as dumping a ton of information—with little concise focus on what the investment community would refer to as materiality.

The Scorecard addresses sustainability disclosure with two KSIs.

KSI 7.1: Company Posture Regarding ESG Materiality. As mentioned in Chapter 7 (Environmental Stewardship: The "E" in ESG), ESG materiality refers to the most significant sustainability issues that could have an impact on future company profitability. For the clear majority of companies, there are fewer than five truly material ESG issues; for many industry sectors, there is only one or two. The range of company posture on materiality follows.

KSI	Stage 1	Stage 2	Stage 3	Stage 4
Company Posture Regarding ESG Materiality	Basic materiality assessment— mostly in own operations	Robust materiality assessment— full value chain (often long list of issues)	Sharp focus on critical few truly material issues; taking bold steps to cut impacts	Viewed as a model company across industry vis-à-vis its materiality focus

Virtually every major company today that reports ESG issues publicly has conducted at least some kind of materiality assessment. And, the clear majority of companies fall into Stage 2; they follow the Global Reporting Initiative (GRI) guidance and issue a matrix or some other figure with a long list of important (to some stakeholder) issues. Few companies focus on the critical few (one to three for most companies) truly material issues. Some leading examples include:

- **Ford:** The global auto company utilizes a highly detailed materiality analysis that was reviewed by a stakeholder team. They use a materiality matrix to determine potential impact of all materiality issues.[i]

- **Gap:** The company conducted a materiality analysis, identifying (among other things) corporate governance and radical transparency as two key material issues.[ii]

KSI 7.2: Communication and Disclosure of Material ESG Impacts. External stakeholders simply want concise, fully transparent communication and disclosure focused on the handful of most material ESG issues. Seems simple; yet, the clear majority of companies fail that test. This is the dividing line between companies in Stages 1 and 2—and those in Stage 3 or beyond.

KSI	Stage 1	Stage 2	Stage 3	Stage 4
Communication and Disclosure of Material ESG Impacts	Disclose required info; compliance focus plus a few other key issues	Annual progress review; follow commonly accepted framework; impose basic "S" requirements on suppliers	Blunt, candid disclosure of full value chain material impacts; impose "S" criteria on suppliers; use "S" product labels	Robust, balanced report—consistent with circular economy principles; full life-cycle impacts quantified and explained

As noted earlier in Chapter 14 (KSI 4.8: Accounting for Most Material Externalities), a 2018 research report published by The Conference Board (titled "Total Impact Valuation: Overview of Current Practices") identified fourteen companies globally that are leading the way in calculating and communicating to stakeholders the total economic, environmental, and social impacts of their companies—across the full value chain. AkzoNobel, BASF, LaFargeHolcim, Samsung, and Volvo were among the companies featured in that report.[iii]

Some examples of how companies have disclosed material issues include:
- **Exxon Mobil:** The oil giant published details of its stranded assets—the value (in Exxon's case) of oil and gas fields that it might not be able to exploit if there were a high carbon price or tough rules on greenhouse gas emissions. Exxon did not report this because it had "gone green" but rather because it was heading off a shareholder resolution.[iv]
- **Ford:** As noted in Chapter 3, in what was a bold move at the time, Bill Ford disclosed in the company's 2003–2004 Sustainability Report that, "approximately 90 percent of a vehicle's lifecycle greenhouse gas emissions are attributable to CO2 emitted during customer vehicle use."[v]

- **IBM:** The company's supplier assessment practice requires audited suppliers to create and submit a Supplier Improvement Plan (SIP) for all incidents of noncompliance discovered.[vi]
- **Puma:** The German footwear company notes that the company must address the activities of its supply chain partners that generate 94 percent of the total environmental impact[vii] and developed the first environmental profit and loss statement in 2012.[viii]
- **Walmart:** As of July 2009, the company requires suppliers to provide information about the environmental impact of their products and to distill the data into sustainability ratings.[ix]

In each of these examples, the companies moved beyond their own operations fenceline and considered the truly material issues across the value chain.

Reporting of Sustainability Progress and Performance

As noted above, companies have been reporting on environmental stewardship and social responsibility for over forty years.

The Scorecard addresses the reporting of sustainability progress and performance with three KSIs: the first two dealing with annual external reports and a second that looks at data assurance and verification.

KSI 7.3: Sustainability in Annual Report. For many years, leading companies—particularly outside the United States—have included detailed ESG information in their annual reports. As one example, Sims Metal Management (the world's largest metal recycling company) has included sustainability information in its annual report since 2000. However, in the United States today, the norm in public company annual reports is for a CEO letter and little more preceding the main 10K portion of the report.

The range of inclusion of ESG matters in the annual report follows.

KSI	Stage 1	Stage 2	Stage 3	Stage 4
Sustainability in Annual Report	Brief mention in CEO letter	Significant mention in CEO letter with few key "S" KPIs	Top material "S" KPIs integrated with key financial metrics	Fully integrated report to society: financial, social, environment

The movement toward integrated reporting—incorporating a detailed report (of ESG issues) to society alongside the conventional financial report to shareholders—has steadily grown. Many examples of excellent integrated reporting best practices can be found; however, the clear majority are from western European and other countries that tend to be out front on ESG issues.[x]

Integrated reports for U.S.-based companies are rare. However, as seen on the Integrated Reporting website, some excellent examples exist.

- **Aegon, Eskom, Marks & Spencer, Novartis; Novo Nordisk; Sasol, and Vancity** (to name just a few) have issued comprehensive integrated reports.
- **AEP; United Technologies; Southwest Airlines** were among the first U.S. companies to issue integrated reports.
- **BP** included key ESG and financial metrics in its annual financial report for many years, starting when John Browne was CEO.
- **Ingersoll Rand** published an integrated 2016 annual report. This is an excellent example of demonstrating how sustainability is fully embedded into corporate growth strategy; how the company is building its product portfolio to deliver that growth; and the metrics in place to drive progress.[xi]

In each of these examples, companies are moving the needle. The U.S. companies are clearly breaking the mold. At a time when the clear majority of U.S. companies issue an annual report consisting of a CEO letter and the 10-K, integrated reporters stand out.

KSI 7.4: Sustainability Report. For the past forty years, often lengthy sustainability reports have evolved. A 2018 report by the Governance and Accountability Institute noted that 85 percent of the S&P 500 companies published a sustainability report (by whatever name) in 2017. This is a dramatic increase over seven years; in 2011, the number of companies publishing such a report was roughly 20 percent.[xii]

Full integration of sustainability/ESG into corporate posture, performance and reporting will be defined ultimately by the death of the separate sustainability report. That may take years; however, that is the direction leading companies are moving.

KSI	Stage 1	Stage 2	Stage 3	Stage 4
Sustainability Report	Update website periodically with ESG data	Updated annually; aligned to industry norms (e.g., TCFD); on website	Clear and transparent reporting; Conforms with common framework	Issued and integrated with Annual Report

Three early reporters from very different corners of the world won plaudits in 2013:[xiii]
- **Bharti Airtel:** The Indian company's first report in 2011–2012 included a "Blueprint for Social Inclusion."

- **Impahla:** The South African company became the country's first carbon neutral garment manufacturer in 2013.
- **ING Bank:** The Polish company provided a thorough presentation of sustainability issues and performance (along with solid creative artwork).

Other examples of early leaders who continue to earn high marks are:
- **Kingfisher:** The sustainable growth plan at Europe's leading home improvement retailer outlines a roadmap to 2025, the next stage in its journey to be a net positive business by 2050.[xiv]
- **Marks and Spencer:** The company's Plan A Report (UK) is a regular award winner.[xv]
- **PUMA:** The German company pioneered reporting of environmental profit and loss information and continues to do so as part of its integrated annual and sustainability report.[xvi]

In each of these examples, the company did not look around its in-country peers to "follow the leader"; they looked outside at best practices and then pushed the envelope even further.

KSI 7.5: Data Assurance/Verification. Since the very early days of sustainability reporting in the late 1890s and 1990s, some leading companies have sought external validation from a respected third party to add further credibility to the report contents. During this period, I was overseeing Arthur D. Little's global environmental management practice and was responsible for authoring or signing off on many of these external assurance statements.

Over the years, companies have enlisted third parties to provide assurance statements at different levels of detail:
- An external opinion about a specific program—typically an aspect of the company's ESG management activities (such as an environment, health, and safety [EHS] audit program or EHS management system).
- An external opinion about the data management process (the methodology by which data is gathered, analyzed and reported).
- An external validation of the actual ESG data itself.

Clearly, the third level of detail is far more involved (and more expensive)—which is a key reason many companies decide it is not worth the money. The range of approaches to assurance is depicted below.

KSI	Stage 1	Stage 2	Stage 3	Stage 4
Data Assurance / Verification	No formal verification	Internal Audit reviews process and verifies selected data	Credible, independent 3rd party review of process and data	Consistent with 3rd party review of financial controls

A recent article ("Sustainability Assurance Services: From a Niche to the Mainstream") describes the current landscape of adopting assurance of environmental, social, and governance (ESG) data. The article notes that European companies are ahead in adopting ESG assurance as sixty one percent of European companies in the S&P Global 1200 include assurance statements in their sustainability reports. The Asia-Pacific region is not far behind, with almost half of the companies in this region including ESG assurance statements in their sustainability reports. Several of the companies mentioned in this article include:[xvii]

- **Lockheed Martin:** The leading aerospace and defense company is among a growing number of companies that obtains independent assurance of its sustainability 2016 report and 21 GRI indicators.[xviii]
- **Walgreens Boots Alliance:** The company's independent assurance of data covers corporate giving and employee diversity, in addition to more common indicators such as CO_2 emissions, energy use and waste.
- **Xylem:** In addition to providing independent assurance of its energy, CO_2 and water metrics, the company also includes assurance for its data on injury frequency and severity.

Transparency

The Scorecard addresses transparency in public disclosure with three KSIs: outreach posture; public policy alignment and approach to advertising and marketing.

KSI 7.6: Outreach Posture, Tools and Techniques. Companies use various means of conveying externally their posture with respect to environmental stewardship, social responsibility, and its strategy to leverage global ESG trends for growth. The range across the four stages is as follows.

KSI	Stage 1	Stage 2	Stage 3	Stage 4
Outreach Posture, Tools and Techniques	Very cautious; "Stay in our comfort zone"	Very candid, balanced reporting of ESG impacts; many outreach channels	Strong and growing "S" messages in social media	Powerful messages from CEO provide focus; multiple ways to reinforce

- **Allergan:** The global pharmaceutical company based in Ireland has published a CSR report since 1994 and has been recognized as one of the most transparent companies. In 2016, they set a 20/20 Challenge: an ambitious goal to reduce its environmental impact 20 percent by 2020.[xix]
- **Coca-Cola:** As part of its outreach, the company discusses water stewardship in press releases once or twice per month.[xx]
- **FedEx:** Mitch Jackson, Vice President of Environmental Affairs & Sustainability, blogs regularly.[xxi]
- **Southwest Airlines:** The airline uses social media as part of its upcycling and repurpose program, which has successfully diverted huge amounts of solid waste (seat covers, life vests, co-mingled waste) out of landfills.[xxii]
- **Zipcar:** The company uses Twitter to discuss the sustainability impacts of their service.[xxiii]

In each of these examples, the company uses a variety of media tools to reach its key stakeholders, and this is all part of a formally developed outreach strategy.

KSI 7.7: Public Policy Alignment with Sustainability Commitments. Few things upset environmental or socially minded NGOs more than when a company touts its great sustainability accomplishments on the one hand—and then the company's government affairs organization lobbies for weaker sustainability laws and regulations on the other hand. The NGO Ceres confronted General Motors head on in the late 1990s on this. GM had been an early endorser of the Ceres principles; however, the company routinely lobbied for weaker fuel economy standards in Washington D.C. Ceres called GM to task as part of the five-year review of the company/NGO relationship.

KSI	Stage 1	Stage 2	Stage 3	Stage 4
Public Policy Alignment with Sustainability Commitments	Cautious; aligned with industry association positions	Join other CEOs on bold policy positions	Blunt, candid disclosure of full value chain impacts	CEO joins peers in driving global sustainability agenda

Related specifically to public policy, BICEP is a Ceres coalition of many leading companies (including Autodesk, eBay, Gap, Etsy, Gap, General Mills, Mars, Nestlé, Nike, Salesforce, Unilever, and others) and has been working for years to pass climate and energy policy.[xxiv]

Two excellent examples of CEOs and company leaders being transparent and candid, supporting ESG and aligning its public policy accordingly, are:

- **DTE:** Formerly known as utility Detroit Edison, the company broke ranks with the general utility sector position on environmental issues. CEO Gerry Anderson stated that, "For many years, the industry has viewed sustainability as a choice between affordability for customers and environmental outcomes. We reject that premise."[xxv]
- **Unilever:** CEO Paul Polman has noted that "We are entering a very interesting period of history where the responsible business world is running ahead of the politicians—taking on a broader role to serve society."[xxvi]

KSI 7.8: Corporate Marketing and Advertising Approach Regarding Sustainability.

Let's face it: corporate advertising and marketing is all about putting your best foot forward as a company and selling the public on how great your company or product is. Thus, when it comes to environmental and social issues, the risk of being accused of "green marketing" is very real.

A considerable amount of sustainability-related activity can be for show. CEOs can be out pitching how green their company is while the core of the business remains mostly unchanged. Some companies (especially large, profitable ones) have the luxury of putting on a good show while not airing their dirty laundry. This represents a serious challenge for external stakeholders: which messages from companies are mostly for marketing purposes and which are genuine commitments to transform the company, even if the tradeoffs are difficult and costly.

The range of practices below illustrates different approaches to transparent marketing.

KSI	Stage 1	Stage 2	Stage 3	Stage 4
Corporate Marketing & Advertising Approach re Sustainability	Being honest— but often viewed by NGOs as "green marketing"	Balanced, truthful, humble approach	Err on the side of caution; emulated by others; earn the respect of NGOs	Ethical marketing credentials and reputation

Several examples of companies working hard to be candid, balanced, and transparent in their advertising follow:

- **Danone:** The French company is tying the brand strongly to sustainability—for example, plant-based plastics and increasing use of recycled packaging.[xxvii]

- **Tesla, Honda** and other auto makers compete for brand kudos as the industry transforms itself—realizing its historic (old-economy) model of churning out cars and trucks is increasingly choking off its own market while "new economy: sustainability transportation options represent future growth opportunities."[xxviii]
- **Toyota:** The Japanese auto company is using pollution-reducing billboards in California. Described as the "catalytic converter" of billboards, they use a titanium dioxide coated vinyl to purify the surrounding air.[xxix]

Advertising is tricky business when it comes to sustainability, but these are a few examples of companies working to align their ESG posture with how they sell products.

How Do Companies Stack Up?

Starting in 2018, we are capturing data from a group of founding participants—invited to use the Scorecard for a company self-assessment and to provide feedback. As we assess the data from the first sixty companies (all Fortune 500 or equivalent), three key messages stand out with respect to ESG disclosure, reporting, and transparency:
- As would be expected, companies fared well on their sustainability reporting—but not where it matters most which is in the annual report. Less than one in four companies rated themselves at 3.0 or higher on ESG in the annual report.
- Companies still have a lot of work to do to focus on materiality, though progress has been made. One-third of companies rate themselves 2.0 or lower; 40 percent rate themselves 3.0 or higher; 20 percent are in the middle at 2.5 rating.
- On external sustainability communications—and alignment with public policy, there is a big gap. Stage 3 is described as "blunt, candid disclosure of full value chain impacts"—and only 18 percent of companies rated themselves at this level (or higher) (see Figure 17.1).

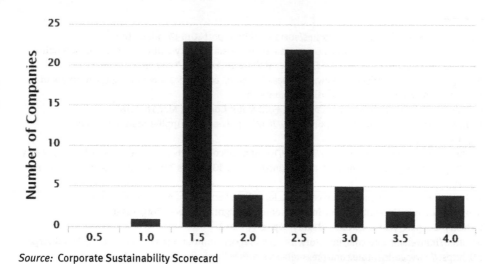

Source: Corporate Sustainability Scorecard

Figure 17.1: Scorecard Data from Sixty Companies on KSI 7.7: External Sustainability Communications Regarding Public Policy

Clearly, plenty of work remains in disclosure and reporting, even after decades of company sustainability reporting.

i https://corporate.ford.com/microsites/sustainability-report-2016-17/index.html

ii http://www.gapincsustainability.com/strategy/our-sustainability-strategy/assessing-materiality

iii Singer, "Total Impact Valuation: Overview of Current Practices," *op cit.*

iv https://www.economist.com/news/business/21599770-companies-are-starting-open-up-about-their-environmental-risks-they-need-do-more-green

v Email to Gib Hedstrom from Jon Coleman, Ford Motor Company; May 11, 2018.

vi https://www.ibm.com/ibm/responsibility/2012/supply-chain/supplier-assessment-and-improvement-plans.html

vii https://www.greenbiz.com/blog/2012/02/10/pumas-eco-impacts-kicks-ball-forward-transparency

viii https://www.greenbiz.com/research/report/2012/02/10/pumas-2010-environmental-profit-loss-report

ix https://www.scientificamerican.com/article/walmart-environmental-impacts-labels/

x http://examples.integratedreporting.org/search_recognized_reports?organisation_industry=&report_year=&award_category=&page_num=2

xi http://ir.ingersollrand.com/investors/financial-reports/annual-reports-and-proxies/default.aspx

xii https://www.ga-institute.com/press-releases/article/flash-report-85-of-sp-500-indexR-companies-publish-sustainability-reports-in-2017.html

xiii https://www.triplepundit.com/2014/01/top-ten-sustainability-reports-2013/

xiv http://www.sustainablebrands.com/news_and_views/leadership/sustainable_brands/kingfisher_continues_path_net_positive_puts_customers

xv http://planareport.marksandspencer.com/

xvi http://about.puma.com/en/sustainability/environment/environmental-profit-and-loss-account

xvii https://www.cpajournal.com/2018/07/20/sustainability-assurance-services/

xviii http://www.lockheedmartin.com/content/dam/lockheed/data/corporate/documents/Sustainability/verification-2016.pdf

xix https://www.greenbiz.com/blog/2014/06/05/do-newsweeks-green-rankings-still-matter

xx https://www.coca-colacompany.com/press-center/press-releases?tagstopics=Water%20Stewardship

xxi https://about.van.fedex.com/blog/sustainability-is-a-team-sport/

xxii https://www.southwestaircommunity.com/t5/Repurposing/bd-p/repurposing

xxiii https://twitter.com/zipcar

xxiv https://www.ceres.org/networks/ceres-policy-network

xxv https://www.newlook.dteenergy.com/wps/wcm/connect/dte-web/dte-pages/ccr/home/ceo-message

xxvi http://www.businessinsider.com/unilever-ceo-paul-polman-the-very-essence-of-capitalism-is-under-threat-2012-6

xxvii http://interbrand.com/best-brands/best-global-brands/2016/ranking/danone/

xxviii http://interbrand.com/best-brands/best-global-brands/2016/sector-overviews/existential-evolution-in-the-auto-category/

xxix http://pressroom.toyota.com/releases/mirai+purifying+billboard+us+campaign.htm.

Chapter 18
Strategic Planning

This chapter begins addressing the second section of the Scorecard—those activities related to corporate strategy and execution. This first chapter focuses on strategic planning—the integration of environmental, social, and governance (ESG) into core planning activities.

Aegon N.V., the multinational insurance company based in the Netherlands, has figured out how to ensure that ESG risks are embedded into the company's strategic planning process. They appointed one individual—Marc van Weede, as Executive Vice President and Global Head of Strategy and Sustainability. The move by Aegon may be a leading indicator of the direction leading companies may be moving—to better integrate environment, social and governance activities with the core of business strategy. It is not surprising that this took place in the Netherlands.

As a country, the Netherlands has long been acutely aware of global climate change and rising sea levels. Many parts of the country are below sea level (protected by dikes and canals) and the country has long been a leader in renewable (especially wind) energy. Furthermore, the relatively large population in a small area makes the Netherlands one of the more densely populated countries in the world (more densely populated than India).[i]

The overarching strategic question that senior executives and board members should be asking is:

Key Question: To what extent are ESG considerations fully embedded in our company's strategic and operational planning processes?

To help answer this key question, the Scorecard analyzes how companies manage and perform in three areas:

- The way the company positions itself regarding ESG issues—overall and as an integral part of its business strategy
- The specific business drivers for sustainability within the company—specifically around reducing cost and risk and enhancing growth and brand
- The extent to which ESG risks and opportunities are incorporated into corporate plans, objectives and budgets

Within each of these areas, executives evaluate their company performance on several key sustainability indicators (KSIs).

DOI 10.1515/9781547400423-018

Sustainability Positioning and Strategy

The Sustainability Scorecard addresses corporate positioning and strategy with respect to sustainability with a single KSI, below.

KSI 8.1: Corporate Sustainability Positioning and Strategy. This is a vitally important KSI; in some ways it sums up the CEO's and C-suite's whole approach to sustainability. The range of approaches varies considerably—as it does with all KSIs.

KSI	Stage 1	Stage 2	Stage 3	Stage 4
Corporate Sustainability Positioning and Strategy	Very basic "S" strategy; sustainability not a key driver of business strategy; aim to "stay in the pack"	Comprehensive "S" strategy; 3–5 year plan tied to business plan; aim to "surprise key competitors"	Robust; road to zero footprint; hard-wired to business strategy; aim to "change the game; leapfrog peers"	No separate sustainability strategy; "S" = integral to corporate strategy; aim to "transform company and industry"

Below are examples of companies that are publicly declaring the direct connection between sustainability and the company's growth strategy. Some (such as GE and IBM) are a bit dated; however, they are important markers in the calendar as ESG issues have grown in importance. Others are new.

- **DuPont:** Before the merger with Dow Chemical, DuPont long stated its aim of " ... creating shareholder and societal value while reducing the environmental and social footprint in the value chains in which we operate ... "[ii]

GE: Then-CEO Jeff Immelt launched *Ecomagination* in 2005. As a part of this strategy, the company is investing in cleaner technology and business innovation, developing solutions to enable economic growth while avoiding emissions and reducing water consumption, committing to reduce the environmental impact in our own operations, and developing strategic partnerships to solve some of the toughest environmental challenges at scale to create a cleaner, faster, smarter tomorrow.[iii]

- **IBM:** The company launched *Smarter Planet* in 2008 as a business strategy, not a sustainability strategy.[iv]
- **Novelis:** The metals company identifies sustainability as a "central component" of business strategy.[v]
- **Marks & Spencer:** Plan A is widely viewed as a leading blueprint for sustainable growth. Plan A is the company's way to help build a sustainable future by being a business that enables its customers to have a positive impact on well-being, communities and the planet through things that Marks & Spencer does.[vi]

- **TD Bank Group:** The company announced a new strategy in late 2017 and early 2018 to support the transition to a low-carbon economy. The Canadian company included a target of CDN$100 billion in low-carbon lending, financing, asset management, and other programs by 2030. Several other banks including Barclays, ING, and Triodos launched similar efforts.[vii]

Each of these company examples illustrate actions to embed sustainability into the core of the company strategic positioning.

Business Drivers for Sustainability Within the Company

In Chapter 6 (Strategy and Execution: The Missing "S" in ESG), we discussed the basic business case for sustainability: embarking on ESG activities where they reduce cost; reduce risk; grow long-term revenue; and enhance brand.

The Scorecard addresses the four key business drivers for sustainability (cost, risk, growth, brand) with KSIs addressing each of these topics.

KSI 8.2: Sustainability Strategy Regarding Cost Reduction. This is the place to start for virtually every company embarking on its sustainability journey. For a company in the early parts of Stage 1, the quickest way to move forward has often been proving that the company can save money by reducing water, waste, packaging, energy, materials, etc. The range of approaches to ESG and cost reduction is depicted below.

KSI	Stage 1	Stage 2	Stage 3	Stage 4
Sustainability Strategy Regarding Cost Reduction	Traditional costing; focus on reduction in footprint (emissions, packaging, waste, etc.)	Relentless approach to cutting waste; often hard-wired to Six-Sigma; Lean, etc.	Utilize **full-cost accounting** across supply chain (e.g., assign cost of carbon)	Explicitly cost key material externalities and offset subsidies; allocate significant CapEx for "S" Projects

The following examples show a deep, enduring commitment to driving toward zero waste over many years.
- **Dell:** The technology company believes that zero waste—producing, consuming and recycling without throwing anything away—is an ethical, cost-efficient, and visionary approach that all manufacturers should employ. And, while absolute zero waste may not be possible in the short term, seven zero waste guiding principles help the company get there.[viii]

- **Dow Chemical:** The huge chemical company generated $160 million in cost savings or new cash flow from projects that are good for business and the environment since 2016.[ix]
- **FedEx:** The package delivery company was able to quantify that its new hybrid fleet of 170 trucks had lowered the company›s fuel spend by 42 percent, while reducing its total emissions by 30 percent.[x]
- **Herman Miller:** The company committed in 2004 to a set of environmental goals that included a zero operational footprint (waste) and 100 percent renewable electrical energy by 2023. Ten years later, the company had largely achieved these goals, having reduced its footprint by 91 percent.[xi]

KSI 8.3: Sustainability Strategy Regarding Risk Reduction. We noted in Chapter 2 (Why Bother?) that the World Economic Forum (WEF) publishes an annual summary of global risks impacting business. (Note when you read the list below that this is from the WEF—not the world environmental forum!)

The latest WEF report looks at five categories of environmental risks: extreme weather events and temperatures; accelerating biodiversity loss; pollution of air, soil and water; failures of climate change mitigation and adaptation; and risks linked to the transition to low carbon. *All these risks ranked highly on both dimensions of likelihood and impact.* All five risks in this category occupy the top-right quadrant of the Global Risks Landscape 2018.

How do companies currently respond to ESG-related risks? The range of approaches is depicted below.

KSI	Stage 1	Stage 2	Stage 3	Stage 4
Sustainability Strategy Regarding Risk Reduction	Analyze ESG risks across supply chain (e.g., 'heat maps')	C-suite reviews key "S" risks—part of enterprise risk assessment	Make portfolio changes to reduce "S" risks across full value chain	Systematic portfolio transformation to reduce "S" risks

Below are several examples of companies that have deliberately focused on reducing risk and reducing material ESG impacts over many years.
- **Allianz:** committed to stop insuring single coal-fired power plants and coal mines, with plans to phase out any coal insurance by 2040.[xii]
- **Coca-Cola** and **Nike** adapted their business strategies to address climate change. Coke's turning point came in 2004 when the company lost a contract in India due to water scarcity. Over the following decade, the disruptive impacts of climate change on water shortages, etc. posed increasing damage to its balance sheet.[xiii]
- **Eurelectric:** Representing 3,500 utilities across Europe with a combined value of over €200bn, Eurelectric pledged no new coal plants after 2020. This pledge

applies to twenty-six of twenty-eight EUY member states (all except Poland and Greece).[xiv]

In each of these examples, the company focused on one of the top one or two most material ESG issues impacting the company and its industry sector—and acted.

KSI 8.4: Sustainability Strategy Regarding Revenue Growth. For most companies, there is a major "ah ha" moment when senior executives suddenly realize that sustainability is not all about "doing less bad"—that this is a way companies can think about driving innovation and growth. That was a defining moment for General Electric in 2005 when (then) CEO Jeff Immelt launched Ecomagination.

However, for most companies (in Stage 1 and Stage 2) they simply are not yet at the point of seeing sustainability as a growth opportunity. The range of responses follows.

KSI	Stage 1	Stage 2	Stage 3	Stage 4
Sustainability Strategy Regarding Revenue Generation	"S" attributes not widely viewed as a revenue driver; respond to customer inquiries; pilot "S" investments	"S"-advantaged **PSS** sales are tallied and reported; work with customers to shape "S" investments	"S" PSS portfolio (or equivalent) is growing with formal, robust criteria; significant investments	Over 50% of sales are "S"-advantaged PSS; "S" drivers dominate growth options

In Chapter 6, we provided examples of how eleven major global companies are building their growth strategy around a portfolio of sustainable products, services and solutions (see Table 6.2.) These companies (BASF, Caterpillar, Dow, DSM, GE, J&J, Kimberly-Clark, Kingfisher, Philips, Siemens, and Toshiba) have all demonstrated impressive results.

Some additional examples of companies driving revenue growth from sustainability include:
– **AkzoNobel:** The Dutch company's goal is to increase Ecopremium solutions revenue to 20 percent by 2020.[xv]
– **Avis Budget Group:** Avis bought car-sharing service Zipcar to complement its rental car business. The acquisition made sense financially (Avis Budget expected significant cost reductions by increasing fleet utilization). It also made sense through the ESG lens; the acquisition thrust Avis into the circular economy business model of the **sharing economy**.[xvi]

- **Eastman:** The chemical company states that sustainability is "foundational to our growth strategy."[xvii] From 2014 to 2017 they were named as one of the World's Most Ethical Companies® by the Ethisphere® Institute.
- **J&J:** The company's *Earthwards* portfolio has grown from only three products in 2009 to 93 products generating $11.5 billion or roughly 16 percent of Johnson & Johnson revenue in 2016. The company aims to have 20 percent of all company revenue coming from Earthwards products by 2020.[xviii]

In each of these examples, the company has found that investing in a defined set of products and services that meet rigorous ESG criteria can focus executive attention on the opportunities for sustainable growth and then drive revenue growth.

KSI 8.5: Sustainability Strategy Regarding Brand and Reputation. Using sustainability to enhance brand and reputation is a result—not a means to an end. What we mean is that if a company sets out to enhance brand or reputation by leveraging its sustainability posture or performance, the actions the company takes often fall into one or more of the previous three (KSI) buckets:
- Significantly reducing the company's footprint—in its own operations and across the supply chain, to thereby cut costs and reduce risks.
- Investing in more sustainable products, services and solutions to drive growth.

When companies do these things—and proactively engage with customers, suppliers, NGOs and other stakeholders, disclosing transparently, then a resulting measure may be enhanced brand or reputation. The range of approaches to this follow.

KSI	Stage 1	Stage 2	Stage 3	Stage 4
Sustainability Strategy Regarding Brand and Reputation	Market current activities in favorable "S" light	Work hard to maximize independent "S" ratings (e.g., CDP, DJSI, Global 100)	Strong track record of industry-leading footprint reduction on material issue(s); "S" positioning aimed at enhancing brand	CEO-led business transformation has "S" at the core; and results in enhanced brand

Below are several examples of companies taking a series of risk reduction and innovation activities that also may have had the added benefit of enhancing brand and reputation.
- **Ford:** EcoBoost™ engine and next generation hybrid technology are helping to lead the path forward with green auto options in the United States.[xix]

- **Nokia:** The Finnish multinational telecommunications and technology company has strong sustainability roots—from internal company dynamics to eco-friendly devices; and they were rated 6 out of 50 of the Greenest Global brands.[xx]
- **Novo Nordisk:** The Danish pharmaceuticals company, aimed to bolster its brand identity through its ESG positioning. Novo developed a blueprint methodology that focused on quantifying the upsides to its business plan—in terms of business growth, and for patients and society. Through Novo's Changing Diabetes program in China, it educated 280,000 patients, trained 55,000 physicians and grew its market share in the insulin market by 23 percent.[xxi]

The Novo Nordisk story is an excellent example of a company focusing on its most material issues; embedding those issues into its business strategy; finding ways to reduce cost and risk while positioning the company for growth and ultimately brand recognition.

Sustainability Inputs to Corporate Planning Process(es)

A key challenge for virtually every chief sustainability officer is to "have a seat at the strategy table"—meaning being part of the inner circle of senior executives that crafts corporate and business unit strategy. Clearly, this is not an issue for Aegon N.V. highlighted at the beginning of this chapter. But in various The Conference Board meetings that I run, including three separate ESG-focused executive councils, this is a constant issue for the clear majority of companies.

The Scorecard addresses integration of sustainability into corporate planning with KSIs focused on three things: risk assessment, scenario planning, and capital expenditure planning.

KSI 8.6: Process for Issues Analysis and Enterprise Risk Management. A May 2018 *Wall Street Journal* article highlighted that an "emerging trend among some big corporations is the melding of their risk and compliance functions with their environmental, social, governance, and human-rights programs." The article noted that Barrick Gold, Novartis AG, Lockheed Martin, and AstraZeneca are among those combining their enterprise risk and sustainability functions.[xxii]

KSI	Stage 1	Stage 2	Stage 3	Stage 4
Process for Issues Analysis and Enterprise Risk Management	Basic process in place to identify and manage "S" issues	ESG issues process is fully integrated with enterprise risk management process	A C-suite member personally manages each material "S" issue	C-suite partners (with customers, suppliers, etc.) to cut material "S" impacts

Lockheed Martin: The company created Sustainability Management Plan based on materiality assessment[xxiii] and later found value in combining its corporate sustainability function with its enterprise risk manage activities.

BlackRock: The world's biggest fund manager, claimed in 2017 that it would vote out directors of companies that fail to address the risks posed to their businesses by climate change. Framing climate change as a "systemic issue," BlackRock said it would vote in favor of proposals on climate risk that "clearly address a gap" which would otherwise lead to material economic disadvantage to the company and its shareholders. BlackRock promised to use its power to get rid of directors who were part of the problem, noting that, "we may vote against the re-election of certain directors where we believe they have not fulfilled that duty, particularly in markets where shareholder proposals are not common."[xxiv]

KSI 8.7: Use of Scenario Planning. Scenario planning is a strategic planning method some organizations use to make flexible long-term plans. There is a saying among those steeped in scenario planning that only one-third of companies use scenario planning as part of their strategy formulation process—and only a third of them do this well. A recent scenario exercise I ran with about thirty-five major companies validated this. (A show of hands indicated that fewer than half had participated in a formal scenario exercise; after several hours many commented that they learned a lot.)

The scenario planning process typically identifies "high impact drivers"(such as major demographic changes) of future business and addresses areas where the company might succeed given what the future might look like. **Shell** is often credited with being the "father of scenario planning." Indeed, Shell has shared its scenarios with the public for years.

KSI	Stage 1	Stage 2	Stage 3	Stage 4
Use of Scenario Planning	Informal	Formal process; includes "S" drivers	Use best-in-class "S" scenarios, including a 2° Celsius (or lower) scenario (aligned with TCFD)	Continuous updating of robust scenarios

A 2018 report noted that banks are moving ahead aggressively with implementing the TCFD[1] recommendation to use scenario planning for climate risk. The report states that 49 percent of banks are implementing climate risk assessments or 2 degrees

---

1 TCFD is the Task Force on Climate-Related Financial Disclosures, discussed earlier in Chapter 5: Governance and Leadership: the "G" in ESG (section titled Investors' Dilemma: Failing the 80/20 Rule).

Celsius scenario analysis (called for by TCFD).[xxv] Other examples of leading practices include:

- **Nike:** The company uses scenario planning to assess impact of ESG issues to inform decision-making.[xxvi]
- **PepsiCo:** In 2009, the company used a scenario planning exercise to map ESG risks and inform its 2030 strategy.[xxvii]
- **Shell:** The company has engaged in scenario planning since the 1970s and led the initial World Business Council for Sustainable Development (WBCSD) scenarios in the late 1990s.[xxviii]

Looking ahead, use of scenario planning is likely to rapidly increase, because of interest from mainstream investors. The 2017 Task Force on Climate Related Financial Disclosures (TCFD)—a voluntary framework for reporting ESG posture and performance to investors—specifically calls for consideration of what a 2° Celsius increase in greenhouse gas emissions (over pre-industrial levels) will mean for the company. (The 2° Celsius increase over preindustrial levels is widely accepted among global climate scientists as a level that would lead to major climate-related problems around the world.)

KSI 8.8: Sustainability Impact of Capital Expenditures. One of the key business decisions the C-suite and (for publicly held companies) the board of directors approves each year is the capital budget—for major improvements in plant and equipment, enhancing the value of the company's assets.

The range of approaches to allocating expense budget to ESG-related improvements follows:

KSI	Stage 1	Stage 2	Stage 3	Stage 4
Sustainability Impact of Capital Expenditures	Traditional metrics; a chunk of CapEx (e.g., ~25% for many sectors) is driven by "S" risks	Growing chunk of CapEx (~ 25–50 % for certain sectors) is driven by "S" risks and opportunities	Major chunk of CapEx (>50 % for certain sectors) is driven by "S" risks and opportunities	Major chunk (often >75 % for certain sectors) of CapEx is driven by "S" risks and opportunities

Information on how companies incorporate ESG factors into capital planning and allocation of capital expenses is not readily available. However, one good example is **AkzoNobel,** the Dutch chemical company. Sustainability is core to the company's decision-making and factored into procurement and capital expenditure decisions.[xxix]

How Do Companies Stack Up?

Starting in 2018, we are capturing data from a group of founding participants—invited to use the Scorecard for a company self-assessment and to provide feedback. As we assess the data from the first sixty companies (all Fortune 500 or equivalent), three key messages stand out:

- Most of the sixty companies rated themselves at Stage 2 or higher on overall corporate sustainability positioning. That means all but 20 percent at least have a comprehensive three- to five-year sustainability strategy tied to business plan.
- Three of four companies (forty-five of the sixty) rated themselves Stage 2 or higher on integration of ESG risks into their company's enterprise risk management process.
- As we might expect because these sixty companies include many leaders, use of scenario planning is only slightly more common than the old rule of thumb suggests. (Recall the common statement among scenario practitioners is that one third of companies do it and one third of them do it well.) Our data indicates that only ten of the sixty companies (17 percent) scored themselves Stage 3 or higher (see Figure 18.1).

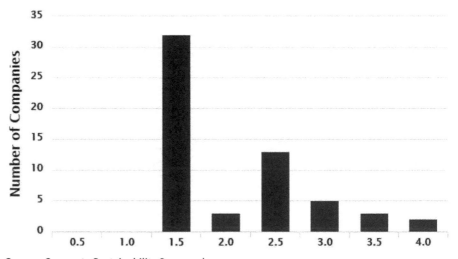

Source: Corporate Sustainability Scorecard

Figure 18.1: Scorecard Data from Sixty Companies on KSI 8.8: Use of Scenario Planning

Scenario planning is an incredibly powerful tool to engage C-suite executives and board members in a deep discussion of ESG and corporate strategy. Revisit "Sustainability Stories from the C-Suite and Boardroom" at the beginning of Chapter 5: Governance and Leadership: the "G" in ESG. The cornerstone of the four-hour board and executive team meeting on ESG issues was a scenario planning exercise developed by the sustainability director. That story proves that it is possible to manage upward ...

i https://en.wikipedia.org/wiki/List_of_countries_and_dependencies_by_population_density
ii "Future Inspired. Sustainable Growth. DuPont 2012 Sustainability Progress Report." http://www.dupont.com/content/dam/assets/corporate-functions/our-approach/sustainability/performance-reporting/articles/documents/DuPont%20Sustainability%20Report%2012%20111612.pdf
iii https://www.ge.com/about-us/ecomagination
iv https://www.ibm.com/smarterplanet/us/en/
v http://novelis.com/sustainability/
vi https://corporate.marksandspencer.com/plan-a
vii http://www.sustainablebrands.com/news_and_views/finance_investment/sustainable_brands/trending_barclays_td_bank_catalyze_low-carbon_e
viii http://www.dell.com/learn/us/en/uscorp1/corp-comm/cr-earth-reduce-reuse-recycle
ix https://www.dow.com/en-us/science-and-sustainability/highlights-and-reporting
x https://www.greenbiz.com/blog/2013/12/04/ceos-struggle-prove-sustainability-value-investors-accenture
xi https://www.hermanmiller.com/our-values/environmental-advocacy/our-vision-and-policy/
xii https://www.reuters.com/article/us-allianz-climatechange/allianz-cuts-back-on-coal-insurance-after-environmentalist-criticism-idUSKBN1I511D
xiii https://www.environmentalleader.com/2014/01/coke-nike-call-climate-change-commercial-threat/
xiv https://www.theguardian.com/environment/2017/apr/05/the-end-of-coal-eu-energy-companies-pledge-no-new-plants-from-2020
xv https://www.akzonobel.com/about-us/how-we-operate/position-statements/eco-premium-solutions
xvi https://www.forbes.com/sites/timworstall/2013/01/02/explaining-the-avis-takeover-of-zipcar/#6eb311b7986b
xvii https://www.eastman.com/Company/Sustainability/Pages/Introduction.aspx
xviii https://www.jnj.com/innovation/earthwards-a-johnson-and-johnson-program-helping-create-a-more-sustainable-world
xix http://interbrand.com/best-brands/best-global-brands/2016/ranking/ford/
xx http://interbrand.com/best-brands/best-global-brands/2014/ranking/nokia/
xxi https://www.greenbiz.com/blog/2013/12/04/ceos-struggle-prove-sustainability-value-investors-accenture
xxii https://blogs.wsj.com/riskandcompliance/2018/05/15/companies-find-value-in-combining-compliance-sustainability/
xxiii https://www.lockheedmartin.com/en-us/who-we-are/sustainability.html
xxiv https://www.independent.co.uk/news/business/news/climate-change-blackrock-manager-threatens-directors-ignore-global-warming-a7631266.html
xxv http://news.bostoncommonasset.com/banking-on-a-low-carbon-future/
xxvi https://about.nike.com/pages/sustainable-innovation
xxvii https://www.forumforthefuture.org/project/pepsico-global-scenarios-and-strategy-2030/overview
xxviii https://www.shell.com/energy-and-innovation/the-energy-future/scenarios.html
xxix https://www.linkedin.com/jobs/view/13614129/

Chapter 19
Innovation, Research, and Development

The second element in the Strategy and Execution section of the Scorecard addresses the extent to which companies embed sustainability into their innovation, research, and development processes.

3M has, for many decades, had a near obsession with eco-efficiency—the systematic reduction in the amount of energy and materials wasted in the full life-cycle creation, use and disposal of goods and services. The company's widely known Pollution Prevention Pays (3P) program has saved many billions of dollars over more than four decades (since its visionary launch in 1975).

More recently, 3M has transitioned its innovation credo from eco-efficiency and waste reduction to innovation and revenue growth. The company launches an average of twenty new products every week—an astonishing feat. And increasingly over the past decade, sustainability has been at the core of the innovation and product development processes.[i]

3M invests nearly 6% of annual sales into R&D to drive a strong and continuous pipeline of new products leveraging 46 technology platforms and serving customers across disparate markets. This investment is tracked rigorously, part of employee compensation, and consistently delivers over 30% of revenues from products introduced in the last 5 years.[ii]

The overarching strategic question that senior executives and board members should be asking with respect to innovation and sustainability is:

Key Question: How are sustainability and ESG issues integrated into innovation research, processes, and investments—ultimately aimed at helping our customers and delivering value to society?

To help answer this key question, the Scorecard analyzes how companies manage and perform in three areas:

- The role innovation plays in the business and the extent to which sustainability is "hard-wired" to innovation
- The processes and methodologies for embedding sustainability into innovation, research and development
- The output of innovation investments

Within each of these areas, executives evaluate their company performance on several key sustainability indicators (KSIs).

DOI 10.1515/9781547400423-019

Role of Sustainability and Innovation

The Scorecard addresses the role of sustainability and innovation with three KSIs: one dealing with the linkage between sustainability and innovation and the next two addressing how environmental, social, and governance (ESG) is embedded into innovation both through material and labor—and through technology.

KSI 9.1: Link Between Sustainability and Innovation. The linkage between sustainability and innovation is profound. Experienced innovation leaders have found that few things can inspire greater imagination and innovation than the opportunity to completely rethink how goods and services delivered to customers can provide the same or greater value with a far lower negative impact on the planet and on society.

The range of ways companies link sustainability and innovation is depicted in the table below.

KSI	Stage 1	Stage 2	Stage 3	Stage 4
Linkage Between Sustainability and Innovation	"S" is informally linked to innovation processes	ESG issues are formally embedded in innovation processes	Innovation is a vital part of culture; goal is to decouple sales growth from footprint	"S" is driver of long-term growth; precautionary principle is central to R&D

Some examples of how global leaders in innovation have embraced sustainability follow:

- **3M:** Innovation is core to 3M's success and the company's "15 percent time program" is a key way sustainability is embedded in the innovation processes.[iii] Launched in 1948, 15 percent of working time from all employees has been used to drive innovation.
- **GE:** The company launched Ecomagination in 2005 to drive innovation and generate growth. Between 2005 and 2012, Ecomagination generated more than $130 billion in revenue—no small feat. Innovation through *Ecomagination "has helped our customers save billions of dollars while significantly reducing their environmental impact."*[iv]
- **SC Johnson:** The company's goal is to continuously improve products to adhere to their Greenlist™ rating system so that products will all use "Better" and "Best" rated ingredients.[v]
- **Tesla:** CEO Elon Musk's goal to accelerate sustainable mobility is a major step in reinventing the entire automotive business model.

The Scorecard descriptor for Stage 4 includes a reference to the **precautionary principle.** The principle implies that there is a social responsibility to protect the public from exposure to harm, when scientific investigation has found a plausible risk. Most companies—especially those in the chemical industry or sectors that rely heavily on chemicals—have historically taken a very dim view (to say the least) of the precautionary principle. However, leading companies have adopted the principle not only as a risk management measure but also as a way to spur innovation.

– **Kaiser Permanente:** As one of the largest not-for-profit health plan in the United States, Kaiser Permanente has adopted the Precautionary Principle to guide both food and chemicals policy.

– **Bristol-Myers Squibb:** The global pharmaceutical company has adopted the Precautionary Principle to guide its use of chemical processes.

In each of these examples, companies have embraced a bold ESG positioning (such as massive reduction in carbon and hazardous materials) to drive further innovation and growth.

KSI 9.2: Sustainable Innovation Through Material and Labor Inputs. One major way to drive sustainable innovation is by rethinking the material and labor inputs to a product or service. The range of ways companies do this follows:

KSI	Stage 1	Stage 2	Stage 3	Stage 4
Sustainable Innovation through Material and Labor Inputs	Regulations are the main ESG driver in evaluating material and labor inputs into new offerings	Processes in place to systematically reduce higher-hazard material and labor inputs; may use some **Life Cycle Assessment (LCA)** tools	Processes in place to eliminate all higher-hazard materials and labor inputs into new products, services and solutions; growing use of LCA	Use LCA to consider ESG impacts of materials and manufacturing; as appropriate, maximize use of "natural" and highly recycled or recyclable materials (as appropriate)

Several examples of how companies have rethought materials and labor follow:

– **Ecovative:** The company produces packaging materials and building insulation that decompose completely in the environment. Its core mission is to envision, develop, produce and market earth friendly materials—to help rid the world of toxic, unsustainable materials. The company is best known for making packaging created from mushrooms. The start-up company quickly caught the attention of Dell and Ikea.[vi]

– **Dell:** The technology shipped the first recycled ocean plastics packaging in its industry in 2017.[vii]

- **LEGO Group:** announced plans in early 2018 to introduce a new product family of plant-based LEGO bricks sourced from sugarcane.[viii]
- **TerraCycle:** The innovative recycling company has become a global leader in recycling hard-to-recycle waste, often converting it into office products.[ix]
- **3M:** The diversified manufacturing company invented a technology that structurally reinforces water pipes, without digging them up.[x]

In each of these examples, the company unleashed its innovation process to completely rethink a product or waste stream or problem—to find a solution that significantly reduces life-cycle environmental impacts.

KSI 9.3: Sustainable Innovation Through Technology. **Toyota** launched the Prius in 1997, arguably ahead of its time. Yet, over many years, the technology behind the Prius has been a success. However, not all technology enhancements result in market success—and the same is true in the sustainability space.

Dow Chemical Company may also have been ahead of its time with its solar shingles business—a great idea and technology that, in the end, did not result in commercial success. Dow created Solar Shingles that are cost effective and easy to install. The company later divested the business in 2016, because of lack of customer demand.[xi] The period 2016 to 2017 were devastating in terms of bankruptcies in the solar business.

The range of approaches to sustainable innovation through technology are depicted below.

KSI	Stage 1	Stage 2	Stage 3	Stage 4
Sustainable Innovation through Technology	Focus on compliance with both existing and new requirements	Use existing technologies to reduce own footprint significantly	Technology focus on suppliers and customers to reduce their footprint	Major investments in disruptive technologies to drive to zero footprint

Some examples of companies that are Stage 3 or better include:
- **Siemens:** The company is one of many companies in the manufacturing, oil, and gas and utility sectors that have started using drone technology for inspections. In Siemens' case, the purpose was inspecting wind farms.[xii]
- **Toyota:** Described as the "catalytic converter" of pollution-reducing billboards, they use a titanium dioxide coated vinyl to purify the surrounding air.[xiii]

In each of these examples the companies are applying new technology to address a fundamental environmental or social challenge.

Processes and Methodologies

The Scorecard addresses processes and methodologies used to embed ESG into innovation with three KSIs: the product development process, innovation tools, and R&D partnerships.

KSI 9.4: Sustainability Innovation Process. This phrase (sustainability innovation process) can be misleading. Hopefully, companies do not have a discrete sustainability innovation process; instead, they systematically incorporate ESG considerations into their main business processes around innovation. The range of approaches across the maturity curve follows.

KSI	Stage 1	Stage 2	Stage 3	Stage 4
Sustainability Innovation Process	Inclusion of ESG attributes in new **products, services and solutions (PSS)** is largely compliance focused; becoming more formal	Company is innovating new PSS offerings that help customers achieve major cuts in footprint and impacts	Very formal; fully integrated; focus = major footprint cuts and/ or mitigated impacts	"S" drives corporate innovation process

In addition to 3M's 15 percent time mentioned above, an excellent example is **Infosys**, India's second largest information technology company. Infosys uses its Sustainable Tomorrow framework to drive resource intensity, which essentially means seeking ways to do more with less, conserve natural resources, eliminate waste, reuse, and recycle raw materials.[xiv]

KSI 9.5: Sustainable Innovation Tools. The Conference Board (and many other leading business organizations) has conducted extensive research about highly innovative companies. During 2017, their latest research ("Signposts of Innovation") specifically analyzed environmental stewardship and social responsibility issues as one of six key signposts of innovation.

Many well-established innovation tools have been used by industry leaders.[xv] A few of these are:
- *Crowd Sourcing*—The general practice of obtaining needed information, financing or services from a large group of people, especially the on-line community.
- *The Stage-Gate Process*—The basic blueprint for managing the new product development process from idea to launch wherein decision "gates" are set up to make decisions about continuation or adaptation of a project.

- *Big Data Customer Analytics*—Examining very large and varied data sets to uncover hidden patterns, etc.

The question for companies is how to tap into these well-established tools to embrace and embed ESG principles—rather than creating a distinct set of sustainability innovation tools.

The range of approaches is depicted below.

KSI	Stage 1	Stage 2	Stage 3	Stage 4
Sustainable Innovation Tools	Traditional for product development process	Pilot various eco-design tools	Tie "S" waste to Lean Six Sigma (zero defects); full use of eco-design tools	Software and tools drive closed-loop processes

Companies use a variety of innovation tools to address environmental and social challenges. A few examples are:

- **Adidas:** The company partnered with Fashion For Good, a global apparel industry initiative that uses a cradle to cradle-inspired, circular approach to product design.[xvi]
- **Starbucks:** The company announced in March 2018 that it is launching the "NextGen Cup Challenge," an innovation accelerator aimed at developing and commercializing fully recyclable and compostable cups. The company is doing this in the Closed Loop Partners' Center for the Circular Economy.[xvii]

In each of these examples, the partnerships will tap into a wide range of innovation tools available, especially leveraging technology and creative thinking of start-up enterprises.

KSI 9.6: *Sustainability R&D Partnerships.* Historically, at many companies the research and development (R&D) activities were carried out behind closed doors. After all, this was the pipeline for future sales growth and competitive differentiation. Thus, the range of partnerships spans from nonexistent to robust.

KSI	Stage 1	Stage 2	Stage 3	Stage 4
Sustainability R&D Partnerships	Rare	Occasional	Open; collaborative	Work with "thought-leaders" - utilize **crowdsourcing**

A few examples of innovative partnerships in the R&D area include:
- **Danone:** The global food company partnered with Nestlé Waters to fund start-up development of 100 percent bio-based bottles.[xviii]
- **IBM:** Over a decade ago, the technology leader used Innovation Jam to bring together employees, families, and customers to innovate. Then CEO Sam Palmisano agreed to put $100 million into promising ideas.[xix]
- **Walmart:** In 2014, the company convened over a dozen CEOs of major companies and CEOs of leading NGOs to sign new commitments accelerating innovation in sustainable agriculture and recycling.[xx]

In each of these examples, companies looked outside their company walls to find partners who could help them move faster, smarter and cheaper than they would have on their own.

Sustainable Innovation Investments

As noted before, General Electric is undergoing some headwinds in 2017 and 2018; however, the company's twelve-year investment in Ecomagination continues. Ecomagination is GE's business strategy to deliver clean technology solutions that drive positive economic and environmental outcomes for GE's customers and the world.

GE has invested a total of $20 billion in cleaner technology solutions; that has returned GE $270 billion in revenues. That gets attention!

The Scorecard addresses sustainable innovation investments with two KSIs: one dealing with the amount of investment and a second that looks at sustainability investment criteria.

KSI 9.7: R&D Investments in Sustainable Products, Services, & Solutions. It is very difficult to distinguish which R&D investments are "ESG driven" and which are not. In reality, projects or technologies that receive these investments may have some aspects that meet environmental or social criteria: does it help save energy? Does it eliminate hazardous materials? And so on.

KSI	Stage 1	Stage 2	Stage 3	Stage 4
R&D Investment in Sustainable Products, Services & Solutions	Likely do not track	< 25% of total R&D investment	~50% of total R&D investment— growing focus on disruptive technologies	~100% of total R&D investment

- **DuPont:** The company doubled its R&D investment from 2007 to 2017 in products with quantifiable environmental benefits and committed another 5B to meet its 2020 goals.[xxi]
- **Skyonic:** The Texas startup is working to convert carbon emissions into revenue streams, taking CO_2 emissions from factories, refineries and power plants and converting them into value-added byproducts that generate cash. [xxii]
- **DSM:** The Dutch chemical company opened America's first cellulosic biofuel plant using corn waste in Iowa in 2014.[xxiii]

In each of these examples, companies allocated a very significant portion of their capital budget to projects that had a strong ESG component.

KSI 9.8: Sustainability Investment Criteria. The range of ways companies think about sustainability investment criteria follows.

KSI	Stage 1	Stage 2	Stage 3	Stage 4
Sustainability Investment Criteria	Respond to customer demands	Pilot new "S" products; anticipate "S" trends	Invest early to create demand from "S" products and positioning	Alter business portfolio driven by "S" trends

Companies tend to treat capital investment decisions—and the criteria that underpins those decisions—as fairly confidential. Clearly, companies like the GE example above have publicly disclosed both the amount of capital investment tied to ESG issues—and the general criteria supporting those investments.

How Do Companies Stack Up?

Starting in 2018, we are capturing data from a group of founding participants—invited to use the Scorecard for a company self-assessment and to provide feedback. As we assess the data from the first sixty companies (all Fortune 500 or equivalent), three key messages stand out:

- In terms of the linkage between sustainability and innovation, the data suggests an even split in three buckets: one third of the companies rated their company at Stage 1.5, meaning ESG issues are not formally embedded in innovation processes. Another third (~20 companies) are in the middle; while the top third rated their company Stage 3 or higher—meaning the goal is to decouple sales growth from footprint.
- Most companies have a formal product development process; yet, the data suggests that nearly one-third of companies are not yet at Stage 2. This means that

group of companies remains largely compliance-focused—rather than strategy and growth focused.

- Only eleven of the sixty companies (18 percent) rated their company as Stage 3 or higher on R&D investment in sustainable products, services and solutions. That means less than 50 percent of total R&D investment is based on ESG criteria (see Figure 19.1).

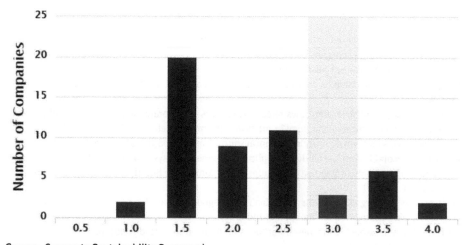

Source: Corporate Sustainability Scorecard

Figure 19.1: Scorecard Data from Sixty Companies on KSI 9.7: R&D Investment in Sustainable Products, Services, & Solutions

Figure 19.1 shows that there is a major opportunity for companies to strengthen the linkages between the R&D organization and those in the company embracing ESG principles.

i https://hbr.org/2012/05/3ms-sustainability-innovation

ii Email from Gayle Schuyller, Vice President and Chief Sustainability Officer, 3M to the author, dated August 22, 2018.

iii https://www.3m.com/3M/en_US/sustainability-us/

iv http://www.sustainablebrands.com/news_and_views/articles/ge-generates-25-billion-revenues-sustainability-investments

v http://www.scjohnson.com/en/commitment/focus-on/greener-products/greenlist.aspx

vi http://www.businessinsider.com/ecovative-turns-mushrooms-into-packaging-ikea-dell-2016-8

vii http://www.dell.com/learn/us/en/uscorp1/press-releases/2017-02-22-dell-announces-ocean-plastics-shipment

viii https://www.lego.com/en-us/aboutus/news-room/2018/march/pfp/

ix https://www.terracycle.com/en-US/about-terracycle

x https://hbr.org/2012/05/3ms-sustainability-innovation

xi https://www.greentechmedia.com/articles/read/dow-chemical-sheds-solar-shingle-business#gs.lyDy=zA

xii https://www.prnewswire.com/news-releases/skyspecs-collaborates-with-siemens-wind-power-for-use-of-automated-drone-technology-in-offshore-turbine-inspections-300414202.html

xiii http://pressroom.toyota.com/releases/mirai+purifying+billboard+us+campaign.htm

xiv http://www.oracle.com/us/products/applications/green/infosys-2049936.html

xv "Insights from Highly Innovative Companies," The Conference Board; Global State of Innovation Survey 2017, p. 11.

xvi https://fashionforgood.com/our_news/fashion-for-good-and-adidas-partner-to-accelerate-and-scale-sustainable-innovation-in-the-apparel-industry/

xvii https://news.starbucks.com/news/starbucks-and-closed-loop-to-develop-recyclable-compostable-cup-solution

xviii https://www.nestle-watersna.com/en/nestle-water-news/pressreleases/nestle-waters-danone-bio-based-bottles

xix https://www.bloomberg.com/news/articles/2006-09-24/crowdsourcing

xx https://news.walmart.com/news-archive/2014/04/29/walmart-convenes-key-partners-at-first-ever-sustainable-product-expo-to-accelerate-supply-chain-innovation

xxi http://www.dupont.com/corporate-functions/sustainability/sustainability-commitments/goals-progress/sustainable-innovation-goal.html

xxii https://www.greenbiz.com/blog/2014/06/09/can-carbon-emissions-become-revenue-stream

xxiii https://thinkprogress.org/americas-first-cellulosic-biofuel-plant-to-use-corn-waste-is-open-in-iowa-1658bb523644/

Chapter 20
Customers and Markets

The third element of the Scorecard in the Strategy and Execution section addresses the relationships with customers. Specifically, this element examines the extent to which a company engages deeply with customers to jointly develop more sustainable solutions.

Ecolab, the global provider of water, hygiene and energy technologies and services to the food, energy, healthcare, industrial and hospitality markets, was honored by the World Environment Center in May 2018, winner of the 34th WEC Gold Medal for International Corporate Achievement in Sustainable Development. The company was recognized for its efforts in global water conservation, sustainability commitments and partnerships, integration of sustainability into the company's core growth strategy, its innovation processes, product development, and customer focus.

Ecolab's approach to customers and markets is a true Stage 4 approach—driving strategic partnerships. Ecolab partnered with Trucost and Microsoft to create the Water Risk Monetizer. This tool provides actionable information to help businesses understand water-related risks and quantify risks in financial terms to inform responsible decisions that enable growth. The tool is available to customers and the public at no cost.[i]

The overarching strategic question that senior executives and board members should be asking is:

Key Question: How are we working with key customers to reduce their full life-cycle impacts and create sustainable solutions?

To help answer this key question, the Scorecard analyzes how companies manage and perform in three areas:
- The sustainability linkages to customers
- Core approach to interacting with customers and to addressing customer needs regarding sustainability
- The role sustainability plays in shaping future market opportunities that deliver value to shareholders and value to society

Within each of these areas, executives evaluate their company performance on several key sustainability indicators (KSIs).

DOI 10.1515/9781547400423-020

Sustainability Linkage to Customers

The Scorecard addresses the overall linkage with customers related to environmental, social, and governance (ESG) with two KSIs.

KSI 10.1: Posture and Interaction with Customers Regarding Sustainability. A key challenge for many corporate sustainability directors in recent years has been the need to fill out often lengthy questionnaires (from customers and other supply chain partners) about various ESG issues. It is not just **Walmart** asking the questions and pressuring its suppliers. Most of the early pressure—dating back to the 1990s—came from European companies, especially in the consumer products sector.

KSI	Stage 1	Stage 2	Stage 3	Stage 4
Posture and Interaction with Customers Regarding Sustainability	Respond to requests; focus is: *Do our customers like our products?*	Educate about "S" attributes; focus is: *Can we help our customers achieve their "S" goals?*	Promote "S" consumption; focus is: *Do our products benefit our customers and society?*	Globally recognized for creating demand for "S" solutions; focus is: *Do our PSS address the world's toughest challenges?*

Several examples of leading practices are:
- **BT:** Formerly known as British Telecom, BT set a 2020 goal to help customers reduce carbon emissions by at least three times the end-to-end carbon impact of BT's business.
- **Google:** The company launched Project Sunroof in 2015, using imagery from Google Maps and Google Earth, 3D modeling, and machine learning to help consumers evaluate solar feasibility for their homes.[ii]

In each of these examples, the companies view customers as a strategic partner when it comes to ESG. They have moved far beyond compliance questionnaires (though those still may exist).

KSI 10.2: Identifying Customers' Sustainability Issues. How can we help our customers meet their sustainability goals and reduce their negative environmental and social impacts? That is the crux of this KSI. The rage of approaches is depicted below.

KSI	Stage 1	Stage 2	Stage 3	Stage 4
Identifying Customers' Sustainability Issues	Respond to customer "S"/ ESG requests	Understand "S"/ ESG goals of key customers	Partner with customers to meet their "'S"/ ESG goals	Partner with customers to jointly create new "S"/ESG solutions

Some innovative ways of partnering with customers on sustainability include:

- **Infosys:** The Indian company partnered with the World Business Council for Sustainable Development (WBCSD) to launch the India Water Tool to help companies better assess their water risks and manage their water usage more efficiently.[iii]
- **Nike:** The Nike+ suite of personal fitness products combines deep understanding of what makes athletes tick with extensive market research data. Nike+ incorporates sensor technologies embedded in running shoes and wearable devices that connect to the web, apps, and social networks.[iv]
- **Ricoh:** The global producer of electronic products is focused on helping its customers reduce energy use, carbon footprint, and use of virgin materials—while also expanding its own business opportunities for product refurbishing, recycling, and new designs.[v]

In most companies, the people who talk to customers daily are not the same people who manage sustainability. When these two groups (and ways of thinking) come together to inquire about customers' ESG challenges, good things can happen.

Core Approach

The Scorecard addresses how companies interact with customers on ESG issues with two KSIs: one dealing with customer partnerships and a second that looks at the nature of customer communications.

KSI 10.3: Customer Partnerships Regarding Sustainability. A company does not need to partner with its customers in order to comply with environmental requirements or manage safe operations. But those are Stage 1 attributes. At the other end of the Scorecard spectrum, companies absolutely need to partner with customers to tackle the larger challenges that extend beyond one company's fence line. The range of practices is depicted below:

KSI	Stage 1	Stage 2	Stage 3	Stage 4
Customer Partnerships Regarding Sustainability	Traditional customer interactions; guidance on safe product use; cut negative impacts	Pilot effort to cut collective footprint; solicit input regarding more "S" products	Significant investment to cut collective footprint & develop more "S" products, services and solutions	Pioneer innovative **closed-loop** business models

Several examples of companies partnering with existing and especially new customers in creative ways embodying ESG principles follow:

- **Natura Cosmeticos:** The number one cosmetics manufacturer in Brazil uses ingredients from the Amazon (though it does not bill itself as a "natural" brand per se), partners with families throughout the region to help them farm sustainably, and packages its products in 100 percent post-consumer recycled containers and so-called green sugar cane ethanol plastic. The company is committed to eco issues and has been given awards for its work.[vi]

- **Coca-Cola:** The company launched EKOCENTER as both a great idea and a magnet for many sustainable solutions. As a cross between a community center and a general store, EKOCENTER units are run mostly by local women entrepreneurs in developing counties—where people at the bottom of the economic pyramid live. Based on community needs, EKOCENTER sells a wide range of products and enables connectivity from solar power. It also facilitates other services from phone charging to financial transactions, provision of safe water and vocational training.[vii]

- **VF Corporation:** The company's North Face subsidiary launched an innovative "Clothes the Loop" program, which allows customers to drop off their unwanted clothing and footwear (any condition, any brand) at retail and outlet stores for proper recycling.[viii]

- **Xerox:** Launched a reforestation program to help its customers offset their paper use by planting new trees in geographic areas of need. The company partnered with technology platform PrintReleaf.[ix]

In these examples, the company started by taking a fresh look at the real needs of current and new customers and partnered with them to create products, services and solutions aligned with ESG.

*KSI 10.4: **Nature of Customer Communications.*** As we look across the spectrum of how companies communicate with customers regarding ESG, the range of practices is as follows:

KSI	Stage 1	Stage 2	Stage 3	Stage 4
Nature of Customer Communications	Feedback on existing products and services	"S" attributes of existing and new products, services and solutions	Joint investments to drive down full value chain footprint	Jointly create or expand market for "S" products, services and solutions

A *Harvard Business Review* article highlighted this powerful intersection between world class customer outreach and sustainability, sharing these examples:[x]

- **Akzo Nobel:** The Dutch company launched a marketing campaign "Let's Color" enlisting volunteers and donating paint to revitalize run-down urban neighborhoods like the favelas in Rio de Janeiro.
- **Unilever:** The company holds a series of globally coordinated and locally delivered internal and external communications events called "Big Moments" to understand customer needs and align around the company's Sustainable Living Plan.

In these examples, the company created a powerful customer outreach program that drives home its sustainability commitment while garnering visibility and brand recognition.

Shaping Future Market Opportunities

The Scorecard addresses the work companies do to shape future market opportunities embedding ESG principles with four KSIs: looking at both existing markets and developing markets—and then looking at both existing product lines and new product families.

KSI 10.5: Selling Sustainability Features into Existing Markets. For companies that transition from seeing sustainability as a risk management play to those seeing it as that plus a revenue growth play, the place to start is often selling sustainability features into existing markets. That was the idea behind GE's launch of Ecomagination in 2005. Yet, most companies have not yet crossed that major hurdle between Stage 2 and Stage 3, as defined below.

KSI	Stage 1	Stage 2	Stage 3	Stage 4
Selling Sustainability Features into Existing Markets	Focus on traditional market segments	Pilot new market segments for "S" product offerings	Growing investment in "S" attributes and products	Transform company to fully align with "S" attributes

A few examples of Stage 3 companies are:
- **Campbell Soup:** The food company has, over the past decade, systematically responded to the broad customer trend toward healthier foods. As one example, the company entered the "packaged fresh" foods category.
- **DTE, NextEra Energy** and other utilities have been deploying smart grid and smart metering capability to its customers.
- **Avis:** As noted earlier, Avis acquired **Zipcar**, which epitomizes the trend toward collaborative consumption.
- **Duke Energy:** The U.S. power company launched a new $62 million solar rebate program in early 2018, which aims to help customers with the upfront cost of installing solar panels on their property.[xi]
- **Patagonia:** The company, through its Common Threads Initiative, encourages customers to purchase used Patagonia products on eBay before buying them new.

KSI 10.6: Selling Sustainability Features into Developing Markets. Most companies do not think of selling to poor people in Africa or various developing economies around the world as representing a key business opportunity. Yet, as the chart in Figure 1.1 in Chapter 1 shows, the doubling of the global middle class does indeed represent a growth opportunity. The range of practices today is as follows:

KSI	Stage 1	Stage 2	Stage 3	Stage 4
Selling Sustainability Features into Developing Markets	New market entry driven by traditional business factors	Repackage existing products around new "S" markets; pilots in underserved markets	Invest in adjacent "S" markets; rapidly grow "S" portfolio; formal partnerships	"S" investments (e.g., mapped to SDGs) provide track record and innovation platform

Some examples of companies that are successfully working to reap the benefits of these developing markets follow:
- **Akzo Nobel:** The Dutch company set a 2020 goal of achieving 20 percent of its revenue from eco-premium solutions that have a downstream sustainability benefit.
- **Allianz:** The insurance company offers a range of product solutions that are specifically tailored to the needs of low-income families. Key markets are developing

countries in Asia, Africa and Latin America where over 50 million low-income people are already reached by financial services from Allianz.[xii]
- **Cisco** and **IBM** see smart grid as representing a $100 billion market opportunity, working with customers including utilities and federal governments.[xiii]
- **Nokia:** In May 2018, the company announced the Smartpur project that aims to develop 500 digitally integrated and sustainable villages across India.[xiv]
- **Schneider Electric:** The French company, a global specialist in energy management and infrastructure operations, is upgrading "smart cities" initiatives, partnering with current and new customers to drive growth.[xv]
- **Yerdle:** This sharing economy startup sees itself as a new kind of retailer, which allows people to trade items for community credit. Yerdle's warehouses are your friends' closets, attics and garages.[xvi]
- **Unilever:** The company's subsidiary Hindustan Lever Ltd. (HLL) developed a washing product for the world's poor people at the "bottom of the economic pyramid" back in 2000–2002, one of the early success stories sometimes captured as "the fortune at the bottom of the pyramid."[xvii]

In each of these examples, the company successfully penetrated developing markets to produce both revenue growth while unlocking a new customer base.

KSI 10.7: Sustainability Attributes in Product Line Extension. It is interesting to look at the clothing industry, especially companies in the outdoor and athletic spaces and the quest to reduce and ultimately eliminate hazardous materials and petroleum-based materials.

KSI	Stage 1	Stage 2	Stage 3	Stage 4
Sustainability Attributes in Product Line Extension	Rarely considers sustainable attributes	Pilot investments in "S" products, services, and solutions	Sustainability is core to product-related business decisions	Launch industry sustainability breakthroughs; lead as market grows

- **Bombardier:** The Canadian aerospace company launched a new family of fuel-efficient airlines. At the time of the product launch, these game-changing aircraft emitted up to 20 percent less CO_2 and up to 50 percent less NOx, flew four times quieter, and delivered dramatic energy savings—up to 20 percent fuel burn advantage as well as up to 15 percent improved cash operating costs versus current in-production aircraft of similar size.[xviii]
- **Levi Strauss:** The company created Water<LessTM Jeans, which use up to 96 percent less water than conventional methods. Levi systematically rethought water consumption at every step of its production process.[xix]

In each of these examples, the companies created an extension of an existing product line—that had significantly less environmental impact across the full life cycle than the traditional product line.

KSI 10.8: New Sustainable Product Families. Sustainability spurs innovation—which in turn offers the opportunity to launch new product lines or product families. Most companies are in Stage 1 (rarely invest) or Stage 2 (pilot investments in green or healthy product lines) as depicted below.

KSI	Stage 1	Stage 2	Stage 3	Stage 4
New Sustainable Product Families	Rarely invest in new "S" products, services or solutions (PSS)	Pilot investments in sustainable PSS	Multi-year investments in "S" PSS families	Preserve or restore **ecosystem services**

Several examples of Stage 3 practices follow:
- **Alcoa:** In 2011, the company created what some called a self-cleaning, smog-eating building material. The company's Reynobond with EcoClean building panels actually cleans the surrounding air.[xx]
- **H&M:** The UK-based clothing retailer developed a "Conscious Exclusive" collection driving toward a more sustainable fashion future. The collection uses recycled "shoreline waste" in new clothing.[xxi]
- **Toyota:** As the world knows, Toyota developed the first mass-produced hybrid vehicle (the Prius), launched in 1997.[xxii]

In each of these examples, the company launched a new line—with significantly lighter (negative) environmental or social impacts compared with similar traditional products.

How Do Companies Stack Up?

Starting in 2018, we are capturing data from a group of founding participants—invited to use the Scorecard for a company self-assessment and to provide feedback. As we assess the data from the first 60 companies (all Fortune 500 or equivalent), three key messages stand out:
- Companies are fairly far down the path of identifying their customer's sustainability issues; nearly four of five companies (78 percent) rated their company Stage 2 or higher (meaning they understand their customer's ESG goals); and over half (55 percent) rated their company Stage 3 or higher.

- When it comes to partnering with customers to jointly cut full life-cycle footprint, companies are not as far along. Two of five companies (42 percent) rated their company Stage 2 or lower. Only one in six (17 percent) rated their company Stage 3.5 or Stage 4.
- Companies are not yet reaping the revenue benefits of selling sustainability features into existing markets. Fewer than one in four (23 percent) rated their company higher than Stage 3; though another 30 percent rated their company Stage 2.5 or Stage 3 (see Figure 20.1).

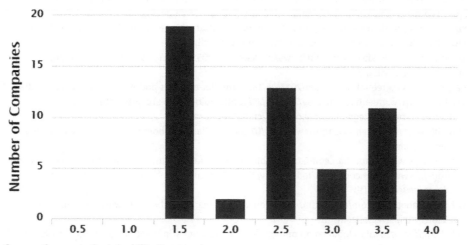

Source: Corporate Sustainability Scorecard

Figure 20.1: Scorecard Data from Sixty Companies on KSI 10.5: Selling Sustainability Features into Existing Markets

Selling ESG features into both existing and new markets—with both existing and new product lines—is likely to represent a massive business opportunity in the coming years.

i https://www.ecolab.com/sustainability/water-risk-monetizer

ii https://blog.google/products/maps/shedding-light-solar-potential-all-50-us-states/

iii https://www.infosys.com/newsroom/features/Pages/india-water-tool.aspx

iv https://hbr.org/2014/07/the-ultimate-marketing-machine

v https://www.conference-board.org/blog/postdetail.cfm?post=6454

vi https://www.racked.com/2017/5/8/15543720/natura-brasil-brazil-beauty

vii ttps://www.coca-colacompany.com/stories/2016-points-of-intersection

viii http://www.uefa.com/insideuefa/social-responsibility/news/newsid=2555915.html

ix https://www.news.xerox.com/news/Xerox-and-PrintReleaf-partnership-replants-global-forests

x https://hbr.org/2014/07/the-ultimate-marketing-machine

xi https://news.duke-energy.com/releases/duke-energy-s-62-million-solar-rebate-program-approved-for-north-carolina-residential-business-and-nonprofit-customers

xii https://www.allianz.com/en/products_solutions/sustainable_solutions/emerging-consumers/

xiii https://www.cnet.com/news/cisco-smart-grid-will-eclipse-size-of-internet/

xiv https://www.nokia.com/en_int/news/releases/2018/05/16/nokia-to-develop-500-digitally-integrated-smart-villages

xv https://www.greenbiz.com/blog/2013/06/18/schneider-electrics-bottoms-approach-smart-cities

xvi https://www.greenbiz.com/blog/2013/11/25/yerdle-cofounders-share-insights-sharing

xvii https://www.strategy-business.com/article/11518?pg=all

xviii https://www.greenbiz.com/news/2008/07/16/canadian-firm-bombardier-launches-green-planes-program

xix https://www.theguardian.com/sustainable-business/levi-rethinking-traditional-process-water

xx https://www.forbes.com/sites/toddwoody/2011/05/09/alcoas-self-cleaning-smog-eating-buildings/#49cee5076f18

xxi http://about.hm.com/en/media/news/general-2017/recycled-shoreline-waste-in-h-ms-new-conscious-exclusive-collect.html

xxii http://www.toyota-global.com/company/toyota_traditions/innovation/nov2008_feb2009_1.html

Chapter 21
Products, Services, and Solutions

The final Scorecard element in the Strategy and Execution section focuses on specific company offerings: the **products, services, and solutions (PSS)** the company currently sells and plans to sell in the future.

Autodesk makes software for people who make things. Thus, if you have ever admired a towering skyscraper, used a smartphone or watched a great movie, chances are you have experienced Autodesk. But the special ingredient of the company is the way it has embedded environmental and social issues into their product portfolio.

A true global leader, Autodesk aims nothing short of leading the way with sustainable, forward-thinking business practices. The company is committed to helping designers and engineers create a future where we all live well and within the limits of the planet. The company and leadership recognize that they have an opportunity to influence the future of everything that gets designed and made, and they take that responsibility seriously.

With a growing group of companies like Autodesk leading the way, the overarching strategic question that senior executives and board members should be asking is:

Key Question: How deeply are ESG risks and opportunities embedded in our evolving portfolio of products, services, and solution (PSS) offerings?

To help answer this key question, the Scorecard analyzes how companies manage and perform in three areas:
- The basic product positioning of the company
- The product development process
- The extent to which sustainability principles are incorporated formally into existing products; services and solutions

Within each of these areas, executives evaluate their company performance on several key sustainability indicators (KSIs).

Basic Product Positioning

The Scorecard addresses basic product positioning regarding environmental, social, and governance (ESG) with two KSIs: one dealing with the core business model and a second that looks at the societal value of PSS.

DOI 10.1515/9781547400423-021

KSI 11.1: PSS Model. **Xerox** was several decades ahead of its time when, in the early 1990s, the company altered its business model to lease copiers instead of selling them. After all, no business or individual truly wants to own a copy machine; we all just want to have a means to create dependable, excellent quality copies whenever we want them.

A key question for companies today is this: do our customers truly want our products—or do they actually just want the service delivered by those products? This KSI is about the extent to which companies have rethought their basic product offering model; do they churn out products that may get used for a while and then end up in a landfill? Or are they migrating toward offering products as well as services and solutions. The range of practices follows:

KSI	Stage 1	Stage 2	Stage 3	Stage 4
Products, Services, and Solutions (PSS) Model	Traditional focus on selling products	Move to more "S" and lighter-footprint products	Grow sustainable ("S") services and solutions; "S" is fully integrated into PSS; exit less "S" products	Fully closed loop supply chain; move increasingly to services and solutions

Several examples of companies that have (for whatever reason—which may not be ESG-driven) adopted a Stage 3 or higher PSS model.

-   **Airbnb:** The young "sharing economy" company grew from start-up to the world's largest hotel chain in eight years—owning no rooms and a testament to the growing popularity of what has been called "collaborative consumption"—the sharing, swapping, and renting of one's possessions.[i]
-   **JP Morgan Chase:** The bank reported in May 2018 that it had facilitated $60 billion in clean financing since 2016.[ii]
-   **Michelin:** The French company has a history of operating with an innovative mindset in order to stay resilient and relevant in the highly competitive business of manufacturing tires. The company recently began selling tires as a service, creating a separate division (Michelin Solutions) leading to eco-efficiency solutions.
-   **London Taxi Company:** A company whose name says it all opened UK's first dedicated electric vehicle factory.[iii]

In each of these examples, the company has been rethinking the fundamental way products in their sector have meet customer needs over many decades—and launched a new, healthier, or greener solution.

KSI 11.2: Societal Value of PSS. These days, the phrase "doing well by doing good" is increasingly used by company executives—either informally in internal company discussions or in public. The basic idea is simple: we can do well as a company (be profitable and successful) by also doing good things for society and the planet. Not surprisingly, companies vary considerably in the extent to which they position their offerings as such. The range of approaches is depicted below.

KSI	Stage 1	Stage 2	Stage 3	Stage 4
Societal Value of Products, Services, and Solutions	Viewed in traditional ways: value = to shareholders	Value = to shareholders and to society; offerings mapped/aligned to SDGs and/or SDG concepts/ intent	Societal value of offerings is visible and widely understood; part of vision, values	Societal value of offerings is front and center; for example, restores **ecosystem services** or address a major social problem

A growing list of major companies have bold carbon reduction goals that drive a net benefit to society.[iv] Some examples:

- **Alcoa:** Before it split into two companies, the global aluminum manufacturer set a goal of enabling carbon savings from the use phase of the company's products that are three times the emissions from the production of those products.
- **AT&T:** The telecommunications giant aims to enable carbon savings ten times the footprint of its operations by 2025.
- **Dow:** By 2025, Dow's products will offset three times more CO_2 than they emit throughout their life cycle.
- **Ericsson:** The Swedish multinational networking and telecommunications company has a goal of reducing societal carbon emissions by a factor of two in relation to the carbon emissions from Ericsson's own activities—by implementing smart meters, smart transport, and related information technology solutions.
- **NEC:** The Japanese multinational provider of information technology services aims to attain a level of CO_2 reduction that is five times the total volume of CO_2 emissions from its entire supply chain in fiscal year 2020.
- **NTT:** The Japan Telegraph and Telephone Corporation has a 2020 goal of societal emissions reductions enabled by its products that are over five times more than the company's own emissions.

Other companies have taken a different approach to broad goals benefiting society.

- **Kingfisher:** The UK home improvement company has set the goal of giving back more than it takes from the ecosystem through reforestation, net energy generation and creating products that reduce waste.[v]

- **Porsche:** The auto company announced a new goal in 2018 to grow its fleet of electric cars to 50 percent of its sales by 2025.[vi]

In both of these examples, the company is decades into evolving its PSS portfolio to align with the emerging needs of society and constraints of the planet.

The Product Development Process

The Scorecard addresses integration of sustainability into product development with two KSIs: one dealing with the product development process and a second looking at product design.

Product development refers to the entire process from concept, market analysis, costing, scheduling, testing, handling the manufacturing process, and all other aspects of getting a product into the market. *Product design* refers to the process of simply designing a product itself.

KSI 11.3: Sustainability in the Product Development Process. Every company that churns out products has a formal product development process. The issue here is to what extent ESG issues are integrated into that process. The range of maturity follows:

KSI	Stage 1	Stage 2	Stage 3	Stage 4
Sustainability in the Product Development Process	Basic "Stage Gate" process with "S" issues considered during the process	"S"/ESG risks and impacts are essentially "bolted-on" to the product development process	"S"/ESG issues, risks, and opportunities are assessed at an early stage and "woven-in" at each key step	"S" criteria are sufficiently important to provide "go/no-go" decision early in the process

Several examples of Stage 3 or higher companies follow:
- **3M:** Over its past several CEOs, 3M has worked to balance creativity and efficiency in its product development process, within the Six Sigma framework that was brought to the company from GE when Jim McNerney arrived as CEO.[vii]
- **Danone:** As noted earlier, the company partnered with Nestlé Waters to fund start-up development of 100% bio-based bottles.[viii]
- **Schneider Electric:** The French company rates about two-thirds of its products with its Green Premium ecolabel, which means minimal use of hazardous substances, product carbon profiles, end-of-life management for optimized recycling.[ix]

In each of these examples, the companies have taken active steps to embed sustainability criteria, analyses, and reviews into the existing product development process.

KSI 11.4: Sustainability in Product Design. In Chapter 6, we listed a group of companies that have a green or healthy portfolio of products (see Table 6.2). In each case, the products or services in the sustainable portfolio meet certain rigorous criteria. And, in most cases the company's goal is to increase the number of products (and percentage of total offerings) in this sustainable portfolio over time. The way they do this is through product design, where the range of current approaches is as follows:

KSI	Stage 1	Stage 2	Stage 3	Stage 4
Sustainability in Product Design	Consider "S" attributes indirectly	Formally consider full life-cycle impacts	Systematically grow "S" PSS as % of sales; **closed-loop design**	Breakthrough solutions to tough global problem(s)

Several examples of companies incorporating sustainability into product design follow:

- **Amcor:** The global packaging company has pledged to design 100 percent of its packaging to be recyclable or reusable by 2025.[x]
- **Schneider Electric:** (France) is upgrading infrastructure for "smart cities" initiatives.[xi]
- **Interface:** The company announced in June 2018 that all of its products are carbon neutral across the entire product lifecycle.[xii]
- **Shaw Industries:** The company's EcoWorx carpet offers ingredient transparency through Cradle to Cradle *Certification*[TM], Health Product Declarations, and Declare registration.[xiii]

These companies illustrate the power of integrating environmental stewardship and social responsibility thinking into the often well-established product development process. In many companies, this involves breaking down some internal barriers, but the results can be striking.

Existing PSS

The Scorecard addresses how companies integrate ESG into existing portfolio of offerings with four KSIs, addressing product rating; product quality and safety, product sustainability audits and product advertising and marketing.

KSI 11.5: Product Sustainability Rating Process. Over the past several decades, two main types of sustainability rating processes have evolved:
- Company-specific schemes for evaluating (rating) their products or product families

- General, industry-wide schemes available to companies in a certain industry sector or to any companies

In both cases, there may be a formal rating scheme in use: a simple scoring system or means of grouping products into main buckets.

KSI	Stage 1	Stage 2	Stage 3	Stage 4
Product Sustainability Rating Process	N/A or informal	Simple, basic scheme for rating product "S" impacts (e.g., green chemistry principles)	Formal risk mapping drives product portfolio changes	Drives product and business portfolio changes

Several examples of leading practices follow:
- **SC Johnson:** The company developed its Greenlist™ Process in 2001 to evaluate all ingredients used in its products. The program is a science-based, four-step evaluation that looks at both hazard and risk, grounded in best-in-class data collection.[xiv]
- **Schneider Electric:** The French company was selected by the Sustainable Apparel Coalition to develop a web-based sustainability assessment tool called the Higg Index. The web-based tool measures the ESG impacts of apparel and footwear products and encourages supply chain transparency.[xv]
- **Nike:** The athletic apparel company found itself in the crosshairs of NGOs over working conditions at some facilities in its huge supply chain in the late 1990s. Since then, the focus on embedding ESG into product design has been relentless. Nike established its "Considered Design Index" in 2009; the company-wide program that incorporates green principles into Nike's design guidelines. The result is products with more environmentally friendly materials, few toxics, and less waste. [xvi]
- **LG Electronics:** The South Korean company wants to make energy efficiency the centerpiece of its competitive differentiation strategy. Global demand for the company's energy efficient products has grown; 2012 sales jumped 75 percent for its "Energy Star Most Efficient" products.[xvii]
- **DSM:** The Dutch plastic company has developed **Cradle to Cradle** systems since 2008 and several of its products are certified with the C2C distinction.[xviii]

The examples above illustrate different ways a few leading companies have embedded ESG into the design and development of their existing product portfolio.

KSI 11.6: Product Quality and Safety. Companies have been focused on product quality and product safety for generations. The auto sector embodies both quality and safety concerns; for consumer products that are (or could be) ingested, product quality is of ultimate importance. The issue for sustainability is the extent to which these traditional business processes have been expanded to address a broader set of ESG issues. The range of approaches is depicted below.

KSI	Stage 1	Stage 2	Stage 3	Stage 4
Product Quality and Safety	Regulation/legal driven	Apply standards globally; candid, balanced disclosure	Priority on product durability (vs. disposable)	Close to "ideally sustainable" PSS

Several examples of companies that have expanded their product safety and quality programs to incorporate ESG follow:

- **Air Products:** The industrial gas company has a longstanding commitment to safety, health, and environment that the company then leveraged to extend into broader ESG positioning.[xix]
- **Toro:** The lawnmower company is committed to developing innovative and safe products that yield performance productivity and environmental benefits for their customers.
- **Unilever:** The company's approach to product safety and quality is hard-wired to its Sustainable Living Plan; the commitment to customers is to provide branded products and services that are safe and to innovate based on sound science.[xx]

KSI 11.7: Product Sustainability Audits. The apparel and technology sectors have led the way on product sustainability audits—mostly as a result of high profile ESG issues in their supply chains. **Nike** found this in the 1990s; **Apple** learned its lesson over the past decade following news of environmental and human rights abuses at Foxconn—a contract supplier in China.

KSI	Stage 1	Stage 2	Stage 3	Stage 4
Product Sustainability Audits	No formal product audits; ensure compliance with laws and customer demands	Product stewardship review program; systematically review and address negative "S" aspects	Audit vs. robust ESG criteria; review product portfolio vs. societal needs, benefits	Quantify "S" and financial benefits for existing and new PSS

Adidas is an excellent example of a Stage 3 approach. The company has used supplier audits to manage risk for a number of years. In 2013, the company issued sixty-six warning letters to suppliers across fourteen countries, and terminated nine manufacturing agreements for social and environmental compliance. Adidas uses the Higg index and sources fewer parts for shoes and uses waste materials for certain components of production.[xxi]

KSI 11.8: Product Marketing and Advertising. When it comes to marketing or advertising and sustainability, this is tricky territory. We addressed this at a corporate level in Chapter 17 (Disclosure, Reporting, and Transparency) under KSI 7.8 (Corporate Marketing and Advertising Approach to Sustainability). This KSI relates to product marketing and advertising. This is tricky because the main purpose of advertising is to sell stuff—to convince the public that your company and product is great.

The range of approaches is depicted below.

KSI	Stage 1	Stage 2	Stage 3	Stage 4
Product Marketing & Advertising	Safe and responsible use; selectively quiet on product risks	Beyond compliance; limited focus on full value-chain impacts	Conveys full life-cycle impacts; transparent regarding "S" impacts	Fully transparent; use **LCA** and share **cradle to cradle** impacts

Staples offers a variety of eco-friendly products that meet specific criteria. The criteria include: meeting one or more third-party environmental standards or certifications; containing 30 percent or more post-consumer recycled content; made with 30 percent or more agricultural residues, rapidly renewable materials or bio-based alternatives.[xxii]

How Do Companies Stack Up?

Starting in 2018, we are capturing data from a group of founding participants—invited to use the Scorecard for a company self-assessment and to provide feedback. As we assess the data from the first sixty companies (all Fortune 500 or equivalent), three key messages stand out:
- Seventy percent of the companies rated themselves Stage 2 or higher, meaning they are moving toward more sustainable, lighter footprint products. A third of the companies rated their company Stage 3 or higher.
- Companies are certainly integrating sustainability into their product development processes. The ratings were fairly evenly distributed: one third rated their company Stage 1 or 1.5; another third rated their company Stage 2 or 2.5; with the balance rating their company Stage 3 or higher.

– Companies appear to be taking a bit of a "wait and see" approach to acting on their product sustainability rating scheme. Most companies have at least a basic scheme for rating product environmental and social impacts. However, only seven of sixty (12 percent) rated their company Stage 3 or higher (see Figure 21.1).

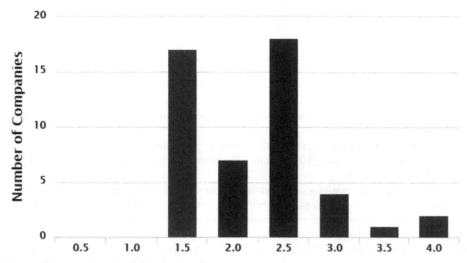

Source: Corporate Sustainability Scorecard

Figure 21.1: Scorecard Data from Sixty Companies on KSI 11.5: Product Sustainability Rating Process

Since GE launched Ecomagination in 2005, much has changed. A long list of major global companies are growing their large sustainable product portfolios. Meanwhile, many mainstream companies are steadily embedding ESG thinking and features into their product development and design processes.

i https://www.telegraph.co.uk/technology/news/9525267/Airbnb-The-story-behind-the-1.3bn-room-letting-website.html

ii https://www.jpmorganchase.com/corporate/Corporate-Responsibility/document/jpmc-cr-esg-report-2017.pdf

iii http://www.wired.co.uk/article/london-taxi-company-electric-vehicles-uk

iv "Estimating and reporting the comparative emissions impacts of products," World Resources Institute; Draft WRI working paper; May 2015.

v https://www.theguardian.com/sustainable-business/sustainability-case-studies-kingfisher-environmental-philosophy

vi https://www.bloomberg.com/news/articles/2018-04-25/porsche-doubles-target-for-deliveries-of-electric-cars-by-2025

vii https://www.bloomberg.com/news/articles/2007-06-10/at-3m-a-struggle-between-efficiency-and-creativity

viii https://www.nestle-watersna.com/en/nestle-water-news/pressreleases/nestle-waters-danone-bio-based-bottles

ix https://www.schneider-electric.com/en/work/support/green-premium/

x https://www.amcor.com/about/media-centre/news/amcor-is-first-global-packaging-company-pledging-to-develop-all-its

xi https://www.greenbiz.com/blog/2013/06/18/schneider-electrics-bottoms-approach-smart-cities

xii http://www.interface.com/US/en-US/about/press-room/Carbon-Neutral-Floors-Release-en_US

xiii https://www.shawcontract.com/en-us/sustainability/product-innovation/ecoworx

xiv http://www.scjohnson.com/en/commitment/focus-on/greener-products/greenlist.aspx

xv https://www.environmentalleader.com/2013/09/schneider-electric-to-develop-web-based-higg-index/

xvi https://www.greenbiz.com/blog/2009/10/19/considered-design-closing-loop

xvii https://www.greenbiz.com/blog/2013/06/21/lg-turns-volume-its-energy-and-climate-strategy

xviii https://www.theguardian.com/sustainable-business/businesses-waste-resource-cradle-to-cradle

xix http://www.airproducts.com/Company/Sustainability/environment-health-and-safety.aspx

xx https://www.unilever.com/sustainable-living/what-matters-to-you/product-safety-and-quality.html

xxi http://www.sustainablebrands.com/news_and_views/supply_chain/mike_hower/adidas_supplier_audit_coverage_reached_75_2013

xxii https://www.staples.com/sbd/cre/marketing/sustainability-center/shop-green-products/?icid=SustProducts:topnav:2:PRODUCTS:

Chapter 22
Environmental Footprint—Operations

The next three chapters address the environmental stewardship portion of the Score-card. As mentioned in Chapter 7 (Environmental Stewardship) the Scorecard and these three chapters are organized around the value chain in three broad buckets: suppliers, operations, products. We start with operations since that is the typical starting point for virtually all companies.

Xerox has, since the early 1990s, had a goal of producing waste-free products in waste-free facilities that promote waste-free customer workplaces. Such a simple idea. Xerox's aim is to design products, packaging and supplies that make efficient use of resources, minimize waste, reuse material where feasible, and recycle what can not be reused. To achieve this goal, the company has:

– Created a collection and reuse/recycling program for spent imaging supplies
– Instituted a product takeback and recycling program
– Set and worked toward waste-free goals in their operations
– Invested in technologies that reduce the creation of waste

Xerox, at the same time, was one of the early adopters of what today are commonly referred to as "circular economy" business models, one of which is shifting from selling products to selling services.[1] From its first product launch in 1959, Xerox focused on leasing its copiers to customers rather than selling them.

When it comes to evaluating the environmental impact of your company opera-tions, the overarching strategic question that senior executives and board members should be asking is:

Key Question: How deeply and robustly are we managing and reducing the environmental risks asso-ciated with our operations?

To help answer this key question, the Scorecard analyzes how companies manage and perform in three areas:

– Managing purchased resource inputs—all those things that enter your property at the factory gate (or equivalent)
– Managing your own physical environmental footprint (within your property boundaries)
– Managing nonproduct outputs—all the things that leave your operation at the end of production, other than the products themselves

Within each of these areas, executives evaluate their company performance on several key sustainability indicators (KSIs).

DOI 10.1515/9781547400423-022

Managing Purchased Resource Inputs

For any company, a very large portion of the environmental impact of your operations is directly tied to the stuff you purchase and that comes in through the facility gate. The Scorecard addresses these purchased resource inputs with five KSIs: dealing with chemicals, energy, materials (both human-made and natural), and water.

KSI 12.1: Chemical Substances Sourced. Much of the pressure to reduce the use of hazardous chemical substances has come from Europe. While the United States and most other developed countries have laws and regulations for use and disposition of hazardous substances, Europe has been at the forefront, especially since 2006 when the European Union regulation was promulgated. The Registration, Evaluation, Authorization, and Restriction of Chemicals (REACH) regulation addresses the production and use of chemical substances, and their potential impacts on both human health and the environment.

While not every company is impacted by REACH, many are. The range of company approaches to this is as follows.

KSI	Stage 1	Stage 2	Stage 3	Stage 4
Chemical Substances Sourced	Comply with regulations	Comply globally with toughest standard (e.g., **REACH**)	Actively phasing out higher toxicity chemicals	Align with **green chemistry** principles

Many companies have taken the initiative to reduce or phase out hazardous chemicals. For example:
- **Kering:** The global luxury group based in France has committed to phase out all hazardous chemicals by 2020.[ii]
- **Levi Strauss:** The company launched a new operating model that digitized their denim finish design and development. The expectation is that this will eliminate thousands of chemical formulations from the jeans finishing process.[iii]
- **Nike:** The company committed in 2011 to zero discharge of hazardous chemicals by 2020 and published its roadmap to achieve that target.[iv] Nike reported in May 2018 that it had achieved 98 percent compliance with its Nike Restricted Substance List in FY16/17.[v]

KSI 12.2: Energy Purchased (Scope 2). The environmental impact of purchased energy (for fuel, electricity, transport, etc.) is principally its greenhouse gas (GHG) emissions—which are referred to as Scope 2. Scope 2 GHG emissions result from the generation of electricity, heat, or steam purchased by a company from a utility provider.

Purchased energy is vitally important for virtually all industry sectors. For some, such as mining, metal fabrication and heavy manufacturing, energy is a major component of the cost of goods sold. As a result, for many companies, even a small percentage reduction in money spent on energy can be a very large number. Thus, it is no surprise that many companies have discovered that cutting GHG emissions can save money.

The range of approaches companies take to purchased fuels, electricity and other energy sources is depicted below:

KSI	Stage 1	Stage 2	Stage 3	Stage 4
Energy Purchased (e.g., fuel, electricity, transport, etc.)—Scope 2 Emissions	Some energy efficiency programs; most is conventional sources (oil, gas, coal) with < 10% renewables	Very strong energy efficiency; renewables growing to ~10–30% of total energy used	A leader in energy efficiency; renewables growing to ~30–60% of total energy used	Approaching zero nonrenewable energy used over next 5 years

A growing number of companies are announcing significant accomplishments in the area of renewable energy purchases. Several examples of efforts to dramatically reduce energy consumption follow:

- **Allianz Capital Partners:** The diversified active investment management company based in Germany exceeded €2 billion in renewable energy investments made by 2014.[vi]
- **Bloomberg, Facebook, General Motors, Hewlett-Packard, Intel, Johnson & Johnson, Mars, Novelis, Procter & Gamble, REI, Sprint**, and **Walmart** released a set of principles in July 2014 aimed at making it easier for companies to buy more renewable energy.[vii]
- **Curtis Packaging:** The small, privately held producer of luxury packaging products uses 100 percent certified renewable energy and is carbon neutral.[viii]
- **FedEx:** The company set 2020 reduction goals including 30 percent aircraft emission reduction.[ix]
- **Google:** The company has achieved 100 percent renewables use and committed over $1 billion to renewable energy projects.[x]
- **IKEA:** Committed in 2014 that wind will provide ~1.5x the energy needs of all of IKEA's U.S. operations.[xi]
- **Ingersoll Rand:** The company committed to a 35 percent reduction in GHG footprint, in addition to many other climate commitments, by 2020.[xii]

- **Kohler:** Reported in 2018 that it will now source 100 percent renewable electricity across its eighty-five manufacturing facilities, offices, and warehouses in the United States and Canada.[xiii]
- **Microsoft:** The company achieved carbon neutrality in its company owned operations globally in 2012, using a carbon fee model that charges Microsoft business groups for their carbon footprint. The company also invests in carbon offsets for emissions related to air travel.[xiv]
- **Stockland:** One of the largest diversified property groups in Australia requires each business to meet energy efficiency and climate change mitigation targets in the design, construction, and operation of projects and assets.[xv]
- **Vale:** The Brazilian-based global mining company cut water to suppress dust by 75 percent; reduced GHG emissions 40 percent.[xvi]

In each of these examples, the company made a bold commitment, and they kept with it because it made sound business sense.

KSI 12.3: Materials Sourced: Biological-Based (e.g., forest products, etc.). As mentioned in Chapter 3 (Terminology), most materials flow in one of several value chains: the agricultural value chain is largely biological-based while the metals and petrochemicals value chains are based on human-made materials. The food and beverage sector is largely reliant on the bio-based supply chain, while for other sectors this may represent a relatively small portion of their overall material inputs.

The range of approaches companies take to managing the sourcing of bio-based materials is as depicted below:

KSI	Stage 1	Stage 2	Stage 3	Stage 4
Materials Sourced: Biological-Based (e.g., forest products, etc.)	Compliance focus; incremental reductions; support industry codes	~50% and growing from certified "S" sources (e.g., forests); goals for growing bio-based inputs	~50% bio-based plastics and related materials if demonstrated through life cycle assessment (LCA) to be preferred	100% from certified "S" sources; 100% bio-based plastics and related materials if demonstrated through LCA to be preferred

Below are several companies that have made bold commitments to sourcing biological-based materials.
- **B&Q:** The UK-based home and garden supply store is the first UK company to sustainably source all of its timber products.[xvii]

- **General Mills:** The global food company has committed to sustainably sourcing 100 percent of its top ten priority ingredients by 2020. These ingredients (including oats, wheat, corn, dairy, fiber packaging, cocoa, vanilla, palm oil, sugar cane, and sugar beets) represent 50 percent of the company's total raw materials purchases.[xviii]
- **McDonalds:** Noting a preference for Forest Stewardship Council certification, the company set a goal to source all of its packaging from renewable, recycled, or certified sources by 2025. The company also pledged to make recycling available in all of its restaurants by the same year.[xix]
- **Mondelēz International:** The company committed to sourcing wheat for its biscuit products from 100 percent sustainable sources by 2022.[xx]

In each of these examples, the company focused on one of the major raw materials in its value chain—and achieved impressive results.

KSI 12.4: Materials Sourced: Human-Made (e.g., metals, plastics, etc.). For the vast majority of companies, the preponderance of purchased material that comes in the factory gates is composed of metals, plastics, and other human-made materials. The range of ways companies manage this key sourcing area is as follows:

KSI	Stage 1	Stage 2	Stage 3	Stage 4
Materials Sourced: Human-Made (e.g., metals, plastics, etc.)	Compliance focus; adopt **design for environment** principles; 10–20% recycled content; some resource efficiency efforts	Apply toughest standard globally (e.g., **REACH**); drive efficiency; Reduce / recycle ~25%; 20–50% recycled content	Far beyond compliance; Reduce / recycle ~25–75%; 50–75% recycled content; actively phasing out toxics globally	Approaching closed-loop; 75–100% recycled content; Align with **green chemistry** principles

Novelis the global leader in aluminum rolled products and the world's largest recycler of aluminum, is a terrific example of a Stage 3 plus approach to managing human-made materials in the value chain. Aluminum is the most recyclable substance in the world; it can be recycled again and again without losing its core properties. This is in contrast to recycling of plastics and other materials that normally result in "downcycling"—recycling into a park bench or other product that requires lower specifications.

In 2011, Novelis's then-CEO Phil Martens realized that over two thirds of its raw material came from mining bauxite ore—a very energy-intensive operation. At the same time, he saw a world awash in waste aluminum soda cans and other materials waiting to be recycled. Novelis set the transformational goal in 2011 to source 80 percent of its inputs from recycled sources by 2020. At the time, the company was only sourcing 33 percent recycled materials. This goal represents a massive change for the company, its customers and its industry sector. In 2017, the company achieved a level of 55 percent recycled inputs.[xxi]

Several other 2018 examples include:
- **Dunkin' Donuts:** Polystyrene foam cups have long been a symbol of waste in the United States. However, the company announced on February 7, 2018 that it plans to phase out polystyrene foam cups in its global supply chain by 2020. The company currently uses paper cups in the majority of its international markets.[xxii]
- **Evian:** The bottled water brand pledged to make all of its plastic bottles from 100 percent recycled plastic by 2025.[xxiii]

KSI 12.5: Water Sourced. We would expect beverage companies globally to manage water resources efficiently and carefully—and they do. But they are not alone. With increasing pressures on quality and quantity of potable water around the world, many companies have stepped up their water conservation efforts. The range of approaches is as follows:

KSI	Stage 1	Stage 2	Stage 3	Stage 4
Water Sourced	Compliance focus; incremental reduction	Significant reductions achieved	Selectively **water-neutral** operations	Fully water-neutral operations

Several examples of impressive water conservation efforts follow:
- **Biogen:** The company achieved a 69 percent reduction in water intensity[1] in 2015, 86 percent of the 2020 goal.[xxiv]
- **Coca-Cola:** The company has been working diligently—especially in the past decade—with communities globally on water usage.[xxv]
- **Kimberly Clark:** The company achieved its 2015 water reduction goal of 25 percent. This goal was one of a suite of robust 2015 sustainability goals the company had set years earlier.[xxvi]

---

[1] Companies typically adopt one of two broad types of footprint reduction goals: absolute reductions or reductions in (e.g., water or carbon) intensity. The latter refers to volume of emissions per level of production (e.g., volume of water used per unit of product produced).

Managing Own Physical Footprint

Once all of the materials come inside the factory gate, companies manage the environmental impact of their operations in a pretty simply way: by managing all of the manufacturing, assembly and related operations that take place inside buildings and the environmental impacts on the surrounding land. Thus, the Scorecard addresses a company's own physical footprint with KSIs representing these two aspects.

KSI 12.6: Buildings and Equipment. When the United States Green Building Council (USGBC) launched its Leadership in Energy and Environmental Design (LEED) standards, few knew what the result would be. The standard was first developed in the early 1990s, but over the past twenty-five years, the growth in the use of this green building certification program has been remarkable. More companies every day make claims about LEED certified buildings.

The range of approaches companies take to managing the environmental footprint of their buildings and equipment is as follows:

KSI	Stage 1	Stage 2	Stage 3	Stage 4
Buildings and Equipment	Focus on reducing energy; some recycling	Major initiative driven by **LEED** standards	Aggressive retrofits; new buildings LEED	~100% owned/ leased buildings are zero net energy within 5 years

Below are several examples of strong practices in managing the environmental impact of buildings.
- **Bloomberg:** The financial services company has seventeen office buildings that achieved LEED (Leadership in Energy and Environmental Design) Platinum and another eighteen that achieved LEED Gold.[xxvii]
- **Unilever:** The company has, since 2013, been building new factories that are at least 50 percent more efficient and sustainable than the average for its other facilities in the same category.[xxviii]

KSI 12.7: Land Management. This KSI refers to any land management activity affecting biodiversity, forest products, remediation and restoration. For many companies, managing the land they own from an environmental stewardship perspective involves incremental actions: cutting down on pesticides and herbicides; planting trees in the parking lots; converting lawn to fields; avoiding negative impacts on streams and local biodiversity. It also means cleaning up (remediating) the messes from legacy operations—called Superfund sites in the United States. These represent Stage 1 in the Scorecard below.

KSI	Stage 1	Stage 2	Stage 3	Stage 4
Land Management (e.g., biodiversity, forest products, remediation and restoration)		Promote and invest in **brownfield redevelopment**	Selectively restore habitats	Aggressively restore and protect habitat

Two examples of how a leading company is managing its approach to land, going far beyond compliance and remediation to actually restoring and protecting habitats, are:

- **IKEA:** The Dutch company set a roadmap back in 2012 to be "forest positive" through a wide range of targets including renewable energy, recycling, waste management, and "green" product sourcing.[xxix]
- **Kingfisher:** The UK company set a goal as part of the company's sustainable growth plan to be net positive—to create more forest than it uses, help customers build homes, create more energy than they consume, and ensure that every product will enable a net positive lifestyle.[xxx]

In these two examples, the company takes a very broad—even global—approach to ensuring stewardship of land potentially impacted by its operations across the full value chain.

Managing Nonproduct Outputs

Thus far, we have looked at the stuff that comes into the factory from the outside (managed purchase inputs) and the company operations footprint (buildings, equipment, and land). The third bucket of own operations environmental footprint is managing the stuff that goes out the other side—other than the products—following on-site manufacturing, assembly or other operation. Think of all of these nonproduct outputs as emissions and waste.

The Scorecard addresses how companies manage nonproduct outputs with four KSIs: GHG emissions; other emissions; waste generation, and water discharges.

KSI 12.8: GHG Emissions (Scope 1). Scope 1 GHG emissions are direct emissions from sources that are owned or controlled by the company. The way companies manage these Scope 1 GHG emissions is depicted below.

KSI	Stage 1	Stage 2	Stage 3	Stage 4
Greenhouse Gas (GHG) Emissions (Scope 1)	10–20% reduction goals	On target for 20–50% reduction from baseline year	On target for 50–80% reduction from baseline year	On target for being carbon neutral—or carbon negative

Several examples of companies that have made significant reductions in GHG emissions are as follows:

- **Adobe Systems:** The company claims to be carbon neutral in United States and will be 100 percent renewable energy by 2035.[xxxi]
- **Boise Cascade:** The manufacturer of engineered wood products learned in 2013 that it could cut CO_2 emissions 60 percent by switching from road to rail.[xxxii]
- **BT:** The company's Net Good goal: customers cut GHG emissions by 3x BT's 2020 carbon impact.[xxxiii]
- **O2:** As the trading name for **Telefónica Europe,** a European telecommunications provider, O2 launched its Think Big Blueprint—a plan for people and the planet—that will deliver carbon reductions for customers 10x the impact of O2's network.[xxxiv]
- **Samsung:** The South Korean electronics giant cut GHG emissions 57 percent since 2008 and 2013.[xxxv]

In each of these examples, the company set a very bold goal, one they honestly were not sure they could achieve. The results are impressive.

KSI 12.9: Other Emissions. GHG are not the only emissions of significance for many companies. For many decades—dating back to the 1970s in the United States—companies have been subjected to national, regional, and local air pollution control requirements. The Stage 1 companies manage for compliance; Stage 2 companies look around at the different countries where they have operations and make a deliberate decision to impose the toughest standard globally—even if it exceeds the local requirements.

KSI	Stage 1	Stage 2	Stage 3	Stage 4
Other Emissions	Manage for compliance	Manage to toughest standards globally	Zero discharge of hazardous substances	Emissions are benign and continually reduced

Xerox has been systematically reducing its air emissions for over twenty years, in addition to accomplishing very significant GHG reductions.[xxxvi]

KSI 12.10: Waste Generation. 3M "wrote the book" on reducing waste—and literally hundreds of companies globally have followed suit. In 1975 3M launched a pioneering program called Pollution Prevention Pays, which empowers 3Mers to find creative ways to make the company more efficient. This initiative continues today, and has led to 15,000 projects that have prevented two million tons of air, water, and waste pollution.[xxxvii]

KSI	Stage 1	Stage 2	Stage 3	Stage 4
Waste Generation	Goals to reduce waste; steady progress	Very significant focus on waste reduction; significant success to date	Pockets of zero waste to landfill and 100% recycling	Zero waste to landfill and 100% recycling; zero hazardous waste

Zero waste has been an ambition of many companies for decades—including companies that create massive amounts of waste. **DuPont** set a zero waste goal in the 1990s; **Walmart** had zero waste as one of its three main ambitions in 2005 when then-CEO Lee Scott launched the company on its sustainability journey. AT&T more recently set a zero waste goal for 100 company facilities by the end of 2020. A few other examples:

- **Chipotle Mexican Grill:** The company achieved a 40 percent waste diversion rate (waste diverted from landfills) in 2017 and announced a goal to increase that to 50 percent by 2020.[xxxviii]
- **Ecolab:** The company helped customers eliminate 26.4 million pounds of waste in 2015.[xxxix]
- **HP Inc.:** The company achieved TRUE (Total Resource Use and Efficiency) Zero Waste certification for its Palo Alto, CA corporate headquarters in 2018.[xl]
- **Nestlé:** The company achieved zero waste disposal status at 253 factories worldwide by the end of 2017.[xli]
- **Subaru:** The company embarked on company-wide zero waste initiatives in 2012. In just two years, Subaru transformed its automotive assembly plant in Lafayette, Indiana into the first zero-landfill factory in the United States.[xlii]

KSI 12.11: Water Discharges. The stage for water concerns was set long ago. In "The Rime of the Ancient Mariner" author Samuel Taylor Coleridge said, "Water, water everywhere, and all the boards did shrink; Water, water everywhere, Nor any drop to drink." And as Ben Franklin said, "When the well is dry we know the value of water."

In the early months of 2018, the city of Cape Town in South Africa came into the headlines as the city approached "Day Zero"—the day when literally the city taps in the city run dry and people start lining up (queuing) for water. That gets attention! The date is now pushed back to 2019.

KSI	Stage 1	Stage 2	Stage 3	Stage 4
Water Discharges	Manage for compliance	Manage to toughest standards globally	Discharges cleaner than water sourced	Net neutral impact on stressed aquifer supply

Two excellent examples of ways companies are working to be excellent stewards of fresh water supplies globally are:

– **Coca-Cola:** The company is working to replenish water supplies and improve the quality of water they discharge to the environment. The company does this in two primary ways:

   o   Replenish the water used in global sales volume back to communities and nature through water projects outside the company's manufacturing plant boundaries; and

   o   Return the water used to make its beverages back to communities and nature after it is appropriately treated.[xliii]

– **Ecolab, General Mills, Nestlé, Sealed Air**, and **Veolia** are among the companies driving the Alliance for Water Stewardship—the organization behind the development of a global standard for defining water stewardship.[xliv]

– **NRG Energy:** The power company reduced water withdrawal by 40 percent in 2017, achieving its 2030 goal more than a decade ahead of schedule.[xlv]

Cape Town is just an early and visible indicator of fresh water challenges. Until it hits close to home, most people go on about their daily lives. This is another example of poor pricing mechanisms.

How Do Companies Stack Up?

Starting in 2018, we are capturing data from a group of founding participants—invited to use the Scorecard for a company self-assessment and to provide feedback. As we assess the data from the first 60 companies (all Fortune 500 or equivalent), three key messages stand out:

– Waste reduction has been around for a half century (witness 3M's Pollution Prevent Pays program). However, even a group of sixty well-established companies rate themselves as only above average. More than one third rate themselves Stage 1 or 1.5. Another third rate themselves Stage 2 or 2.5 while a final third rate their company Stage 3 or higher.

– With all the focus on purchased energy, it is not surprising that two thirds of the companies rate themselves Stage 2 or higher, with a quarter of them rating their company Stage 3 or higher. Another third rate their company Stage 1 or 1.5.

–   When it comes to human-made materials sourced, nearly half of the companies (47 percent) rated themselves Stage 1.5. The other half are scattered between Stage 2 and Stage 4 as depicted in Figure 22.1.

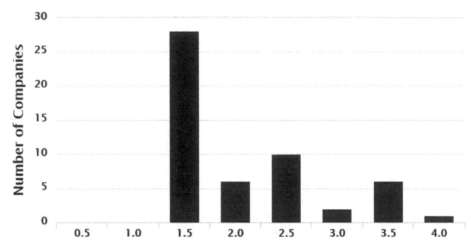

Source: Corporate Sustainability Scorecard

Figure 22.1: Scorecard Data from Sixty Companies on KSI 12.4: Materials Source: Human-Made (e.g., metals, plastics, etc.)

When we look at Figure 22.1, it seems that the circular economy may be a pipe dream. Clearly, companies today are a long way from the Stage 3 descriptor (reduce/recycle 25–75 percent; using materials with 50–75 percent recycled content; and actively phasing out toxics globally).

i Peter Lacy and Jakob Rutqvist, *Waste to Wealth*, Palgrave MacMillan, 2015

ii http://www.kering.com/en/sustainability/targets

iii http://www.levistrauss.com/wp-content/uploads/2018/02/Project-FLX-Press-Release_Sustainability.pdf

iv https://news.nike.com/news/nike-roadmap-toward-zero-discharge-of-hazardous-chemicals

v https://sustainability.nike.com/

vi https://www.allianz.com/en/press/news/financials/stakes_investments/141110_investment-in-renewable-energy-exceeds-two-billion.html/

vii https://www.greenbiz.com/blog/2014/07/11/GM-HP-Walmart-others-demand-simpler-buying- renewables?mkt_tok=3RkMMJWWfF9wsRojuq%2FKZKXonjHpfsX56%2BwsXaK1lMI%2F0ER3fOvrPUfG jI4FSsJjI%2BSLDwEYGJlv6SgFSLHEMa5qw7gMXRQ%3D

viii http://www.curtispackaging.com/environmental-stewardship/renewable-electricity/

ix http://www.fedex.com/bt/about/sustainability/environment.html

x https://environment.google/

xi https://www.greenbiz.com/blog/2014/07/01/ikea-microsoft-google-invest-in-wind-energy

xii https://company.ingersollrand.com/strengths/sustainability/our-climate-commitment.html

xiii https://www.prnewswire.com/news-releases/kohler-co-announces-wind-power-investment-300608992.html

xiv https://www.microsoft.com/en-us/environment/carbon

xv ttps://www.stockland.com.au/about-stockland/sustainability

xvi http://www.vale.com/EN/aboutvale/sustainability/Pages/default.aspx#agua

xvii https://www.diy.com/one-planet-home/forest-friendly

xviii https://www.2degreesnetwork.com/groups/2degrees-community/resources/general-mills-commits-sustainable-sourcing-half-its-raw-materials-by-2020/

xix http://news.mcdonalds.com/Corporate/manual-releases/By-2025-all-of-McDonald-s-Packaging-to-Come-from-R

xx https://ir.mondelezinternational.com/news-releases/news-release-details/mondelez-international-expands-its-sustainable-wheat-program

xxi http://investors.novelis.com/2017-10-03-Novelis-Reaches-Key-Sustainability-Goals-Ahead-of-Target

xxii https://news.dunkindonuts.com/news/dunkin-donuts-to-eliminate-foam-cups-worldwide-in-2020

xxiii https://www.businesswire.com/news/home/20180118005342/en/evian%C2%AE-Transforms-Approach-Plastic-100-Circular-Brand

xxiv https://www.biogen.com/content/dam/corporate/en_us/pdfs/.../BiogenCCR2015.pdf

xxv https://www.coca-colacompany.com/water-stewardship-replenish-report

xxvi http://investor.kimberly-clark.com/news-releases/news-release-details/kimberly-clark-corporation-concludes-5-year-sustainability

xxvii https://www.bloomberg.com/careers/blog/offices-leading-leed/

xxviii https://www.greenbiz.com/blog/2013/10/30/unilever-sweetens-ice-cream-factory-leed

xxix

xxx https://www.kingfisher.com/sustainability/index.asp?pageid=251

xxxi https://theblog.adobe.com/leading-the-way-to-a-low-carbon-sustainable-future/

xxxii https://www.environmentalleader.com/2013/09/boise-switches-to-rail-cuts-co2-emissions-60/

xxxiii https://www.edie.net/news/5/BT-reveals-strong-desire-to-be-Net-Positive-frontrunner-/

xxxiv https://news.o2.co.uk/?press-release=o2-sets-out-think-big-blueprint-its-plan-for-people-and-the-planet

xxxv https://www.environmentalleader.com/2013/10/standards-compliance-briefing-samsungs-iso-50001-csxs-leed-whitewave/

xxxvi https://www.xerox.com/corporate-citizenship/2016/sustainability/environmental-impact.html

xxxvii https://www.3m.com/3M/en_US/sustainability-us/

xxxviii https://ir.chipotle.com/news-releases/news-release-details/chipotle-sets-new-goal-drive-environmental-sustainability

xxxix https://investor.ecolab.com/news-and-events/press-releases/2016/06-20-2016-140537133

xl http://www.csrwire.com/press_releases/40966-HP-Inc-Named-First-Technology-Company-in-California-to-Achieve-TRUE-Zero-Waste-Certification

xli https://www.nestle.com/asset-library/documents/library/documents/corporate_social_responsibility/nestle-csv-full-report-2017-en.pdf

xlii https://www.scientificamerican.com/custom-media/scjohnson-transparent-by-design/zerowastefactory/

xliii https://www.coca-colacompany.com/stories/treating-and-recycling-wastewater

xliv https://www.greenbiz.com/blog/2014/08/04/10-companies-innovating-water-making-waves-water-innovation

xlv http://investors.nrg.com/phoenix.zhtml?c=121544&p=irol-newsArticle&ID=2345060

Chapter 23
Environmental Impacts—Supply Chain

The second Scorecard element in the Environmental Stewardship section addresses environmental impacts across the full supply chain, with a particular focus on suppliers. This complements the previous chapter focused on a company's own operations and the next chapter focused on its products.

Dell is a leader in supply chain sustainability. While this chapter focuses specifically on environmental stewardship aspects, Dell's commitment, programs, and performance apply equally on the social side.

Dell's philosophy is simple: "We operate in a world with many different cultures, countries and levels of economic development. Even in this diverse world, we believe there are some standards that are universal —including respect for workers, communities and the environment—and meeting these standards is a condition of doing business with Dell."[1]

Dell requires suppliers not just to comply with all applicable laws and regulations. The company also imposes requirements on itself and its suppliers, each supported by formal policies in the following areas:
- Responsible sourcing—up the supply chain
- Supplier diversity and nondiscrimination
- Sustainability reporting and transparency
- Continuous improvement
- Supplier engagement, capability building, and assessment
- Quarterly business reviews

As companies consider their environmental impacts across the supply chain, the overarching strategic question that senior executives and board members should be asking is:

Key Question: How deeply and robustly are we managing and reducing the environmental risks associated with the company's full supply chain impacts?

To help answer this key question, the Scorecard analyzes how companies manage and perform in three areas:
- Posture and management processes
- Addressing the most material supply chain environmental impacts
- The nature and extent of supply chain partnerships

Within each of these areas, executives evaluate their company performance on several key sustainability indicators (KSIs).

DOI 10.1515/9781547400423-023

Posture and Management Processes

So long as your suppliers comply with the law and stay out of the headlines (for negative reasons), do you care how they manage their environmental impacts? Increasingly, the answer is yes.

The Scorecard addresses the overall posture and management approach to supplier environmental impacts with four KSIs. It starts with the overall posture—and then looks at standards of performance, measuring, and verifying that performance.

KSI 13.1: Posture Regarding Supplier Environmental Footprint. Before the turn of the century, many companies focused predominantly on environmental impacts within their fence line—in their own operations. They did not bother so much with what their suppliers did—that was their problem.

Among the early drivers of supplier environmental oversight came from the chemical sector. In 1999, Mattel, at the time the world's largest toy maker, announced an initiative aimed at making its plastic toys out of environmentally friendly, organically based materials derived from edible oils and plant starches. The announcement was hailed as "revolutionary" by Greenpeace, the international environmental group that had campaigned against the use of toys made with phthalates—substances added to plastics to increase flexibility, durability, and longevity.

KSI	Stage 1	Stage 2	Stage 3	Stage 4
Posture Regarding Supplier Environmental Footprint	Manage for compliance; goal is low cost	Manage risks; goal is to improve productivity	Responsible sourcing; partner to cut footprint; goal is industry leader	Collaborate around growth opportunities

In 2005, **Walmart** was the 200-pound gorilla of the consumer products sector. When Walmart asked questions, suppliers responded immediately. Thus, it is no surprise the Walmart's 2005 launch into sustainability caught the world's attention.

Walmart CEO Lee Scott announced goals in 2005: to be supplied 100 percent by renewable energy, to create zero waste, and to sell products that sustain resources and the environment. Eleven years later, current CEO Doug McMillon reported progress on those goals and provided a roadmap for the next several years.[ii]

Walmart (as of July 2009) rates suppliers on environmental impact of their products.[iii]

KSI 13.2: Standards for Supplier Environmental Footprint. A growing number of companies impose requirements on their suppliers related to environmental issues and impacts. The range of approaches is depicted below.

KSI	Stage 1	Stage 2	Stage 3	Stage 4
Standards for Supplier Environmental Footprint	Adopt industry standards; traditional; business/ compliance requirements; supplier risk analysis	Formal "S" procurement policy; lead industry efforts to standardize	Basic "S" requirements: all suppliers; drive improved supplier "S" performance	Lead cross-industry standards; best-in-class across industry; "S" requirements non-negotiable

Several leading company examples follow:
- **Sainsbury:** The UK company developed the first dairy industry carbon footprint measurement system in 2008 to help farmers reduce energy costs and the full life cycle carbon impacts.[iv]
- **Nike:** The apparel company unveiled its (then) new Manufacturing Index (MI) in 2012, a factory rating system designed to help the company evaluate its manufacturing partners.[v]
- **Philips:** The Dutch multinational technology company requires all suppliers to conform to the Supplier Sustainability Declaration, in a bid to help the company's suppliers improve their social and environmental performance.[vi]

In each of these examples the company set some stringent demands on their suppliers—driving improved environmental performance across the value chain. While some larger suppliers may have a competitive edge given their size and scale to meet additional requirements, smaller more nimble start-up companies can also have an edge because they are not burdened by that same size and scale.

KSI 13.3: Measuring Supplier Environmental Footprint. It is one thing to add some wording to a purchasing contract specifying certain things a supplier must do vis-à-vis environmental performance. It is quite another to measure that performance. The range of ways companies approach this follows.

KSI	Stage 1	Stage 2	Stage 3	Stage 4
Measuring Supplier Environmental Footprint	Rely primarily on supplier reports	Require "S" KPIs of their major (suppliers; train buyers on "S"	Publicize supplier names and "S" KPIs (all suppliers)	Fully transparent regarding supplier "S" risks and performance

Two examples of strong measurement of supplier environmental performance are:
- **CH2M Hill:** The engineering company has a supply chain sustainability strategy for evaluating and selecting products. The company expects its suppliers to

endorse CH2M's commitment to corporate social responsibility, including fair labor and operating practices, environmental protection, diversity, and supplier development.[vii]

- **Walmart:** Tracks environmental impacts from the source.[viii]

KSI 13.4: Verifying Supplier Environmental Footprint. Some companies go a step further than setting standards and measuring performance. They also find some way to assure or verify the results. The range of practices is depicted below:

KSI	Stage 1	Stage 2	Stage 3	Stage 4
Verifying Supplier Environmental Footprint	Conventional contract requirements including self-audits	Basic "S" contract requirements	Third-party audits—Tier 1+; "S" included in buyer performance	Partnership reviews with most suppliers; build supplier "S" capacity

The Sustainable Supply Chain Initiative, launched in 2018, provides buyers and suppliers with guidance on which third-party auditing and certification schemes are available to address key environmental, social, and governance (ESG) requirements. The goal is to apply robust verification practices.[ix] This is an industry-wide initiative; some examples of individual company initiatives follow:

- **Adidas:** The athletic apparel company conducted 1,346 supplier audits in 2013, resulting in sixty-six warning letters and nine terminations.[x]
- **Anvil Knitwear:** The company launched Track My Tee, which allows people to see the path their shirt took from farm to store, along with advice on how to lower each shirt's life cycle emissions.[xi]
- **Sun Hung Kai Properties:** The Chinese company has suppliers verify sustainably sourced materials.[xii]
- The **Electronic Industry Citizenship Coalition** developed a social and environmental audit process to both certify auditors and drive consistency in the auditing process.[xiii]

In each of these examples, the company adopted an approach to provide added assurance that the suppliers are following the rules imposed by the customer. However, a downside of these verification schemes is that they can place an undue burden on small companies and essentially "force the little guys out."

Addressing the Most Material Supply Chain Environmental Impacts

In the section above, we reviewed how companies manage their key suppliers and others in their supply chain: the posture, setting standards, measuring, and verifying results. In this section we focus on the most material supply chain environmental impacts.

The key here is the word "material." In Chapter 7 (Environmental Stewardship: The "E" in ESG), we referenced the German Environment Ministry study that identifies the three most material sustainability issues (environmental or social) for more than sixty industry sectors. For companies that have not yet conducted a formal materiality assessment (also discussed in Chapter 7), a good place to start is to review the materiality assessment of your competitors and to review this German study.

The Scorecard addresses these material environmental impacts in the supply chain with five KSIs: one dealing with biodiversity, upstream and downstream greenhouse gas (GHG) emissions (Scope 3), materials, toxics, and water.

KSI 13.5: Supplier Impacts: Biodiversity. Does the mahogany wood used in your conference room come from cutting old growth trees in the Amazon rainforest? Does the fish you serve in your cafeteria come from depleted or heavily stressed fisheries? Increasingly, these are the kinds of questions companies are being asked—from employees, from community groups or other nongovernmental organizations (NGOs), from customers or even from investors. The range of approaches companies take to answering the questions follow:

KSI	Stage 1	Stage 2	Stage 3	Stage 4
Supplier Impacts: Biodiversity	Avoid problems; assess key impacts	Assess and systematically reduce impacts	Invest in biodiversity	100% "S" sourcing; independently verified

A few examples of companies taking a leading position on supply chain biodiversity follow.

- **Compass Group:** The world's leading caterer based in the UK implements a "Fish to Avoid" list that supports the Marine Conservation Society's guidance on endangered species to avoid.[xiv]
- **General Mills:** The global food company reported in May 2018 that it had sustainably sourced 76 percent of its ten priority ingredients during 2017.[xv]
- **Hershey:** The privately-held chocolate company sourced 100 percent certified palm oil ahead of its 2015 commitment.[xvi]
- **Natura Cosmeticos:** The Brazilian company is a founding member of the Union for Bioethical Trade.[xvii]

KSI 13.6: Upstream and Downstream GHG Emissions (Scope 3). Scope 3 GHG emissions are from sources not owned or directly controlled by the company but are related to the company activities. They include employee travel and commuting, contracted waste disposal. It also can result from transportation and distribution loses associated with purchased electricity. The range of approaches companies take to managing Scope 3 GHG emissions is depicted below.

KSI	Stage 1	Stage 2	Stage 3	Stage 4
Upstream and Downstream GHG Emissions (Scope 3)	Do not place a significant focus on Scope 3 GHG emissions	Basic efforts to quantify and reduce Scope 3 emissions	Strong goals and metrics in place to cut Scope 3 GHG emissions	Active collaboration with suppliers and others to cut Scope 3 GHG emissions

- **Apple:** The company secured a pledge from component supplier **Ibiden** to use 100 percent renewable energy, a new milestone for both Apple and Japan.[xviii]
- **Boeing** and **South African Airways** signed a Memorandum of Understanding promoting sustainable aviation, partnering to launch the development of aviation biofuel supply chain in Southern Africa.[xix]
- **HP:** Prior to its split into two companies, HP announced a (then) new requirement in 2013 for first-tier suppliers to cut GHG emissions intensity 20 percent (2010 to 2020). This was a first for the information technology industry.[xx]
- **Nestlé** (Switzerland), **Sainsbury's** (UK), and the **Co-operative Group** began a partnership in 2013 to decrease the supply chain footprint of products with the most GHG emissions, product waste, water, energy, and resource use.[xxi]

These examples illustrate how some leading companies in different industry sectors are driving down carbon emissions across their value chain.

KSI 13.7: Supplier Impacts: Materials. Mentioned above was whether you knew the source of the mahogany in your conference room or the fish served in your cafeteria. What do you know about the origin of all other materials sourced, especially the non-bio-based materials?

KSI	Stage 1	Stage 2	Stage 3	Stage 4
Supplier Impacts: Materials	Understand source of all major materials; purchase recycled materials	Actively manage "S" sourcing; "de-select" hazardous materials; Tier 1 supplier focus	Sustainably source most major materials; limited engagement beyond Tier 1 suppliers	**Closed-loop** focus; source 100% "S" materials; active tracing and engagement with upstream suppliers all the way to resource extraction

A few examples:

- **Dell:** The information technology (IT) company announced two IT industry firsts in 2014: launching a carbon-negative packaging and using UL-Environment certified closed-loop recycled plastics in manufacturing its computers.[xxii]
- **IKEA:** The well-known household products company announced in 2018 that it had acquired 25,000 acres of forestland in Alabama to support the sustainable production of resources used by the company.[xxiii]
- **Nike:** The company announced in its FY16/17 Sustainable Business Report that the company had sourced the most recycled polyester in its industry for the fourth year in a row. Nike equated this to diverting nearly five billion plastic water bottles from landfill between 2012 and 2018.[xxiv]
- **Staples:** The Boston-based office supply company deployed use of On-Demand Packaging in 2014, allowing the company to create a customer package for every single less-than-full order it ships. The more efficiently sized packaging reduced 25,000 metric tons of CO_2.[xxv]

KSI 13.8: Supplier Impacts: Toxics. In the last chapter, we mentioned the significant impact of the European REACH regulation, addressing the production and use of chemical substances. The issue for companies is not only which chemical substances you use in your own operations, but also about the impacts of those substances throughout the supply chain. The range of approaches follows.

KSI	Stage 1	Stage 2	Stage 3	Stage 4
Supplier Impacts: Toxics	Compliance with REACH, etc.	Tier 1 supplier list of requirements; systematically avoid key toxics	Green chemistry leader; working aggressively toward goal of eliminating toxics	Approaching goal of eliminating toxics

- **Adidas, Nike, Levi Strauss, Puma, C&A, Esprit, G-Star Raw, H&M, Inditex, Jack Wolfskin, Li Ning, & New Balance,** members of the Zero Discharge of Hazardous Chemicals Group agreed to publish a list of chemical substances targeted for phase out by 2015—part of a plan to eliminate hazardous chemicals from their supply chains by 2020.[xxvi]
- **H&M:** The UK company teamed up with eleven other companies in 2018 in an effort dubbed Project Effective. The collaboration aimed to produce more sustainable fibers and plastics for commercial use—and to increase adoption of sustainable materials—by using renewable feedstocks and bio based technologies. One of the key objectives of Project Effective is to develop a more sustainable nylon.[xxvii]
- **SC Johnson:** In its twenty-sixth annual sustainability report published in 2018 for FY17, the company included a close look inside the criteria it uses for its Greenlist material selection program. Greenlist, formalized in 2001, is SC Johnson's peer-reviewed, science-based program that evaluates the effects on human health and the environment for every ingredient the company uses.[xxviii]

KSI 13.9: Supplier Impacts: Water. If water is a vital ingredient in your product (as the beverage industry knows)—or if water is the lifeblood of your operation (agriculture), your business strategy incorporates water. For many other industry sectors, water is an expense item—either a stand-alone expense or folded into building rental costs. The range of approaches to managing water resources varies widely, as illustrated below.

KSI	Stage 1	Stage 2	Stage 3	Stage 4
Supplier Impacts: Water	Compliance focus with Tier 1 suppliers	Slash supplier water use	Industry leader (e.g., "irrigate the crop; not the land")	Water-neutral

- **Keurig Green Mountain:** Recognizing that water is a critical resource of strategic importance to its business, stakeholders, and the communities in which it operates, Keurig developed a comprehensive Water Policy that addresses access and protects resources.[xxix]
- **Sainsbury:** The UK company's approach to its supply chain focuses on areas of water vulnerability.[xxx]

Nature and Extent of Supplier Sustainability Partnerships

Are the suppliers of products and services your company purchases viewed as strategic partners or simply as the successful (typically low cost; high or acceptable quality) provider? The answer is likely some of each.

The Scorecard addresses the nature and extent of supplier sustainability partnerships with two KSIs: one dealing with the extent to which companies engage with suppliers on sustainability and a second that looks at setting goals with—and for—your suppliers and others in your supply chain.

KSI 13.10: Engaging with Suppliers on Sustainability. Companies are facing growing pressure to reduce their environmental impacts. This pressure often results in passing along the To Do list to others in your supply chain, as depicted below.

KSI	Stage 1	Stage 2	Stage 3	Stage 4
Engaging with Suppliers on Sustainability	Respond as needed	Stay in the pack; engage proactively with key Tier 1 suppliers	Partner with key suppliers to engage upstream supply tiers; collaborate with peer companies to align expectations	Partner with most suppliers throughout the supply chain; collaborate with industry groups to enforce common supplier standards

A Global Supply Chain Report in 2018, authored by DCP and McKinsey) identified a group of fifty-eight leading companies (out of more than 3,300 analyzed) that led the way on supplier engagement. These fifty-eight companies were recognized on CSP's Supplier Engagement Leaderboard for their work with suppliers to reduce emissions and lower environmental risks in the supply chain.[xxxi] Some additional leading examples are:

- **Coca-Cola:** The company hosted a Supplier Sustainability Summit in 2009 to participate with senior management in a discussion about the need for business to embed sustainability as a critical element of its growth plans. The company held an earlier summit two years earlier; however, 2009 was the first time the sole focus was on how we can work together to improve our businesses, promote innovation and create a climate for mutual success by focusing on a shared vision of sustainability.[xxxii]

- **HP:** Over several decades, the company has built a robust set of supplier and peer education programs over the past decade. These are supported by formal company policies on wages and benefits, supplier code of conduct, responsible minerals and supplier environmental performance.[xxxiii]

*KSI 13.11: **Setting Sustainability Goals with Suppliers.*** It is challenging enough to set sustainability goals for our own company; why bother setting goals with suppliers? The answer is that it only makes sense when there is a sound business reason, typically to jointly reduce or manage risk or to partner on a business growth opportunity. The range of practices follows.

KSI	Stage 1	Stage 2	Stage 3	Stage 4
Setting Sustainability Goals with Suppliers	Comply with industry standards	Pockets of collaboration in joint goal-setting	Joint customer-supplier goals: risk focus	Joint customer-supplier goals: opportunity focus

Below are a few companies leading the way.

- **Baxter:** As one of the early leaders, the healthcare company set 2015 supply chain goals for sustainable purchasing and fleet emissions.[xxxiv]
- **HP:** The company set its industry's first supply chain goal in 2013—a 20 percent decrease in first-tier manufacturing and product transportation-related GHG emissions by 2020, compared with 2010.[xxxv]

How Do Companies Stack Up?

Starting in 2018, we are capturing data from a group of founding participants—invited to use the Scorecard for a company self-assessment and to provide feedback. As we assess the data from the first 60 companies (all Fortune 500 or equivalent), three key messages stand out:

- Companies are doing a fairly impressive job engaging with suppliers (KSI 13.10). Just over three in four rated their company at Stage 2.5 or higher, indicating strong outreach and engagement.
- Interestingly, companies' overall posture with respect to suppliers is evenly split—with roughly one third each rated Stage 1.5 to Stage 2; Stage 2.5 to Stage 3; and Stage 3.5 to Stage 4. Those are strong marks; however, focus is clearly on risk management. Only one in four are moving toward true responsible sourcing and beginning to collaborate around growth opportunities.
- When it comes to setting sustainability goals with suppliers (KSI 13.11), companies rate themselves quite far behind. Only eleven rated their company Stage 3 or higher (18 percent) with another sixteen rating their company Stage 2.5. Nearly half rated their company Stage 1.5 (see Figure 23.1).

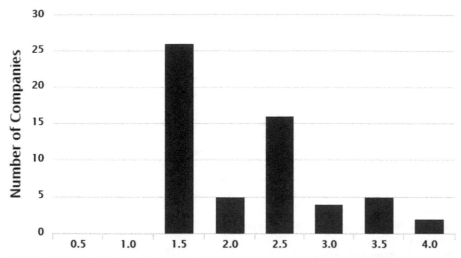

Source: Corporate Sustainability Scorecard

Figure 23.1: Scorecard Data from Sixty Companies on KSI 13.11: Setting Sustainability Goals with Suppliers

The move toward full life-cycle responsibility for the environmental impacts associated with your company's operations and products has grown in recent years. With continued advances in technology, coupled with demands for transparency, this trend will likely accelerate in the coming years.

i http://www.dell.com/learn/us/en/uscorp1/cr-social-responsibility?s=corp
ii https://news.walmart.com/2016/11/04/walmart-offers-new-vision-for-the-companys-role-in-society
iii https://www.scientificamerican.com/article/walmart-environmental-impacts-labels/
iv https://www.theguardian.com/sustainable-business/sustainability-case-studies-sainsburys-farmers-support-groups
v https://news.thomasnet.com/imt/2012/05/14/nikes-sustainability-strategy-reshapes-a-global-manufacturing-network
vi https://www.philips.com/a-w/about/company/suppliers/supplier-sustainability.html
vii https://www.ch2m.com/who-we-are/what-guides-us/sccr/supply-chain-management
viii https://www.greenbiz.com/blog/2012/04/19/why-walmarts-better-supplier-scorecard-big-deal
ix https://www.theconsumergoodsforum.com/press_releases/the-consumer-goods-forum-announces-new-benchmarking-and-recognition-initiative-for-sustainability-standards/
x http://www.sustainablebrands.com/news_and_views/supply_chain/mike_hower/adidas_supplier_audit_coverage_reached_75_2013
xi https://www.greenbiz.com/news/2010/08/05/bringing-organic-tees-masses
xii https://www.shkp.com/Html/CSR/SHKP_SR_2017_EN.pdf

xiii www.eiccoalition.org/media/docs/EICC_Strategic_Vision_Summary_2015.pdf

xiv https://www.compass-group.co.uk/responsibility/sourcing/responsibly-sourced-fish/

xv https://www.generalmills.com/en/News/NewsReleases/Library/2018/April/GRR-2018-4-19

xvi https://www.environmentalleader.com/2013/12/hershey-supply-chain-100-traceable-sustainable-palm-oil-by-2014/

xvii https://www.greenbiz.com/blog/2014/02/04/natura-cosmetics-sustainability-amazon

xviii https://www.apple.com/newsroom/2017/03/apple-takes-supplier-clean-energy-program-to-japan.html

xix https://www.marketwatch.com/story/boeing-south-african-airways-launch-sustainable-aviation-biofuel-effort-in-southern-africa-2013-10-10

xx http://www8.hp.com/us/en/hp-news/press-release.html?id=1489007#.WxLVPu4vx1t

xxi http://www.sustainablebrands.com/news_and_views/co-op-nestle-sainsburys-reduce-supply-chain-footprint

xxii https://www.environmentalleader.com/2014/05/dell-builds-pc-from-recycled-plastic-electronics/

xxiii https://www.ikea.com/us/en/about_ikea/newsitem/020118-IKEA-Group-aquires-forest-in_alabama

xxiv https://sustainability.nike.com/

xxv https://www.greenerpackage.com/source_reduction/staples_deploys_-demand_custom_case_making

xxvi https://www.environmentalleader.com/tag/new-balance/

xxvii https://www.environmentalleader.com/2018/05/partnership-hopes-to-develop-and-drive-adoption-of-more-sustainable-nylon/

xxviii https://www.environmentalleader.com/2018/04/sc-johnson-transparency/

xxix http://www.keuriggreenmountain.com/en/Sustainability/ReportsAndDisclosures/WaterPolicy.aspx

xxx https://www.about.sainsburys.co.uk/making-a-difference/our-values

xxxi https://www.cdp.net/en/research/global-reports/global-supply-chain-report-2018

xxxii http://supply-chain.unglobalcompact.org/site/article/70

xxxiii http://www8.hp.com/us/en/hp-information/global-citizenship/society/supplychain.html

xxxiv https://www.baxter.com/our-story/corporate-responsibility

xxxv http://www8.hp.com/us/en/hp-information/global-citizenship/society/supplychain.html

Chapter 24
Environmental Impacts—Products

The third and final element in the environmental section of the Scorecard addresses products, specifically the environmental impacts of products throughout their life cycle.

PPG, the Pittsburg-based global coatings company, commissioned a customer survey in 2012. In the survey, PPG asked architects about the trend toward building-integrated clean energy sources—materials with green benefits that replace conventional building and construction materials. The result of the survey was that this trend toward green products was expected to grow.

PPG's focus on reducing environmental impact includes helping customers improve their environmental performance. The company has long been committed to developing sustainable technologies, such as waterborne liquid coatings, chromate-free powder coatings, and low-VOC formulations. PPG's goal is to achieve 40 percent of yearly sales from sustainable-advantaged products by 2025.

The overarching strategic question that senior executives and board members should be asking with respect to the environmental impacts of their products is:

Key Question: How deeply and robustly are we managing and reducing the environmental risks associated with our products, services, and other offerings?

To help answer this key question, the Scorecard analyzes how companies manage and perform in three areas:
- Overall approach to product stewardship, defined below
- Product design process—specifically evaluating key product attributes
- End-of-life product management, referring to what happens to the product after customer use

Within each of these areas, executives evaluate their company performance on several key sustainability indicators (KSIs).

Overall Product Stewardship Approach

Product stewardship is defined as an environmental management strategy that means whoever designs, produces, sells, or uses a product takes responsibility for minimizing the product's environmental impact throughout all stages of the products' life cycle, including end-of-life management.

The overall approach to product stewardship is very industry-specific. The chemical industry, responding to extensive external concern and pressure in the 1980s,

DOI 10.1515/9781547400423-024

launched an industry-wide product stewardship initiative as part of the Responsible Care program. At the other extreme, the utility sector—which essentially sells electrons that consumers can not see, touch or feel, evolved over the ensuing decades without being under the spotlight. That has increasingly changed because of the carbon impact of its electric power generation.

The Scorecard addresses a company's overall product stewardship approach with three KSIs: one dealing with overall philosophy and strategy; a second that looks at product risk and life cycle assessment (LCA) and the third evaluating the use of industry codes, standards certifications, and ecolabels.

KSI 14.1: Product Stewardship Philosophy and Strategy. Regardless of the industry sector, companies today (large and small, private and public) are coming under increasing pressure to transparently communicate the full life-cycle environmental (and social) impacts of their products, services and solutions.

KSI	Stage 1	Stage 2	Stage 3	Stage 4
Product Stewardship Philosophy	Risk and compliance focused; understand full life-cycle environmental risks	Implement basic Implement basic **design for environment (DfE)** criteria; pilot "S" products	Publicly accept full life cycle responsibility and accountability; C-suite-led greening of product portfolio, partnering with customers	Green or healthy products growing, recognized, and performing well

Two examples of an advanced product stewardship philosophy are:
– **Coca-Cola:** The company announced a goal in 2018 to collect and recycle a bottle or can for each one that it sells globally by 2030.[i]
– **Desso:** The Dutch carpet company adopted a "cradle to cradle" approach in 2007.[ii]

KSI 14.2: Product Risk/LCA. Product **life cycle assessments**, commonly referred to as LCAs, have been around since the 1980s or earlier. In the early years (decades), LCAs tended to be extremely detailed, involved, quantitative analyses, costing significant amounts of money to conduct. In later years, more streamlined versions of LCAs became available. As we look across companies today, the range of approaches companies take to analyzing their product risk via LCAs or other means is depicted below.

KSI	Stage 1	Stage 2	Stage 3	Stage 4
Product Risk/ Life Cycle Assessment	Selectively use LCA software for high-risk products with high business impact	Streamlined LCA for key product lines/families to identify key risks	Full LCA on key (> 25% of) products; LCA is core to new "S" product efforts	**Cradle to cradle** scorecard or equivalent on most/ all products, services, and solutions (PSS)

- **Deere:** The company's 2018 eco-efficiency goals include product LCAs.[iii]
- **Kimberly-Clark:** The company performed an LCA on alternative fibers to reduce the demand on forests.[iv]
- **SC Johnson:** The company's Greenlist™ process, discussed in the last chapter, involves a product risk rating scheme. Each material is rated on a scale of zero to three.[v]

KSI 14.3: Use of Industry Codes, Standards, Certifications, Ecolabels. Ecolabelling is a voluntary method of environmental performance certification and labelling that is practiced around the world. An ecolabel identifies products or services proven to be environmentally preferable overall, within a specific product or service category.

Ecolabels are contrasted with "green" symbols or claim statements that are developed by companies (manufacturers or service providers). The most credible labels are awarded by an impartial third party.

The range of ways companies use industry codes, standards, certifications, and ecolabels is as follows.

KSI	Stage 1	Stage 2	Stage 3	Stage 4
Use of Industry Codes, Standards, Certifications, Ecolabels	Comply	Actively promote	Lead or co-lead product sustainability initiatives within industry sector	Model across all industry sectors

Listed below are some examples of companies that have established their own certification programs, in addition to the many companies that utilize external schemes.

- **Croda:** The UK ingredient supplier is committed to reducing its contribution to deforestation and any resultant impacts on climate change and biodiversity. The company committed to having 100 percent sustainable palm oil certification of all supply chains by 2015.[vi]
- **Kroger:** The company's Sustainable Seafood Policy furnishes procurement standards.[vii]

- **Nike:** The company spent seven years and $6 million developing the Environmental Apparel Design Tool, a Web-based portal that uses a scoring system to rate a product's environmental impact.[viii]
- **Walmart:** The company announced in 2009 that it would launch a Sustainability Index. The company also created a Sustainability Consortium, a group of academics and others with the ambitious agenda of establishing the scientific standards to measure the sustainability of consumer products.[ix]

These examples illustrate the different approaches companies have taken to obtain validation of claims regarding product environmental attributes.

Product Design Process

The first part of this chapter looked at a company's overall product stewardship approach. We now look at the specific environmental issues involved in the product design process.

Think about any product and start asking questions about it—What's in it? Can you trace the stuff back to its source? What's the carbon impact before it gets to my company gate? What happens to it after my customers dispose of it?

The Scorecard addresses environmental impacts associated with products in the product design process with seven KSIs, dealing with traceability, energy efficiency, materials use, durability, biodegradability, recyclability, water-use efficiency.

KSI 14.4: Product Traceability. Do you know where your product came from? 3M now traces the paper that goes into Post-It Notes and other 3M products down to the individual forest where the trees were harvested.

Blockchain technology may prove to be a breakthrough when it comes to tracing products across the supply chain. Blockchain, the same technology that underlies bitcoin, collects and stores information, and can be especially useful in tough-to track industry sectors such as luxury goods (furs and diamonds). The technology makes it more difficult to conceal corruption.

The range of practices regarding product traceability today is depicted below.

KSI	Stage 1	Stage 2	Stage 3	Stage 4
Product Traceability	Not a major focus	Key materials are from traceable sources	All material inputs are from traceable sources	Fully traceable (e.g., "from farm to fork")

Examples of some leading practices in tracing a product's materials and labor to its source are listed below.

- **3M:** The company now traces the sourcing of its paper purchased for use in Post-it Notes and other products to ensure they come from sources that protect forests and respect the rights of workers and people who live in or may depend on forests for their livelihood. 3M now only accepts virgin fiber that can be traced to the forest source, proven that it is obtained legally.[x]
- **Campbell Soup:** The company announced in 2016 its support for mandatory genetically modified organisms (GMO) labelling to establish a single labelling standard for foods derived from GMOs.[xi]
- **Hershey:** The company committed in 2013 to source 100 percent certified palm oil. The company achieved 100 percent traceable and sustainably sourced palm oil by the end of 2014.[xii]
- **IBM:** The company is experimenting with blockchain technology to transform visibility and traceability in complex, often opaque supply chains. IBM partnered with Walmart in 2017 to address food safety in the global supply chain.
- **Patagonia:** The company uses 100 percent traceable down, a by-product of the food industry, through an audit process; certified to the Global Traceable Down Standard.[xiii]

KSI 14.5: Product Energy Efficiency. When GE then-CEO Jeff Immelt launched Eco-magination in 2005, product energy efficiency was at the core of the idea and the major initiative. Immelt's premise was very simple: if GE provides its customers with products that are the same or better quality (than a competitor's similar product) at the same or lower cost—and if the GE product also is more energy efficient (saving customers money throughout the life cycle), then GE will win more customers and grow sales.

KSI	Stage 1	Stage 2	Stage 3	Stage 4
Product Energy Efficiency	Not a major priority; focus is on low cost	Research and map customer energy efficiency goals	Increase product energy efficiency ~25–50%	All products designed for maximum energy efficiency

The information technology sector has had many early leaders—working hard on product energy efficiency.

- **HP:** Most of the company's environmental footprint occurs in its supply chain and when customers use its products. Together, these phases account for 94 percent of HP's carbon footprint. Thus, for decades, the company has designed products for energy efficiency, materials innovation, and recyclability.[xiv]
- **EMC:** Though the company has since been acquired by **Dell**, EMC was noted for driving energy efficient product design to save money for its customers, drive efficiency, and reduce the carbon footprint.[xv]

KSI 14.6: *Product Materials Use.* As discussed in Chapter 22, many companies have managed their chemical substances sourced (KSI 12.1) responding to the REACH regulation and related rules. Some companies have chosen to extend their product materials focus to their supply chain, as discussed in the last chapter (KSI 13.8). It also extends to the products and services your company produces. The range of practices is depicted below.

KSI	Stage 1	Stage 2	Stage 3	Stage 4
Product Materials Use	Compliance focus	Prioritized list of toxics	Systematic reduction of toxics	Zero toxics; maximize recycled content

- **Adidas:** The company (whose brands include Reebok and TaylorMade) committed in 2011 to the goal of zero discharge of hazardous chemicals from its supply chain via all pathways, with a 2020 deadline.[xvi]
- **Herman Miller:** The office and home furnishings company uses a "Design for the Environment" matrix when creating products.[xvii]

KSI 14.7: *Product Durability.* How long does your product last? Do you want it to last a long time—or the opposite ... do you want it to conveniently start to go downhill after a year or two so your customer purchases a new one?

This is one of the stickiest issues associated with sustainability—because it starkly contrasts the old economy model (take-make-waste) from the new economy one (where product durability is good).

In the early years following World War II, some products were built to last. Remember Maytag appliances (and the advertisements on television about the very lonely Maytag repair person? However, during the past 30–50 years, the phrase "built-in obsolescence" has described the norm for many industry sectors, especially those selling consumer products. We live in the throw-away society. Christmas lights might last one season. Cars go downhill after five to six years; people use Swiffers instead of brooms; iPhones get replaced every eighteen months. The list is endless. Contrast this with the "new economy" approach Xerox and others have pioneered—the bold and perhaps risky move of wanting your product to last as long as possible (and making your money by servicing that product).

The range of approaches companies take to product durability follow:

KSI	Stage 1	Stage 2	Stage 3	Stage 4
Product Durability	Cheapest; disposable	Confront the conflict: durable vs. disposable	Systematically reducing disposables and increasing durability	Model performer across industry sectors

Electrolux, the Swedish appliance company, has been working to simplify its products, increase the use of modular parts and components, and make their materials and components more serviceable and reusable. A few other examples of leaders in product durability include:

- **Autodesk:** The American multinational software company teaches sustainability workshops on improving product durability.[xviii]
- **DuPont:** The company's weathering systems are certified for product durability.[xix]

Again, this issue of product durability is very tricky. It strikes at the heart of what I call the *sustainability transformation.* Sooner or later, communities, regions, and even countries run out of space to throw things away. The transition to having products last longer and then be recycled or reused has been slow to arrive.

KSI 14.8: Product Biodegradability. Ray Anderson, founder and former CEO of Interface Carpets, launched his entire sustainability campaign because of a "spear through the heart" he learned about his business. A proud CEO of high quality carpets—that took a matter of hours or days to manufacture; had a typical useful life of a handful of years—and then took 20,000 years to decompose in a landfill. The opposite of biodegradable.

The range of practices in product biodegradability are depicted below.

KSI	Stage 1	Stage 2	Stage 3	Stage 4
Product Biodegradability	Not a major consideration	Explicit for few products	Explicit for most products	100% (as applicable)

Below are a few examples of companies creating biodegradable products or packaging.

- **Ecovative Design:** The company makes 100 percent compostable packing material created from mushrooms.[xx]
- **Danone:** The company partnered with Nestlé Waters to fund a start-up of 100 percent bio-based bottles.[xxi]
- **Reebok:** The global athletic footwear and apparel company announced in early 2017 its "Cotton + Corn" sustainable products initiative, including the planned

launch of its 100 percent compostable shoe, made with a cotton upper part and a sole made from a corn-based plastic substitute. (The intent is that the shoes will last roughly as long as conventional ones; however, they will be able to decompose after use far more quickly.)[xxii]

KSI 14.9: *Product Recyclability/Reusability.* Do your company's products end up in a landfill at the end of their useful life? Or can they be designed in a manner that they can be disassembled into component parts and reused or recycled after their normal customer use?

KSI	Stage 1	Stage 2	Stage 3	Stage 4
Product Recyclability and Reusability	Not typically considered	Explicit for few products	Explicit for most products	100% (as applicable)

- **Shaw Industries:** The U.S. carpet company collects carpets across the United States; 80 percent can be closed-loop recycled.[xxiii]
- **Nestlé Waters North America:** Continuing its sustainability efforts, the company has developed a water bottle made from 100 percent food grade recycled plastic.[xxiv]
- **Oreck:** The maker of commercial vacuums, air purifiers and cleaning solutions features product quality and durability.

KSI 14.10: *Product Water-Use Efficiency.* The importance of owning products that are especially water-efficient can vary dramatically depending on (1) freshwater availability in the region the product is being used; and (2) the cost of water in that locale. If water is plentiful and cheap (as it has been in many places the past hundred years, then why bother with water efficient products? If you live in Cape Town, South Africa in 2018, this is a big deal.

KSI	Stage 1	Stage 2	Stage 3	Stage 4
Product Water-Use Efficiency	Low cost; research and map customer goals	Increase product water use efficiency ~10–20%	Increase product water use efficiency ~25% plus	All products designed for minimum water use

The WaterSense Labeling system, launched by the U.S. Environmental Protection Agency, is designed to identify products that use the least amount of water—from irrigation systems to bathroom appliances. The system specifies water efficiency and performance and is backed by independent, third-party certification.[xxv]

End-of-Life Product Management

Why do you care what happens to your product after your customer takes owner-ship of it? Companies selling to Walmart had to address this following the company's strong supply chain push starting in 2005.

The Scorecard addresses how companies manage product environmental impacts at the end of the product's useful life. Two KSIs are used: one dealing with packaging; and a second that looks at end-of-life product responsibility.

KSI 14.11: Packaging. In the days of cheap landfill disposal, getting rid of some extra packaging material was just a cost of doing business. But increasingly customers are pushing back, asking why the supplier needs to use all that packaging; whether it can be recycled; and similar questions. As a result, the range of approaches companies are taking to product packaging are as follows:

KSI	Stage 1	Stage 2	Stage 3	Stage 4
Packaging	Renewable, recyclable or reusable packaging is not a major focus	~25–50% of packaging is renewable, recyclable, and/or reusable	~50–75% or packaging is renewable, recyclable, and/or reusable	100% of packaging is renewable or recyclable

- **Dell:** The technology company has been using recycled ocean plastics in packag-ing. This effort is borne out of the global challenge; addressing an estimated five trillion pieces of plastics in the oceans that never break down completely.[xxvi] Dell also launched carbon-negative packaging and is using UL-Environment certified closed-loop recycled plastics in the manufacturing of computers.[xxvii]
- **Hasbro:** The global play and entertainment company announced in early 2018 its plans to incorporate 30 percent plant-based material into its product packaging starting in 2019.[xxviii]
- **McDonalds:** The company will phase out the use of foam packaging globally by the end of 2018. The company reports that foam packaging represents 2 percent of its packaging globally.[xxix]
- **Nestlé:** The company announced in April 2018 that it plans to make 100 percent of its packaging recyclable or reusable by 2025.
- **Nike:** The athletic apparel company partnered with circular economy firm Miniwiz to create sustainable packaging.[xxx]
- **SC Johnson:** In a move to offer consumers a green choice, the company expanded its Mini line of concentrated cleaners that can be used in refillable bottles.[xxxi]

KSI 14.12: End-of-Life Product Responsibility. Increasingly, companies are finding that they own responsibility for the products they manufacture—from raw material extraction right through to what happens to the products (and waste) at the end of the useful life. The range of approaches companies take to end-of-life product management are depicted below.

KSI	Stage 1	Stage 2	Stage 3	Stage 4
End-of-life Product Responsibility	Compliance-focus; no added product recycling or reuse	Take back and manage ~25–50%; follow industry code of conduct (e.g., WEEE)	Take back and manage ~50–75%; leader in own industry	100% closed-loop; leader across all industries

Below are several examples of leading practices.

- **Best Buy, LG Electronics, Panasonic, Samsung, Sharp, Sprint** and **Staples, Dell, Sony, Nokia** joined U.S. EPA's Sustainable Materials Management Electronics Challenge in 2012, and committed to 100 percent certified refurbishing/recycling of used electronics they collect.[xxxii]
- **BMW Recyclers LLC:** The used auto parts dealer specializing in the reuse of original BMW parts and vehicles.[xxxiii]
- **Cisco:** The global technology company has a robust product takeback program to reduce the environmental impact of electronics.[xxxiv]
- **Garnier:** This second largest brand of the L'Oréal Group plans to divert 10 million beauty products from landfills in 2017. To make a positive impact on the planet, Garnier and DoSomething.org, the largest organization for young people and social change, have teamed up to launch *Rinse, Recycle, Repeat,* a national campaign and college campus competition to educate America's youth about the importance of recycling beauty product empties.[xxxv]
- **Kimberly-Clark:** The consumer products company concluded a five-year sustainability initiative in 2016. Among many accomplishments, the company had diverted 95.6 percent of manufacturing waste from landfills as of December 2015. The company's new 2022 goal is to extend the zero waste mindset to all solid wastes.[xxxvi]
- **Sprint:** The telecommunications company has been an industry leader in phone recycling; its buyback program lets you earn up to $300 when you trade in your device, regardless of what carrier it is from.[xxxvii]

How Do Companies Stack Up?

Starting in 2018, we are capturing data from a group of founding participants—invited to use the Scorecard for a company self-assessment and to provide feedback.

As we assess the data from the first 60 companies (all Fortune 500 or equivalent), the first thing to note is that for almost a sixty quarter of the companies, some or all of the product environmental issues were noted as not applicable. In our group of sixty companies, roughly fifteen were comprised of utilities (sell electrons), commercial and professional service firms (sell professional services) banks, or transport firms. Of the (three quarters or so) of companies that rated themselves on product issues, three key messages stand out:

– The overall product stewardship philosophy and strategy (KSI 14.1) is notably bimodal, with majority of companies rated 1.5 (33 percent) or 2.5 (41 percent). Only five companies (11 percent) rated their companies at Stage 3 or higher.
– On the KSI 14.2, Product Risk/LCA, the bell curve is skewed notably left, with the peak and most companies rated at Stage 1.5 (22 companies or 50%). The trailing edge of the curve higher than Stage 1 had only 19 companies split across five ratings between Stage 2 and Stage 4.
– Responsibility for products at the end of their useful life (KSI 14.12, End-of-Life Product Responsibility) also showed a bell curve shifted notably left, as depicted in Figure 24.1. One third rated their company at Stage 1.5 or lower, essentially a "compliance-plus" posture of adhering to industry codes of conduct plus taking responsibility for a portion of your company's products at the end of their useful life. Only seven companies (12 percent) rated themselves at Stage 3 or higher.

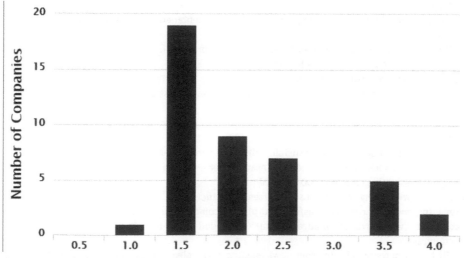

Source: Corporate Sustainability Scorecard

Figure 24.1: Scorecard Data from Sixty Companies on KSI 14.12: End-of-Life Product Responsibility

Information technology companies, as you might expect, are leading the way with product take-back and end-of-life product management. (These companies often have limited hardware and have very good information about their customer base.) We can expect other industry sectors to follow suit.

———

i https://www.coca-colacompany.com/worldwithoutwaste
ii https://www.theguardian.com/sustainable-business/cradle-to-cradle-desso-carpet-tiles-innovation
iii http://www.deere.com/en_US/docs/html/brochures/publication.html?id=956f8978#1
iv http://www.kimberly-clark.com/sustainability/planet/fibersourcing.aspx
v http://www.scjohnson.com/en/commitment/focus-on/greener-products/greenlist.aspx
vi https://www.croda.com/en-gb/sustainability/material-areas/product-stewardship/palm-oil
vii http://sustainability.kroger.com/2020-goals.html
viii https://www.bizjournals.com/portland/blog/sbo/2010/11/nike-releases-green-design-tool.html?page=all
ix https://www.greenbiz.com/blog/2009/08/17/inside-walmarts-sustainability-consortium
x https://www.3m.com/3M/en_US/sustainability-us/policies-reports/sustainable-forestry/
xi https://www.campbellsoupcompany.com/newsroom/news/2016/01/07/labeling/
xii https://www.thehersheycompany.com/en_us/news-center/blog/hersheys-palm-oil-sustainability-journey.html
xiii http://www.patagonia.com/traceable-down.html
xiv http://www8.hp.com/us/en/hp-information/environment/design-for-environment.html#.U88mORZiAnA
xv https://www.emc.com/corporate/sustainability/sustaining-ecosystems/products.htm
xvi https://www.environmentalleader.com/2014/06/adidas-kicks-up-pfc-free-pledge-partners-with-bluesign/
xvii https://www.hermanmiller.com/our-values/environmental-advocacy/design-for-the-environment/
xviii https://www.autodesk.com/search?sn=en_US&qt=product+durability&p=0
xix http://www2.dupont.com/Weathering_Systems/en_US/
xx https://www.ecovativedesign.com/
xxi https://www.nestle-watersna.com/en/nestle-water-news/pressreleases/nestle-waters-danone-bio-based-bottles
xxii https://www.usatoday.com/story/money/2017/04/23/earth-friendly-sneakers-new-reeboks-biogradable/100568292/
xxiii https://shawfloors.com/shaw-sustainability/post-consumer-carpet-recycling
xxiv https://www.nestle-watersna.com/en/nestle-water-news/pressreleases/nestl-pure-life-launches-new-bottle-made-from-100-recycled-plastic
xxv https://www.epa.gov/watersense/watersense-products
xxvi http://www.dell.com/learn/us/en/uscorp1/corp-comm/ocean-plastics
xxvii https://www.environmentalleader.com/2014/05/dell-builds-pc-from-recycled-plastic-electronics/
xxviii https://newsroom.hasbro.com/news-releases/news-release-details/hasbro-roll-out-plant-based-packaging

xxix http://www.businessinsider.com/mcdonalds-ditches-foam-cups-packaging-2018-1

xxx https://www.environmentalleader.com/2017/03/nike-circular-economy-firm-miniwiz-develop-sustainable-packaging-trash/

xxxi https://www.plasticstoday.com/content/sc-johnson-expands-its-line-concentrated-cleaner-refills/44026370117128

xxxii https://www.environmentalleader.com/2012/09/best-buy-lg-panasonic-join-epa-electronics-recycling-challenge/

xxxiii http://www.recyclebmws.com/

xxxiv https://www.cisco.com/c/en/us/about/product-innovation-stewardship/product-recycling.html

xxxv https://www.prnewswire.com/news-releases/garnier-and-dosomethingorg-launch-rinse-recycle-repeat-campaign-with-youtube-personality-remi-cruz-to-raise-awareness-about-the-positive-impact-of-bathroom-recycling-on-the-environment-300418239.html

xxxvi http://investor.kimberly-clark.com/news-releases/news-release-details/kimberly-clark-corporation-concludes-5-year-sustainability

xxxvii https://www.sprint.com/en/support/solutions/services/how-do-i-trade-in-turn-in-giveback-or-return-my-device.html

Chapter 25
Own Operations—Workplace

The next three chapters address the social responsibility portion of the Scorecard. As mentioned in Chapter 8 (Social Responsibility: The "S" in ESG) the Scorecard (and these three chapters) are organized around the value chain in three broad buckets: workplace, supply chain social impacts, and community. We start with workplace.

Marriott International achieved recognition as a Fortune 100 Best Company to Work® For every year since 1998 when the list was launched. But that's not all. Marriott has received numerous awards for being a best place to work for parents, for diversity, and for women. The company invests heavily in a workplace culture that is based on trust, fair treatment for all, authentic leadership, and personal connections.

The overarching strategic question that senior executives and board members should be asking with respect to the workplace environment is:

Key Question: How does our workplace environment and supporting programs, incentives, and initiatives engage our employees and others in sustainability issues?

To help answer this key question, the Scorecard analyzes how companies manage and perform in three areas:
- The general workplace environment
- Core workplace programs, related to recruitment and retention, compensation and benefits, safety, and health and wellness
- Capability building initiatives with employees

Within each of these areas, executives evaluate their company performance on several key sustainability indicators (KSIs).

General Workplace Environment

The Scorecard addresses how companies manage the general workplace environment with two KSIs: one dealing with the workplace environment and a second focused on diversity and inclusion.

KSI 15.1: Workplace Environment. In Chapter 15 (Culture and Organization), one of the KSIs (KSI 5.5) measures the "Unwritten Rules of the Game"—which in many ways captures the workplace culture. With respect to the workplace environment more broadly, the range of company approaches is as follows.

DOI 10.1515/9781547400423-025

KSI	Stage 1	Stage 2	Stage 3	Stage 4
Workplace Environment	Employees view company as meeting basic needs; honor individual privacy; focus is mostly "inside the fence line" (company operations)	Employees view company as a very good company to work for; supportive work environment; focus is work, home, and family	Widely viewed as being among best companies to work for in sector; company stands for something meaningful; focus is work, home, family, and community	Employees believe they are helping solve the world's toughest challenges— in a highly supportive work environment; focus is the global community

Entire books, journals, and websites address the actions leading companies take to attract and retain employees. Fortune magazine has issued the Best Companies to Work For since 1998. Here are a few examples of leading benefits that have an important sustainability angle.

- **Cisco:** The company states that *"Our people are part of a global community that values inclusion and diversity."*[i]
- **Costco:** Full insurance benefits are offered to part-time employees after 180 days.[ii]

In each of these examples, the company has been investing seriously to win the war for talent.

KSI 15.2: Diversity and Inclusion. Diversity and inclusion activities represent one of the key governance topics that financial and investor groups analyze. The reason is simple: there is good data for many companies on their diversity and inclusion programs and performance. As a result, many companies are years into deliberate efforts to systematically improve diversity and inclusion. The range of approaches is depicted below.

KSI	Stage 1	Stage 2	Stage 3	Stage 4
Diversity and Inclusion	Public commitments, (e.g., equal opportunity) programs and training	Strong measures and programs; top 50% in industry sector	Diverse board; less-diverse C-suite and executive ranks	Highly diverse board, C-suite, executive and staff ranks; recognized for diversity excellence

A few examples of leading companies include:

- **H&M:** The Swedish fashion retailer focused on affordable, sustainable and good quality fashion, is a leader in diversity. Fifty-eight percent of management board and 41 percent of top leadership are held by women.[iii]
- **Marriott:** The largest of the conventional hotel groups has one of the most diverse and inclusive workforces and has been named one of the World's Best Multinational workplaces by Great Place to Work—the world's largest annual study of workplace excellence.[iv]
- **Sodexo:** The leading provider of integrated food, facilities management and other services, has been consistently recognized as a best place to work, including one of the Top Companies for Diversity.[v]

In each of these examples, investing in diversity and inclusion is not simply done to improve standings in external ratings (though that can help attract talent); it is a core strategic priority of the company.

Core Workplace Programs

The Scorecard addresses the core workplace programs companies have (vis-à-vis environmental, social, and governance [ESG]) with four KSIs: focused on recruitment and retention; compensation and benefits; safety; and health and wellness.

KSI 15.3: Role of Sustainability in Recruitment and Retention. The "war for talent" is very real. In The Conference Board's annual C-suite Challenge Survey (previously called the CEO Challenge Survey), human capital has been the number one challenge for CEOs globally for the past six years. Increasingly, having a robust story to tell about ESG and sustainability is a key way companies attract talent.

KSI	Stage 1	Stage 2	Stage 3	Stage 4
Role of Sustainability in Recruitment and Retention	Traditional approach	Deliberate focus on "S" expertise and passion	Rated among best companies to work for by millennials	"S" expertise and proven success are rewarded

- **Kaiser Permanente:** One of the largest not-for-profit health plans in the U.S. has a strong commitment to supplier diversity and was recognized by DiversityInc's 2017 as a top company for diversity, recruitment, supplier diversity, mentoring.[vi]
- **Salesforce:** The company building the tallest building in San Francisco (Salesforce Tower) considers the environment to be a key stakeholder. This message is part of the company's talent recruitment efforts.

KSI 15.4: Linkage of Sustainability to Compensation and Benefits. With human capital rating as the number one CEO challenge for the past years in The Conference Board's annual C-suite survey, it follows that companies are increasingly rethinking their compensation and benefits packages. The range of ways these programs include ESG issues is as follows:

KSI	Stage 1	Stage 2	Stage 3	Stage 4
Linkage of Sustainability to Compensation and Benefits	Growing focus on ESG benefits (e.g., child care, telecommuting, etc.)	Employees can be part of a "S" network with opportunities for "S" learning	Investment and awards for sustainability-related initiatives	"S" is ~10–20% of executive incentive compensation

Prospective employees often hear about Google and Facebook offering unique employee benefits, ranging from free transport to and from work to free bike use and repair and locally sourced foods in company cafes. But they are not the only ones. Here are some other leading companies:

- **Adobe:** The company provides educational assistance, sabbatical programs, home/auto, and pet insurance.[vii]
- **Aetna:** The insurance company claims that 47 percent of its workforce telecommutes, saving ~$78 million a year.[viii]
- **Clif Bar:** The food supplier offers child care on-site for employees at their headquarters in Emeryville, CA. The company also incentivizes employees to buy fuel-efficient cars and make eco improvements.[ix]
- **Chesapeake Energy Corp:** The company offers on-site child care at their Oklahoma City headquarters.[x]
- **Dell:** The company aims for 50 percent of its global workforce to be telecommuting by 2020. [xi]
- **Salesforce.com:** The company offers career coaching and mentoring; paid volunteer time, customized training; matching donations; education reimbursement; and more.[xii]

These are some of the companies linking ESG to compensation and benefits.

KSI 15.5: Safety Programs and Performance. Most large companies—especially those in "heavy industry" (extractive industries, industrials, materials sectors such as chemicals, metals, and forest products) and others have had a corporate officer overseeing environment, health, and safety for the better part of a generation. Virtually every one of these individuals (and their executive leadership) is passionately focused on worker safety.

KSI	Stage 1	Stage 2	Stage 3	Stage 4
Safety Programs and Performance	Generally consistent with peers	Top half: own sector (e.g., OHSAS 18001)	Top quartile: all industry	Best in class: all industry

I am not going to list individual companies here, since many hundreds or more are outstanding in their management of safety. One company has stood out over the decades: Dupont's "best in class" safety record ultimately led to the company developing its own training service which is essentially a consultancy available to assist other companies.[xiii]

KSI 15.6: Health, Wellness, and Promotion of Sustainable Lifestyles. The statistics on the obesity epidemic—both in the United States and globally, are staggering. Obesity is one of the biggest drivers of preventable chronic diseases and healthcare costs in the United States. Currently, estimates for obesity range from $147 billion to $210 billion per year in the United States—in the same range as tobacco.

KSI	Stage 1	Stage 2	Stage 3	Stage 4
Health; Wellness; and Promotion of Sustainable Lifestyles	Insurance coverage; exercise rooms; formal voluntary programs; healthy food offerings	Formal programs incented; health risk appraisals; ~50% healthy food offerings	Formal health and wellness programs are available to ~90% of employees; ~75% healthy food offerings	Best in class; available to 100% of employees; healthy food offerings; maximum locally-sourced

One recent study highlighted seven companies with epic wellness programs:[xiv] Among those companies highlighted, Accenture has a wide variety of programs—tailored to the rigorous lifestyle associated with consulting. Asana pays employees to take a nap and offers daily yoga programs as well as unlimited paid time off to help employees achieve work-life balance. Draper, a manufacturing company, holds a ten-week weight loss challenges with cash prizes. Intuit has a well-known Fit for Life program.

A few other examples:
- **Badger:** The family-owned small company producing natural and certified organic body care products provides free organic lunch to their employees every day of the week.[xv]
- **Cisco:** The company unveiled a LEED Gold health center in 2008 called the Life-Connections Center, providing an array of services to enhance employees' life balance.[xvi]

Sustainability Capability-Building Initiatives

The Scorecard addresses programs and initiatives companies have to build capability around sustainability in the workplace with two KSIs: one dealing with training and staff development; and a second that looks at employee engagement.

KSI 15.7: Sustainability Training and Staff Development. Companies adopt a range of approaches to training the workforce on social issues. Virtually all companies offer (or require) some type of safety training, but beyond that companies vary widely as depicted below.

KSI	Stage 1	Stage 2	Stage 3	Stage 4
Sustainability Training and Staff Development	All employees undergo basic safety, ethics, diversity etc. training; formal "S" skills development; hire "S" interns	"S-101" short course for all staff; rotating assignments; promote career mobility and life-long "S" learning	Formal for executive team; encourage and fund "S" learning; part of 360 reviews and leadership development	Formal "S" education program for C-suite & Board; high-potential staff "S" assignments

A few examples of leading sustainability training programs include:
- **Accenture:** The professional service company's Sustainability Academy is a flexible, online learning environment designed to improve the skills and performance of professionals who support their organization's sustainability agenda.[xvii]
- **Adidas:** The athletic apparel company offers several levels of development programs for managers under the company's Functional Trainee Program. One of the core subject areas is sustainability.[xviii]

These companies invest heavily in training and staff development—and work hard to fully integrate sustainability/ESG issues into the core curriculum.

KSI 15.8: Employee Engagement with Sustainability. Employees can be an incredible source of ideas, energy, talent, and innovation. For many companies, the workforce is an untapped (certainly not fully-tapped) resource. The range of current approaches is depicted below.

KSI	Stage 1	Stage 2	Stage 3	Stage 4
Employee Engagement with Sustainability	Employee engagement largely based on own initiative	CEO-endorsed; core set of "S" teams / networks, awards & recognition	CEO-led; broad "S"; network and teams; volunteering, incentives	Reputation for being among the best

One of the best examples of a successful employee engagement program is Walmart. The company engages their 2.1 million employees through *My Sustainability Plan*, a platform whose simple interface allowed employees to state where they wanted to have an impact, and how—and then showed them their impact. The platform uses a gaming experience that spurs individual pride while encouraging communication among people around the world in a personal, authentic way. Twenty thousand U.S. associates quit smoking and shed a collective 184,000 pounds.[xix]

In another example, NextEra Energy, the world's largest utility company based in Florida that generates more wind and solar energy than any other company in the world, has a deliberate and continuous focus on employee engagement. In the company's sixth engagement survey in 2016, 90 percent of employees participated, up from 62 percent in 2014.[xx]

In both of these examples, the company sees employee engagement as a powerful tool to attract and retain talent—and to further the company's reputation.

How Do Companies Stack Up?

Starting in 2018, we are capturing data from a group of founding participants—invited to use the Scorecard for a company self-assessment and to provide feedback. As we assess the data about social responsibility in the workplace from the first sixty companies (all Fortune 500 or equivalent), we not surprisingly find that many companies are very strong in safety programs and performance. Likewise, diversity and inclusion is a growing strength across industry sectors. However, three key messages stand out:

- In recruitment and retention (KSI 15.3: Role of Sustainability in Recruitment and Retention), ratings are spread around, with highest numbers at Stage 2.5 (32 percent) and Stage 1.5 (21 percent). One third rated their company at Stage 3 or higher.
- On the subject of employee engagement with sustainability (KSI 15.8), nearly half (42 percent) rated their company at Stage 1.5. The balance were spread between Stage 2 and Stage 4, with nearly a third (32 percent) rating their company at Stage 3 or higher.
- A key opportunity for companies is in the area of sustainability training and staff development (KSI 15.8). Nearly two thirds (65 percent) rated their company at

Stage 1.5, offering some sustainability training and career opportunities, but falling short of robust programs promoting career mobility around ESG. Only four companies were at Stage 3 or higher (see Figure 25.1).

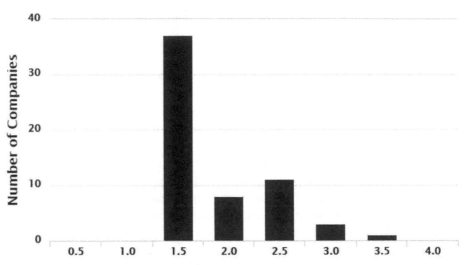

Source: Corporate Sustainability Scorecard

Figure 25.1: Scorecard Data from Sixty Companies on KSI 15.8: Sustainability Training and Staff Development

With the global "war for talent" continuing and growing, we can expect companies to increasingly position their companies as ESG leaders in order to attract the best and brightest of the Gen Y (millennial) and Gen Z (centennial) generations.

i https://www.cisco.com/c/en/us/about/csr/impact/our-people.html

ii https://www.costco.com/benefits.html

iii https://www.huffingtonpost.com/entry/gender-equality-fashion-equality_us_57604b13e4b0e4fe5143e857

iv https://www.marriott.com/diversity/corporate-diversity.mi

v https://www.sodexousa.com/home/media/news-releases/newsListArea/news-releases/sodexo-recognized-as-top-company.html

vi https://www.kaiserpermanentejobs.org/diversity-and-inclusion/

vii https://benefits.adobe.com/

viii https://www.reuters.com/article/us-yahoo-telecommuting-aetna/in-telecommuting-debate-aetna-sticks-by-big-at-home-workforce-idUSBRE92006820130301

ix https://www.bizjournals.com/sanfrancisco/blog/real-estate/2012/08/companies-bring-childcare-onsite.html?page=all

x http://www.chkcdc.com/

xi http://austin.culturemap.com/news/innovation/11-24-13-dell-austin-region-largest-employer-telecommuting/

xii https://www.salesforce.com/company/careers/

xiii http://www.dupont.com/content/dam/dupont/products-and-services/consulting-services-and-process-technologies/consulting-services-and-process-technologies-landing/documents/DnA_USA_Brochure_06192012.pdf

xiv https://www.monster.com/career-advice/article/companies-good-wellness-programs

xv http://www.bcorporation.net/community/ws-badger-co-inc

xvi https://newsroom.cisco.com/press-release-content?type=webcontent&articleId=4592347

xvii https://www.youtube.com/watch?v=PYFsvtAQO4I

xviii https://careers.adidas-group.com/teams/future-talents/functional-trainee-program

xix http://www.sustainablebrands.com/news_and_views/organizational_change/carol_cone/stop_engaging_%E2%80%93_start_fulfilling_new_era_employee_en

xx http://www.nexteraenergy.com/sustainability/employees/engagement.html

Chapter 26
Supply Chain Social Impacts

The second Scorecard element in the Social Responsibility section addresses a company's social impacts across its supply chain. This chapter will bear some resemblance to Chapter 22, which focused on supply chain environmental impacts.

For over 130 years, Johnson & Johnson has been committed to social responsibility. This commitment was codified when Robert Wood Johnson, former chairman of J&J, wrote Our Credo in 1943. This document captured the company's responsibilities to its customers, employees, communities, and stockholders long before anyone ever heard of the term "corporate social responsibility." J&J's Credo is still very much relevant 75 years later, as the company continues its efforts to help more people, in more places live healthier lives. Also worth noting, J&J extends these responsibilities beyond its own operations, seeking to work with suppliers who share a common commitment to operate responsibly.

The overarching strategic question that senior executives and board members should be asking with respect to its supply chain social impacts is:

Key Question: How deeply and robustly are we managing and reducing the social risks associated with the full supply chain impacts?

To help answer this key question, the Scorecard analyzes how companies manage and perform in three areas:
- Posture and management processes—basically how does a company approach labor, working conditions, and other social issues in its supply chain
- How companies address the most material issues in the supply chain
- Ways companies work with their suppliers to build capability

Within each of these areas, executives evaluate their company performance on several key sustainability indicators (KSIs).

Posture and Management Processes

The story of how Nike managed human rights situations over the past twenty-five years illustrates the complexity, the challenges, and many successful actions a company can take. We touch on this below, as the Scorecard addresses company posture and management processes regarding supply chain social impacts with four KSIs addressing: overall philosophy; risk assessment; responsible sourcing and assurance.

DOI 10.1515/9781547400423-026

KSI 16.1: Sustainability Philosophy Regarding the Supply Chain. For Nike, problems started in 1991 when activists reported poor working conditions and low wages in Nike's supply chain. Things got worse during the 1990s until, in 1998, then-CEO Phil Knight boldly and transparently stated, "The Nike product has become synonymous with slave wages, forced overtime and arbitrary abuse." He set to fix the situation. Other companies have learned from Nike; the range of current approaches is as follows.

KSI	Stage 1	Stage 2	Stage 3	Stage 4
Sustainability Philosophy Regarding Supply Chain	Quality; cost; dependability; compliance	Long-term partner; training and incentives to suppliers	Capability-building; joint learning; joint development of "S" solutions	Leading supply chain transformation

Nike established a Board Committee, under the outstanding leadership of Jil Ker Conway, a widely respected woman who was President of Smith College at the time. Nike created the Fair Labor Association, a nonprofit group to establish independent monitoring. Nike conducted 600 factory audits between 2002 and 2004. Since then, the company has continued many initiatives and programs to strengthen its supply chain responsibility.[i]

Nike announced in 2014 that its moonshot ambition is to double its business while halving the company's environmental impact. (This essentially followed the earlier bold launch of Unilever's Sustainable Living Plan in 2010 by CEO Paul Polman.) To achieve this moonshot goal, Nike assesses root causes and seeks systemic change in supply chain operations.[ii]

Two other examples of companies active in this space include:
- **ASML Holding NV:** The Dutch company provides chipmakers with hardware, software and silicon, aims to "virtually integrate" suppliers as part of the company's "value sourcing" strategy. ASML shares skills and processes, with the aim of working as a single enterprise.[iii]
- **Ford:** The company's commitment to managing sustainability throughout the entire supply chain was triggered in no small part by Bill Ford's (then bold and transparent) statement in the company's 2003–2004 Sustainability Report that the clear majority of Ford's greenhouse gas (GHG) emissions came from customers driving the company's vehicles—and that Ford planned to take responsibility for that.[iv]

In each of these examples, the company's CEO and C-suite recognize that they are responsible, like it or not, for the full impacts on society not just of their own operations but also of the entire life cycle (from mine face to landfill—or from farm to fork as the sayings go).

KSI 16.2: Supply Chain Risk Assessment and Management. In Chapter 13, we discussed how companies assess their supplier's *environmental* impacts. This KSI is similar on the *social* side, where the range of company approaches is as follows:

KSI	Stage 1	Stage 2	Stage 3	Stage 4
Supply Chain Risk Assessment and Risk Management	Basic due-diligence; focus on compliance in own operations and > 50% JVs	Formal risk assessment addresses "S" risks across supply chain	KPIs require robust "S" controls and systems across full value chain	Actively responsible for "S" impacts across full value chain and in communities where we operate

Below are several examples:

- **HP, Baxter, Lowe's**, and **Johnson & Johnson** were early leaders reducing the GHG footprint of their supply chains. One of the ways the companies worked with their suppliers was by diverting road transport to rail.[v]
- **Kone:** The global elevator and escalator company based in Finland has a supplier management system that includes oversight of ethics, environmental impact, strict labor guidelines, clear health and safety requirements, and a strong management system to oversee CSR KPIs, accountability and control of operational risks.[vi]

KSI 16.3: Responsible Sourcing. It has been interesting to watch how the term "responsible sourcing" has evolved in recent years. The term refers to looking beyond the traditional aspects of cost, quality, and delivery time in purchase decisions—and focusing on ethics, labor, social, and environmental aspects. The range of company activity is:

KSI	Stage 1	Stage 2	Stage 3	Stage 4
Responsible Sourcing	Emphasize local talent in purchasing and hiring decisions	Formal responsible sourcing program and criteria; support local "S" entrepreneurs	Measure, track and report "S" sourcing, aiming for net positive impacts	Global leader in responsible sourcing

A few examples of especially strong responsible sourcing practices are:

- **ASML Holding NV:** The Dutch company trained procurement managers on the Electronic Industry Citizenship Coalition® Code of Conduct corporate responsibility, addressing conflict minerals, and human trafficking issues.[vii]
- Visible consumer products companies including **Unilever, Patagonia, Starbucks**, and **Gap** are widely seen as especially strong in responsible sourcing.
- Information technology companies including **Apple, Dell, IBM**, and **HP** have learned from past mistakes and become industry leaders.

KSI 16.4: Supply Chain Auditing and Assurance. In Chapter 13 we discussed the assurance activities companies undertake on *environmental* performance across the supply chain. The same basic process applies on the social responsibility front, where the range of practices is as follows:

KSI	Stage 1	Stage 2	Stage 3	Stage 4
Supply Chain Auditing and Assurance	Require compliance assurance	Periodic external audits of key suppliers	Robust program of independent audits across supply chain	Publish audit findings and use to strengthen full supply chain "S" performance

Some examples of strong assurance programs are:
- **Dell:** The privately-held company ensures that all Tier 1 suppliers publish a sustainability report.[viii]
- **Siemens:** The German-based global industrial giant performs external sustainability audits for supply chain partners.[ix]

Addressing the Most Material Supply Chain Impacts

The Scorecard addresses how companies address the most material supply chain social impacts with three KSIs: one dealing with human rights; a second that looks at labor relations and labor issues; and a third evaluating the approach to animal rights.

It is worth noting that the Corporate Sustainability Scorecard is designed to apply to all industry sectors—ranging from banks to mining companies; from chemical manufacturers to food companies. As such, the Scorecard can not be sharply focused on the key issues in any one sector. This section of the Scorecard illustrates this dilemma. The three topics listed below broadly apply to many sectors—but certainly not all.

KSI 16.5: Human Rights—Including Indigenous People. The United Nations Declaration on Human Rights was adopted by the United Nations General Assembly at its third session in December 1948. The Declaration consists of thirty articles affirming an individual's rights, and has been endorsed by many companies and organizations globally.

Depicted below is the range of company practices related to human rights:

KSI	Stage 1	Stage 2	Stage 3	Stage 4
Human Rights— including Indigenous People	Compliance with laws, regulations and global conventions; consistent with industry peers	Strong set of principles and requirements; endorse UN Global Compact	Endorse UN Declaration on Human Rights; a leading industry advocate	Viewed as among the best in all of industry

The Nike story described above is as good an example as any as to how a company has worked diligently over many years, in fact decades, to become a leader across the supply chain on human rights issues.

KSI 16.6: Labor Relations and Labor Issues. In many developed countries, labor issues and labor relations represent a key corporate function. The area is vitally important and often a major cost item.

KSI	Stage 1	Stage 2	Stage 3	Stage 4
Labor Relations and Labor Issues	Basic, structured relations with trade unions; consistent with industry sector peers	Structured relations with employee reps; support UN declaration re child/forced labor	Public commitment; strong labor relations; endorse UN declaration re child/forced labor	Viewed as among the best in all of industry; on a mission to eradicate child/forced labor

Among the leading companies are:
- **Nestlé:** The global consumer products company conducted an internal investigation of its Thai fish supply chains in 2014 and found forced labor practices. Nestlé stopped the practice, reported it online, and compelled other companies that source fish in Thailand to follow suit.[x]
- **Patagonia:** Tackling the issue of worker welfare in its supply chain in some unique ways, the company announced in 2014 that it would plan to sell different styles of Fair Trade Certified apparel, made by a supplier called Pratibha using organic cotton farms. Patagonia also has third party audit every three years to review its corporate social responsibility (CSR) program.[xi]

–   **Unilever:** Working with Oxfam, the global consumer products company analyzed Supply Chain labor rights in Vietnam and developed a set of principles to guide a stronger path ahead in supply chain labor.[xii]

KSI 16.7: Animal Rights. The issue of animal rights is of critical importance in some industry sectors, and essentially not applicable in others. The range of approaches companies take is depicted below.

KSI	Stage 1	Stage 2	Stage 3	Stage 4
Animal Rights	Compliance with laws, regulations, and global conventions	Acknowledge and take strong industry role addressing needs	Invest considerably as leading industry advocate	A leading solution provider, growing globally

Here are several examples of companies recognized for leadership in this area:[xiii]

–   **Marks and Spencer:** The U.K. retail giant may be best known in sustainability circles for its Plan A agenda noted separately in this book, but its internal animal welfare standard is robust—insisting that animals be respected at all stages of their lives: on the farm, during transportation, and at the place of slaughter.
–   **McDonalds:** Some may be surprised to see McDonalds listed here since back in the 1990s the fast-food chain was often targeted for alleged mistreatment of animals in its supply chain. In 2013, the company switched to 100 percent sustainable fish and pledges to source sustainable beef and cage-free eggs. The transition is slow but the Humane Society of the United States called the cage-free egg move a "watershed moment for animal welfare."

Supply Chain Partnerships

The Scorecard addresses supply chain partnerships with respect to corporate social responsibility with a single KSI that looks at supplier capability building.

KSI 16.8: Supplier Capability Building. Here is the core question: is it your responsibility to help your suppliers build their own CSR capabilities, programs and initiatives? The answer is likely driven by two things: (1) shared highly material issue; and (2) risk or vulnerability associated with poor performance regarding that issue. The range of practices is as follows:

KSI	Stage 1	Stage 2	Stage 3	Stage 4
Supplier Capability Building	Ensure quality, dependability and compliance	Partnerships with leading nongovernmental organizations (NGOs) to address major industry-wide environmental, social, and governance (ESG) issues	Leading efforts at transforming the supply chain to eliminate negative ESG impacts	Collaborating with suppliers and other companies to jointly be leading solution providers, globally

Several examples of leading practices include:
- **DuPont:** The chemical company worked with APICS, self-described as the world's leading community for end-to-end supply chain excellence, on a multi-year Supply Chain Transformation Project.
- **Hershey:** The company helped found CocoaAction, supporting sustainable development in supplier communities.
- **SAP:** The technology leader developed an "open" course in sustainability, pulling together the lessons learned from its own program as well as its sustainability software. SAP offers a free sustainability course (openSAP); 14,500 enrolled in the first five weeks.[xiv]

In each of these examples, the company reached into its bank of supply chain partners, investing in the partnership for clear business benefits, as well as brand or reputation benefits.

How Do Companies Stack Up?

Starting in 2018, we are capturing data from a group of founding participants—invited to use the Scorecard for a company self-assessment and to provide feedback. As we assess the data from the first sixty companies (all Fortune 500 or equivalent), three key messages stand out:
- On companies' sustainability philosophy regarding supply chain partners on social issues (KSI 16.1, Sustainability Philosophy re Supply Chain), two of every five companies (41 percent) rated themselves at Stage 1.5. A similar number (37 percent) rated their company at Stage 2.5 or Stage 3 with another nine companies at Stage 3.5 or Stage 4.
- On KSI 16.2 (Supply Chain Risk Assessment & Management), companies, the vast majority of companies are between Stage 1.5 and Stage 2.5: 29 percent at Stage 1.5;

22 percent at Stage 2; 32 percent at Stage 2.5. Only 10 companies rated themselves Stage 3 or higher.

– On Supplier Capability Building (KSI 16.8), the story is similar but even more skewed toward Stage 1. Nearly half (47 percent) of the companies rated themselves Stage 1.5. Notably, six companies rated themselves Stage 4, including several information technology companies, an industrial and a materials company (see Figure 26.1).

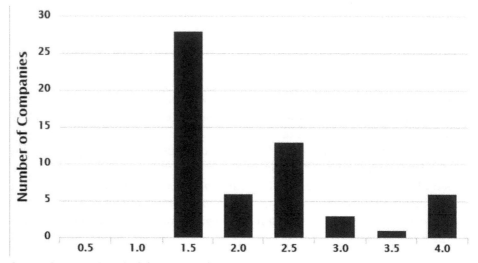

Source: Corporate Sustainability Scorecard

Figure 26.1: Scorecard Data from Sixty Companies on KSI 16.8: Supplier Capability Building

The opportunity to learn from supply chain partners is clear from the data above—and Figure 26.1.

i http://www.businessinsider.com/how-nike-solved-its-sweatshop-problem-2013-5

ii https://news.nike.com/news/sustainable-innovation

iii https://www.asml.com/asml/show.do?lang=EN&ctx=50049&dfp_fragment=suppliers_1

iv https://corporate.ford.com/microsites/sustainability-report-2016-17/index.html

v https://sloanreview.mit.edu/article/greening-transportation-in-the-supply-chain/

vi http://www.kone.com/en/sustainability/partners-and-societies/

vii https://www.asml.com/asml/show.do?lang=EN&ctx=50049&dfp_fragment=suppliers_1

viii http://www.dell.com/learn/us/en/uscorp1/cr-social-responsibility

ix https://w5.siemens.com/cms/supply-chain-management/en/sustainability/detection/external/pages/audits.aspx

x https://www.theguardian.com/global-development/2015/nov/24/nestle-admits-forced-labour-in-seafood-supply-chain

xi https://www.greenbiz.com/blog/2013/10/30/patagonia-weaves-fair-trade-supply-chain

xii https://policy-practice.oxfam.org.uk/blog/2016/07/labour-rights-in-unilever-vietnam-supply-chain-what-has-changed-since-the-first-oxfam-study

xiii https://www.triplepundit.com/2017/04/corporate-animal-welfare/

xiv https://www.greenbiz.com/blog/2014/06/18/sap-extends-free-sustainability-lessons-other-businesses

Chapter 27
Community Investment

The final element in the Social Responsibility section of the Scorecard (and of the entire Scorecard) addresses the broad issue of a company's relationship with the community. The term "community" refers to everything from the local neighbors surrounding a plant to the global community.

Cisco thinks big when it comes to community—aiming to positively impact one billion people by 2025. The company's goal is to inspire and empower a generation of global problem solvers who will thrive in our digital economy. Among Cisco's many programs are:

- *Cisco Networking Academy*—builds IT and career skills that empower people to thrive in the digital economy. Over the last 20 years, the program has changed the lives of over 8 million students in 180 countries.
- *Support for non-profits*—partnering with nonprofit organizations around the world to helping them solve global problems through cash grants, technology, and shared expertise. As of fiscal 2017, more than 230 million people were positively impacted.
- *Cisco Innovate Everywhere Challenge*—a companywide contest designed to bring employees' most innovative ideas to life.
- *Cisco Global Problem Solver Challenge*—launched in 2016 to recognize new innovative solutions that leverage technology for social impact from student entrepreneurs around the world.

The overarching strategic question that senior executives and board members should be asking with respect to their company's relationship with the community is:

Key Question: What types of policies, programs, partnerships, and investments are we making to benefit the communities in which we operate and society at large?

To help answer this key question, the Scorecard analyzes how companies manage and perform in three areas:

- Community policies and programs—the company's overall philosophy, approach, and investments in community activity as well as its philanthropic activities.
- Community investments—the partnerships and different ways of contributing to community development.
- Benefits to society—the ways company efforts contribute to community job creation, revitalization, and general sustainable development.

Within each of these areas, executives evaluate their company performance on several key sustainability indicators (KSIs).

DOI 10.1515/9781547400423-027

Community Policies and Programs

A company's outreach to communities starts with its fundamental philosophy about its role in the community and how it wants to position itself. The Scorecard addresses community policies and programs with two KSIs: one dealing with the company's philosophy and approach to community engagement and a second that looks at philanthropy.

KSI 17.1: Company's Philosophy Regarding "Community." Historically, companies addressed community outreach starting at the local level: sponsoring a local sports team; helping with a city park; and the like. Larger companies operating nationally and globally do this and more. The range of approaches is depicted below.

KSI	Stage 1	Stage 2	Stage 3	Stage 4
Company's Philosophy re "Community"	Focus of community initiatives is predominantly local; focus is "stay in the pack" among industry peers	Focus of community initiatives—and desired impact— is local and regional	Inspire employees to get involved with community initiatives locally, regionally and nationally	Focus of community initiatives— and desired impact—is local, regional, national, and global

Some examples of leading approaches to community support are:
- **Coca-Cola:** The Coca-Cola Foundation was launched in 1984 to address critical community challenges and opportunities. In 2007, the Foundation broadened its support to include global water stewardship programs, fitness and nutrition efforts and community recycling programs. Today, their strategies align with the Company's Sustainability platform and include women's empowerment and entrepreneurship.[i]
- **Intel:** The company's annual Science Talent Search honors the top U.S. students with ideas to solve the world's most vexing problems. *New York Times* columnist and author Thomas Friedman wrote in 2010 about "America's Real Dream Team." Recipient, Alice Wei Zhao of Sheboygan, Wisconsin, chosen by her fellow finalists to be their spokeswoman, summed things up when she told the audience: "Don't sweat about the problems our generation will have to deal with. Believe me, our future is in good hands."[ii]
- **Nike:** The company's goal is to create global impact through innovative, physical-activity. The company's stated purpose: to use the power of sport to move the world forward. "We believe in a fair, sustainable future—one where everyone thrives on a healthy planet and level playing field."[iii]

- **Nielsen:** The CEO stated: "the vitality of a business is closely linked to the health of the markets and communities in which it operates."[iv]
- **Unilever:** CEO Paul Polman has made the company purpose simple and clear: to make sustainable living commonplace. He stated that "We cannot close our eyes to the challenges that the world faces. Business must make an explicit and positive contribution to addressing them."[v]

KSI 17.2: Philanthropy. Corporate philanthropy programs have been around since before the days of Henry Ford. Historically, philanthropy efforts were quite separate from running the business; we run the business to make money and we have philanthropy for all the soft stuff around being a good neighbor.

That has all changed in the past several decades, as the scale and magnitude of global environmental and societal challenges increasingly impact the day-to-day activities of companies. The range of approaches companies take are as depicted below.

KSI	Stage 1	Stage 2	Stage 3	Stage 4
Philanthropy	Generally consistent with peer companies	Pro-bono service; top quartile among peers	Aligned with top few material "S" issues and with sustainable development goals (SDGs); matching gifts	Aligned with the SDGs; a leader in helping to solve the world's toughest challenges

There are hundreds, thousands of examples of companies doing good work via their company philanthropy programs. Below are two noteworthy examples.

- **Microsoft:** The company matched employee 2016 charitable donations for a total of $142 million donated. The company also launched Hack for Good—a community of Microsoft employees with a passion for applying technical and business skills to some of the world's most pressing societal problems. Past projects have included a tool for disrupting sex trafficking.[vi]
- **Intel:** One of the highest tech donors in Silicon Valley, Intel employees volunteered over one million hours in 2016. The Intel Foundation sponsors the most prestigious high school science competition in the U.S., the Intel Science Talent Search. Other programs for girls and women. The Intel Education Service Corps.[vii]

The linkage between philanthropy and sustainability is very strong; traditional philanthropic activities continue today but typically under a broader umbrella of corporate responsibility and sustainability.

Community Investments

There are different ways companies invest in communities they live and work in. The Scorecard addresses the subject of community investments with three KSIs: one dealing with community partnerships, a second focused on employee volunteerism and a third dealing with community infrastructure development.

KSI 17.3: Community Partnerships. A community partnership can be as simple as providing free food at a local event or as complex and involved as Bill Gates fighting polio. The range of company approaches is depicted below.

KSI	Stage 1	Stage 2	Stage 3	Stage 4
Community Partnerships	Local industry groups and sponsorships; selected "safe" NGOs	With broad range of NGOs	Lead effort to tackle a major societal challenge	Best globally (e.g., UNICEF)

In Chapter 16 (and specifically KSI 6.7), we discussed **JPMorgan Chase**'s very significant investment and multi-year partnership with the city of Detroit. The company plans to invest $150 million in Detroit by 2019. Some other examples include:
- **Patagonia:** The outdoor clothing company launched Patagonia Action Works; this online platform connects individuals with local environmental groups.[viii]
- **Sainsbury:** The UK company partnered with Comic Relief back in 1999 with an aim to transform the lives of small producers in Africa. Since then they have developed partnerships between small producers, producer groups, non-governmental organizations, donors and retailers.[ix]

KSI 17.4: Employee Volunteerism in Communities. Should your company encourage employees to volunteer time working with the local community? Should you allow employees to take paid leave to do this? The range of approaches companies take to these and related questions follow.

KSI	Stage 1	Stage 2	Stage 3	Stage 4
Employee Volunteerism in Communities	Limited company sponsored time; consistent with most peer companies	Formal corporate "S" volunteer programs; short-term "S" volunteer projects (days)	Medium-term "S" volunteer projects (weeks/ months); best in sector	Long-term "S" volunteer projects (years); ~40 hours per year paid per employee

Among leading companies providing paid time to volunteer in communities:

- **Autodesk:** The maker of design software, with its long-term commitment to sustainability, gives up to 48 hours paid time per year per employee.
- **Novo Nordisk:** The Danish pharmaceutical company, provides employees 10 days (80 hours) per year to volunteer, organized by the company's Social Awareness teams.
- **NetApp:** Employees have five paid days a year to volunteer in community as part of the company's Volunteer Time Off program.[x]
- **Nu Star:** The Texas-based terminal and pipeline operator gives employees up to 60 hours (7.5 days) per year.
- **Timberland:** Employees receive up to 40 paid community service hours each year. The company's ambitious goal is to have 80 percent of employees engaged in community service; the 2017 result was 42 percent.[xi]

KSI 17.5: Community Infrastructure Development. Mining companies and other extractive resource companies have, by necessity, established the notion of a company town a century ago. The companies might be solely (or largely) responsible for building roads, providing water and other resources, providing housing and schools, and more. Today, the range of ways companies support community infrastructure development is as follows:

KSI	Stage 1	Stage 2	Stage 3	Stage 4
Community Infrastructure Development	Invest locally in enhancing societal value (e.g., schools)	Invest regionally in enhancing societal value (e.g., water treatment)	Invest nationally and globally in enhancing societal value (e.g., STEM)	Invest in a single material issue globally to enhance people's lives

- **Atlas Copco:** The world-leading provider of sustainable productivity solutions based in Sweden launched "Water for All"—the company's main community engagement project, driven on the local level by employees on a voluntary basis. The program is bringing drinking water and sanitation to almost two million people, supporting projects all over the world. One project alone covers 27 villages in India.[xii]
- **IBM:** The company developed a mobile app to allow students and the Brazilian government to track the biodiversity of the Amazon rainforest.[xiii]

Benefits to Society

The Scorecard addresses a company's benefit to society (admittedly a very broad topic—so addressed here in the context of social responsibility) with three KSIs: one dealing with community education and learning, a second dealing with job creation and a third addressing community revitalization.

KSI 17.6: Community Education and Sustainability Learning. Does your company have a role to play in educating the public—likely starting locally—about key material environmental, social, and governance (ESG) issues relevant to your company and the neighbors? The range of approaches is as follows:

KSI	Stage 1	Stage 2	Stage 3	Stage 4
Community Education and Sustainability Learning	Traditional—via philanthropy	Executives support "S" education locally	CEO is a leading advocate nationally (e.g., on STEM)	CEO is a leading advocate globally

Here are a few examples:
- **Dow Chemical:** The global company is offering $100,000 in grants to help local communities divert traditionally nonrecycled plastics from landfills and convert them to energy sources.[xiv]
- **Google:** The company donated $2 million to deliver affordable internet access to rural communities in California.[xv]
- **PG&E:** The California utility signed on to its first community solar project in 2018, allowing customers (including renters and those who are not able to install solar) the option of purchasing up to 100 percent solar energy. The option does not require users to install solar panels.

KSI 17.7: Community Job Creation. Small and mid-size companies are the major creators of community jobs—certainly in the United States but also in many other countries. Many are privately held, family firms with access to technology, knowledge of local customers and the opportunity for speed to market.[xvi]

KSI	Stage 1	Stage 2	Stage 3	Stage 4
Community Job Creation	Consistent with industry peers	A leader in communities where we operate	Among leaders in national efforts in key regions of the world	Full value chain: "from farm to fork"

Two examples of companies spurring local job creation are:
- **Danone:** The French company has committed to promoting the development of a circular economy surrounding its essential resources of plastic, milk and water. The company is partnering with local communities on plastics, with goals to use sustainable (bio-based) resources, optimize packaging weight; send zero plas-

tics to landfill; engage consumers in recycling; and co-create a second life for all plastics.[xvii]
– **Natura Cosmeticos:** The Brazilian company will triple locally sourced raw materials by 2020 while hiring 1,000 researchers for the benefit of the Amazon.[xviii]

KSI 17.8: Community Revitalization. For a company to help revitalize a community can be as simple as cleaning (or clearing the snow on) the sidewalk outside your store or as large as JPMorgan Chase's Detroit investment. The range of approaches is depicted below.

KSI	Stage 1	Stage 2	Stage 3	Stage 4
Community Revitalization	Local support; philanthropy	Lead small and moderate "S" initiatives	Lead major "S" initiative(s); partner to achieve scale impacts	Lead investor in eco-parks, smart cities, etc.

– **Atlas Copco:** The Swedish company developed a leading HIV/AIDS program for nine African countries.[xix]
– **The Hershey Company:** With its core product largely dependent on the cocoa supply chain, Hershey has long been a leader in community outreach. In early 2018, the company unveiled a $500 million investment to boost sustainable cocoa production by 2030 and improve the livelihoods of farmers in local communities in Africa.[xx]
– **Quicken:** The mortgage lender, placing a bet on the revival of the city, provides an incentive for employees to move to Detroit.[xxi]

How Do Companies Stack Up?

Starting in 2018, we are capturing data from a group of founding participants—invited to use the Scorecard for a company self-assessment and to provide feedback. As we assess the data from the first sixty companies (all Fortune 500 or equivalent), three key messages stand out vis-à-vis the role of companies in communities where they operate:
– Philanthropy (KSI 17.2) has been a mature set of offerings by companies for over a century. What is surprising is that nearly half (43 percent) of the companies scored less than Stage 3. The Stage 3 descriptor is that philanthropy is aligned with the company's top few material sustainability issues and SDGs—and companies match employee gifts. Of note, a similar number of companies (46 percent) rated their company either Stage 3.5 or Stage 4—evenly split between the two.

- On community partnerships, the ratings were evenly distributed across the range: Slightly less than one third rated their company Stage 1.5 or Stage 2, with a similar number rating their company Stage 2.5 or Stage 3. Two in five companies (40 percent) rated themselves Stage 3.5 or Stage 4.
- Outreach to communities to share learnings and educate the public about sustainability issues is an area where there is a lot of room for improvement. One third rated their company at Stage 1.5 or lower. Another third rated the company Stage 2 to Stage 3, with one quarter rating their company Stage 3.5 or higher, as depicted in Figure 27.1.

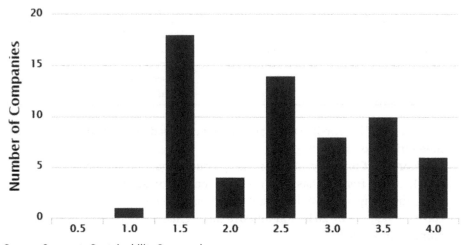

Source: Corporate Sustainability Scorecard

Figure 27.1: Scorecard Data from Sixty Companies on KSI 17.7: Community Education/Sustainability Learning

As the United Nations SDGs continue to gain a stronger foothold in company boardrooms, along with ever present pressure on the bottom line, we can expect companies to increasingly focus their community investments and outreach aligned with the critical few most material ESG issues for the company and its industry sector.

i https://www.coca-colacompany.com/our-company/the-coca-cola-foundation
ii https://www.nytimes.com/2010/03/21/opinion/21friedman.html?_r=0
iii https://sustainability.nike.com
iv http://www.nielsen.com/us/en/about-us/global-responsibility-and-sustainability.html
v https://www.unilever.com/about/who-we-are/our-vision/
vi https://www.microsoft.com/en-us/philanthropies/employee-engagement
vii https://www.intel.com/content/www/us/en/corporate-responsibility/community-involvement.
html
viii https://www.forbes.com/forbes/welcome/?toURL=https://www.forbes.com/sites/
melissaanders/2018/02/07/patagonia-steps-up-environmental-activism-with-dating-site-for-
grassroots-projects/&refURL=&referrer=#79c8de3e556a
ix https://www.comicrelief.com/partners/sainsburys
x https://community.netapp.com/t5/Company/Volunteer-Time-Off-Gaining-Inspiration-by-Giving-
Back/ba-p/82670
xi https://www.timberland.com/responsibility.html?story=1
xii http://www.atlascopcogroup.com/en/about-us/water-for-all
xiii https://www.greenbiz.com/blog/2014/02/18/how-ibm-helps-monitor-biodiversity-amazon
xiv https://www.kab.org/hefty-energybag-grant-program/news-info/press-releases/dow-keep-
america-beautiful-award-100000-2018
xv https://blog.sfgate.com/techchron/2013/10/22/google-grants-2m-to-researchers-bringing-
broadband-to-rural-california/
xvi https://www.forbes.com/sites/allbusiness/2017/02/08/job-creation-in-the-new-political-
economy-small-companies-not-big-companies-create-jobs/2/#546ab51b20a2
xvii https://www.ellenmacarthurfoundation.org/ce100/directory/danone
xviii https://www.greenbiz.com/blog/2014/02/04/natura-cosmetics-sustainability-amazon
xix http://www.atlascopcogroup.com/en/sustainability?/investing-in-health-and-safety/fighting-
hiv-aids
xx https://www.thehersheycompany.com/content/corporate/en_us/news-center/news-detail.
html?2340764
xxi https://www.reuters.com/article/us-usa-detroit-downtown/mortgage-lender-quicken-bets-on-
downtown-detroits-revival-idUSBRE91I00O20130219

Chapter 28
Conclusion: Tomorrow's Elite Corporation

"Business as usual" continues to undergo dramatic change. The sustainability transformation is underway—and it is accelerating. The rapid transformation is being driven by the doubling of the global middle class between 2015 and 2030. This is causing—and will increasingly cause—an unprecedented demand for oil, gas, metals, food, water, land, clean air, and more.

As with earlier massive societal disruptions (like the dawn of the industrial revolution in the late 1800s), this one is messy. Solar companies are going bankrupt as the market for renewable energy solutions grows at a massive scale. Ford is changing more in the current five-year period than the past hundred years combined. Still, investors have not always been rewarded for their new strategy or investments in sustainable mobility.

Everything is up for grabs. Regardless of industry sector, every traditional company must engage in some soul-searching and in fundamental business transformation to survive and thrive. In short, like an Olympic athlete competing on the global stage, they need to become *fit, trim,* and *resilient*.

- *Fit*—exercising new behaviors with skill and coordination.
- *Trim*—embracing the circular economy full stop. They aim to: source 100 percent renewable energy and recycled/recyclable materials; generate zero waste; and sell solutions rather than (or in addition to) products.
- *Resilient*—anticipating major disruptions and building the capacity to innovate and react with speed to those disruptions.

This means learning to operate outside their comfort zone.

Fit: Visualizing Success

Each CEO, board member, and senior executive needs to essentially "turn on its head" the operating philosophy of the past 150 years. Tomorrow's leading companies systematically will shed their old ways of doing business in the "take-make-waste" world. For Ford and other automobile companies, it means completely transforming the business model:

- *From* churning out cars and trucks (where a key metric has been volume of vehicles sold)
- *To* providing customers and consumers with a wide range of sustainable mobility solutions (where the key metric might be vehicle miles covered)

DOI 10.1515/9781547400423-028

This transformation is brutally difficult. It starts at the top, with productive conversations among C-suite executives and in the boardroom. It requires robust governance.

As noted in the Introduction, *the resource revolution represents the biggest business opportunity in a century.* What do we mean by the resource revolution? It means: (1) getting more value out of the stuff we already have; and (2) creating more new value from less stuff. Here are a few examples:

- In many communities, homes (or certainly bedrooms) sit idle for a great majority of the time. *Enter Airbnb.*
- The typical automobile is parked 95 percent of the time. *Enter Uber, Lyft, and a host of new "sustainable mobility solutions."*
- Many women purchase fancy attire that is used only once or a few times. *Enter Rent the Runway.*
- Ray Anderson, the legendary leader of Interface Carpets who became a leading CEO advocate for sustainability, came to a shocking realization: the carpets his company manufactured took only a few days to make; had a useful life of a few years; and then took about 20,000 years or more to decompose (if ever). *Enter the circular economy.*

McKinsey notes that rather than settling for historic resource-productivity improvement rates of one to two percentage points a year, companies need to deliver productivity gains of 50 percent or so every few years.[i] Incremental improvement such as energy efficiency gains of two-to-three percent per year will no longer be sufficient.

Trim: Decoupling Growth and Profitability from Resource Intensity

How can companies grow and make more money but use less energy, fewer materials, and generate less waste? That's the goal of the circular economy.

The circular economy may be the biggest revolution in the global economy since the industrial revolution.[ii] C-suite executives should be asking themselves: *How do we do this? Where do we start? How do we get the timing right? Is there a logical pathway?*

To gain competitive advantage in the emerging circular economy, the C-suite will embrace sustainability in five core ways. Their action list looks like this:

1. **Closed-Loop Supply.** Start by engaging your employees. Tap into the powerful resource base that exists in every enterprise. Take inventory of every material coming into your factory gate. *Put the materials in one of two buckets*: those produced through natural systems and those that are human-made –
   o Natural materials (e.g., agricultural, forest, and fisheries products) should be in a circular loop, such as composting all food, fiber, and natural materials.
   o Human-made materials (e.g., metal, plastic, etc.), wherever possible, should be sourced from renewable materials—and recycled forever.

New and old companies do this today. Microsoft's global operations have been 100 percent carbon neutral since 2012. UPS offers carbon neutral shipping. Novelis is rapidly moving from sourcing 30 percent of its raw material from recycled stock to 80 percent. Dell launched carbon negative packaging. Today, Ecovative, Google, and IKEA invest in renewable energy sourcing on a major scale. DSM, the major Dutch chemical company, produces biofuels and bio-based materials made from cellulosic biomass. Croda and Hershey have achieved 100 percent sustainably sourced palm oil. Curtis Packaging, a family-held paper and packaging company, has sourced 100 percent of its energy from renewable sources for years.

2. **Zero Waste.** On January 24, 2018, Mumbai (Bombay), the largest city in India, banned single use plastics (plastic bags, cups, bottles) and imposed fines of up to 25,000 rupees ($364) and up to three months in jail for offenders. So, what does that mean for companies?

    Once inside the factory gate, place a "wall" around your company's own operations—the things you control. Determine how to drive toward zero waste. This should be the easy part. Many leading companies have twenty–thirty years of experience driving down waste under the "quality" (Lean or Six Sigma) banner. 3M has worked for nearly fifty years at cutting waste through its Pollution Prevention Pays program, which was launched in 1975. DuPont and others followed suit with zero waste ambitions and initiatives. Subaru is among the leaders in its industry.

    Moving toward zero waste employs the same thinking as lean or Six Sigma. However, "zero waste" thinking is applied on a broader scale, such as in these examples: The Nike Flyknit technology redefines performance-engineered footwear. Reebok is launching a 100 percent compostable sneaker. Carpetmakers Shaw Industries and Desso have changed the industry: Shaw Industries launched EcoWorx, a "PVC-free, cradle to cradle certified backing system." Desso's innovative separation technique (Refinity) enables the company to separate the yarn and fibers from the backing–thus greatly enhancing recycling.

3. **Product to Service.** Shifting from selling products to selling services and solutions is nothing new. In the early 1990s, Xerox taught us about *leasing* instead of *selling* copy machines; and the company committed to a vision of "zero waste products from zero waste factories." Xerox was ahead of its time. Such approaches are starting to expand. Though Michelin is in the business of selling tires, the company has come to realize that *customers want safety and mileage, not just tires.* So, Michelin is reinventing itself to sell "mileage" instead of rubber; that is, selling a service rather than a product. Increasingly, customers are driving this shift from product to service. In a recent Conference Board survey, 36 percent of respondents agree that, compared to three years ago, their

companies are more likely to use a pay-per-use service of a product instead of buying the product outright.[iii]

4. **Durability.** Companies are looking to extend the durability of products that may not lend themselves to be sold as a service. This is difficult because we have been living in a disposable society for more than fifty years (especially in the United States). Many businesses have been incented to sell stuff that people use for a while and then throw away. However, future business opportunities lie in finding ways to extend product durability.[iv] Autodesk teaches sustainability workshops on improving product durability. DuPont's weathering systems are certified for product durability. Caterpillar products are designed to support " ... durability that allows for multiple rebuilds, ease of serviceability and reparability...," while John Deere's new L-Series Skidders deliver "best-in-class horsepower as well as improved stability and durability." Cisco's VX Tactical, for example, "designed for portability and ease of use in the field is a high-definition video collaboration system with functions that facilitate remote communication and collaboration in remote environments...providing portability, durability, and other functions."

5. **Waste Recovery.** Waste Management was forced to reinvent itself when it realized its customers wanted to create less waste (not more waste). So, it flipped its business on its head and determined how to grow the company's revenue by helping its customers generate *less waste*—and how to become smarter about the waste they did generate. This represented a 180-degree shift from the company's history of growing sales by growing the volume of waste coming into its treatment, storage, and disposal system. UK apparel company H&M is one of the "biggest users of recycled polyester in the world" noting that one-third of the clothing in the UK goes to landfill. In 2015, thirty-one of thirty-three of the Kroger's manufacturing plants were designated as "zero waste" facilities.

These five core attributes of gaining circular competitive advantage align with the global shift toward the *sharing economy*. While many sharing economy companies may not place sustainability at the core of their mission, these companies are, in fact, accelerating the sustainability transformation.

Resilient: Capacity to Innovate Among Disruptions

Perhaps more than any other trait, the "need to operate outside of its comfort zone" will characterize tomorrow's elite corporation. Why? At its core, sustainability is about not only being fit and trim, but also *resilient*.

Companies must build the capacity to adapt and innovate among disruptions. They need to adopt and embrace what can be an uncomfortable set of assumptions about the world around us:
- "Unlearning" how industrial society has operated for 150 years
- "Charting a new route" to reach the same goal of delivering shareholder value

Going forward, C-suite executives and boards must treat social responsibility and environmental stewardship not as separate functions largely disconnected from strategy, but rather as integral to corporate and business strategy. *In many ways, that is precisely what the Corporate Sustainability Scorecard is all about.*

A Few Words on Climate Change

Climate change—and more specifically the rapid acceleration of levels of greenhouse gases in the atmosphere—is an important and controversial subject. In many ways, it is becoming a defining issue of the early twenty-first century. This is not Greenpeace talking; climate change increasingly pervades many conversations among what we referred to in Chapter 9 as "the new ESG regulators."
- *Economists*: As reported by the World Economic Forum in its annual (2017) update,[v] several of the highest risk megatrends are not only sustainability related but also focused squarely on climate change. Four of the top five risks are: extreme weather events, failure of climate change mitigation and adaptation, water crises, and large-scale involuntary migration.
- *Investors*: The final report titled "Recommendations of the Task Force on Climate-related Financial Disclosures" (TCFD) in June 2017 began with the statement: "One of the most significant, and perhaps most misunderstood, risks that organizations face today relates to climate change." This set the stage for Black-Rock CEO Larry Fink's January 16, 2018 letter to CEOs essentially demanding that they demonstrate how their companies provide value to society.
- *Millennials*: Currently ages twenty-two to thirty-nine (born between 1979 and 1996) this largest of all generations (larger than the baby boomer parents) will access 24 trillion of accessible wealth by 2024. They understand technology; they believe in the environmental threats of climate change, water shortages, and toxics, and they plan to act.

Yet despite its dominance in discourse, climate change is not a stand-alone issue; it in many ways is intricately interwoven with other issues. It is also becoming one of the world's powerful and destabilizing geopolitical forces.

Companies (and any enterprise) can undertake two basic sets of actions to address climate change:

- *Mitigation*: actions to reduce the likely negative impacts of growing greenhouse gas concentrations in the atmosphere.
- *Adaptation*: actions to prepare for managing the potential negative consequences of climate change.

Thirty years ago, these two core responses to climate change could be considered interchangeable. As the *Harvard Business Review* reported in its 2017 article about the U.S. Navy, that window has shut.[vi]

The U.S. Navy realizes that virtually all its operations exist at or near sea level; as such, the land-based operations need to be resilient to potential sea level rises. The Navy also sees the Arctic opening and realizes that it lacks the assets it needs to operate effectively in that region.

In the same way that the U.S. Navy is mitigating its impacts and adapting to the future realities that are ever-present today, each company needs to *be resilient* and *prepare for disruptions*.

The Path Forward

Sometimes individuals, companies, and countries make things too complicated. It is true that sustainability can be complex, challenging, perplexing, and amorphous. The objectives for sustainability include everything from solving climate change and tackling world hunger to protecting human rights and providing access to potable water.

At its core, *sustainability is about leadership*. And many companies are indeed leading. The hundreds of examples throughout this book illustrate examples of individual leadership practices. Moreover, the fact that more than sixty of the Fortune 500 have already utilized the Scorecard tool described in this book is evidence of their keen desire to elevate their sustainability performance, especially around governance and strategy.

Yet, too many companies fail to see the big picture for sustainability. They see ESG issues almost entirely as risks to manage. On the Corporate Sustainability Scorecard, they are in Stage 1. They have yet to view the "power of sustainability" to drive profitable growth and value creation.

The Corporate Sustainability Scorecard C-suite rating system comes in here. Aimed specifically at the C-suite and the board (often via those advising them), the Scorecard can help create the right conversations about governance and leadership, and about strategy and execution.

At some point ...

... the first light bulb goes on in the C-suite or boardroom. Board members "see" the mess that humans are making of the planet and the coming global impact of doubling middle-class consumption on this planet with fixed resources. They think about

stranded assets; and they recognize that sustainability risks and opportunities are several orders of magnitude higher than in the past ...

... *and then a second light bulb goes on.* The executive team begins to see the massive growth of the global middle class not only as a source of risk, but also as a huge business opportunity. They imagine growing a profitable business without consuming nonrenewable resources.

Today's leading companies are positioning themselves to grow and profit from addressing the world's most pressing challenges. As companies transform and realign toward this new overarching goal, *sustainability leadership* in the C-suite and boardroom can be enabled by this simple agenda –

– Anticipate trends
– Understand new and diverse risks
– Determine what it would take to be carbon neutral
– Target zero waste throughout the value chain
– Work with your suppliers and customers to "close the loop" on everything
– Understand the agendas of people who can influence your business
– Inspire your employees
– Prevent nasty surprises
– Be proud to tell your kids what you do

The leaders of today's companies have a choice: ***Will we transform with the times and position our company as a fit, trim, and resilient company of tomorrow? Based on my work with sustainability leaders, I believe we will.***

Game on!

---

i Heck and Rogers, "Are You Ready?" *op cit.*

ii Peter Lacy, "Gaining an Edge from the Circle: Growth, Innovation and Customer Value through the Circular Economy," *Accenture Strategy*, 2015.

iii Thomas Singer, "Business Transformation and the Circular Economy," The Conference Board, Research Report 1628, 2017, p. 21.

iv Singer, "Business Transformation and the Circular Economy, *op cit.*

v "The Global Risks Report 2017, 12th Edition," World Economic Forum, 2017, p. 4. http://www3.weforum.org/docs/GRR17_Report_web.pdf

vi Forest L. Reinhardt and Michael W. Toffel, "Managing Climate Change: Lessons from the U.S. Navy," *Harvard Business Review*, July-August 2017, pp. 103–111.

Appendix A
Definitions

Assurance Letter: Typically, an annual signed statement from business executives (often business presidents) to the CEO stating that operations comply; risks and significant issues are identified and being managed; and processes are in place to ensure consistent implementation of corporate policies and values.

Board: Refers to the external Board of Directors (as with all U.S.-based public corporations); the governing body with oversight fiduciary responsibility for the corporation *[Note: the "Supervisory Board" referred to often in Europe, consisting of the CEO and his/her direct reports, is not part of this section. That is covered under CEO Leadership and Culture and Organization.]*

Brownfield Redevelopment: The expansion, redevelopment or reuse of land and property, which may be complicated by the presence or potential presence of hazardous substances or contaminants.

Carbon Neutral: Having a net zero carbon footprint; achieving net zero carbon emissions by balancing a measured amount of carbon released with an equivalent amount sequestered or offset, or buying enough carbon credits to make up the difference.

Chief Sustainability Officer (CSO): The most senior person in the company with responsibility for overseeing sustainability policy, positioning and activities. Note: the person may or may not be officially designated as the CSO by the company.

Circular Economy: An alternative to the traditional linear economy (make, use, dispose) in which resources remain in use for as long as possible, extracting the maximum value from them while in use, then recover and regenerate products and materials at the end of each product or service life.

Closed-Loop: Also referred to as the circular economy, where materials, at the end of their useful life, are consistently repurposed, recycled, reused, reclaimed, restored, or otherwise converted to some use rather than discharged as waste.

Community of Practice: A group of people who share a common interest (e.g., in sustainability); may evolve naturally or can be created to share knowledge.

Cradle to Cradle: A holistic framework for design of industry, products, buildings, or urban environments that seeks to create systems that are efficient and essentially

DOI 10.1515/9781547400423-029

waste free. (The term Cradle to Cradle is a registered trademark of McDonough Braungart Design Chemistry/MBDC.)

Crowdsourcing: The process of obtaining needed services, ideas, or content by soliciting contributions from a large group of people, especially from an online community, rather than from traditional employees or suppliers.

Design for Environment (DfE): A global movement incorporating environmental motives to improve product design to minimize health and environmental impacts.

Ecosystem Services: Humankind benefits in a multitude of ways from ecosystems (e.g., cleaning drinking water, decomposing wastes, etc.). Collectively, these benefits are known as *ecosystem services*.

ESG (Environmental, Social, and Governance): The term often used by the investment community to refer to what they characterize as the three central factors in measuring the sustainability of an investment in a company or business. In this book and the companion website, the term ESG is used interchangeably with sustainability.

Executive Committee: Refers to direct reports to the CEO charged with overseeing strategy and operations.

Executive Sustainability Council: The senior-level, cross-functional group of executives that many companies must provide a forum for setting policy direction; recommending goals and metrics; deciding priorities; allocating resources; and reviewing progress on key initiatives.

External Sustainability Advisory Board: A group of sustainability experts or thought leaders from various external stakeholder groups, assembled to periodically advise the CEO and CSO.

Externality: The cost or benefit that affects a party who did not choose to incur that cost or benefit. For example, manufacturing activities that cause air pollution or carbon emissions may impose health, cleanup, or other costs on society.

Footprint: A measure of an organization's (or human's) demand on the Earth's ecosystems. Unless otherwise, in this context is used as a measure of the full impact across the supply chain of an organization's operations, including, for example, consumption, use and emissions of energy, materials, resources, water, etc.

Forest Stewardship Council (FSC): An international not for-profit, multi-stakeholder organization established in 1993 to promote responsible management of the world's forests. FSC is a global forest certification system established to promote forest management that is environmentally appropriate, socially beneficial, and economically viable.

Global Reporting Initiative (GRI): A nonprofit organization that produces one of the world's most prevalent standards for sustainability reporting.

Green Chemistry: The design of chemical products and processes that reduce or eliminate the use or generation of hazardous substances across the full life cycle of chemical production, from design and manufacture to product use and disposal.

International Sustainability Charters/Commitments: A global sustainability charter, framework or set of principles such as, for example, the UN Global Compact; UN Declaration on Human Rights; the Precautionary Principle; Green Chemistry Principles; etc. Also includes commitments to global agreements such as the Paris Climate Accord.

Key Business Decisions: The handful of major decisions the CEO and Board make each year—typically involving merger, acquisition or divestiture; large capital expenditure; new product launch; major research and development expenditure, etc.

Key Sustainability Indicators (KSI): Hedstrom Associates uses the term key sustainability indicators to characterize the specific items in our Corporate Sustainability Scorecard C-suite rating system. The Corporate Sustainability Scorecard allows a user to rate a company on about 150 key sustainability indicators.

LEED: Leadership in Energy and Environmental Design is one of the most popular green building certification programs worldwide. It was developed by the nonprofit U.S. Green Building Council.

Life Cycle Assessment (LCA): A technique to assess environmental impacts associated with all the stages of a product's life from-cradle-to-grave (i.e., from raw material extraction through materials processing, manufacture, distribution, use, repair and maintenance, and disposal or recycling). Also known as life-cycle analysis.

Material: Information is material if its omission or misstatement could influence the economic decision of users taken based on the financial statements. (See Materiality.)

Materiality: A concept or convention within the financial community relating to the importance/significance of something relevant to the corporation. Information is material if its omission or misstatement could influence the economic decision of users taken based on the financial statements. Materiality in relation to the inclusion of information in an integrated (financial and sustainability) report refers to matters that "could substantively affect the organization's ability to create value over the short, medium and long term."[1]

Net Neutral (Environmental Impact): Refers to a situation where the sum of the full environmental impacts of an organization—across the full supply chain—is offset by the net reduction in environmental impact caused by use of the company's products, services or solutions.

Net Positive (Environmental Impact): Refers to a situation where the sum of the full environmental impacts of an organization—across the full supply chain—is less than the net reduction in environmental impact caused by use of the company's products, services, or solutions.

NGO (Nongovernmental Organization): An organization that is neither a part of a government nor a conventional for-profit business; seen to represent "civil society."

Precautionary Principle: If an action or policy has a suspected risk of causing harm to the public or to the environment, in the absence of scientific consensus that the action or policy is not harmful, the burden of proof that it is *not* harmful falls on those taking an action.

Products, Services, or Solutions (PSS): Items or services sold by companies that are intended to satisfy a market need. From a sustainability context, shifting from selling products to leasing products or selling services is consistent with moving from a linear ("take–make–waste") system to a closed-loop one whereby products, after their useful life, are recycled, reused, refurbished, or returned to some productive use.

REACH: A European regulation promulgated in 2006 that addresses the production and use of chemical substances, and their potential impacts on both human health and the environment.

Sharing Economy: While there is not one widely agreed definition, the sharing economy involves attempts to make more efficient use of labor and capital resources using information technology that lowers the costs of matching buyer with sellers.

Stakeholder: Individuals or groups of people who can reasonably be expected to be significantly affected by an organization's business activities, outputs, or outcomes, or whose actions can reasonably be expected to significantly affect the ability of the organization to create value over time.
  - o "Internal stakeholders" typically include the organization's governing body, management, employees, and shareholders.

o   "External stakeholders" typically include communities, government, environmental groups, as well as suppliers, customers, and consumers.

Stranded Assets: Assets such as fossil fuel supply that are no longer able to earn an economic return because of changes associated with the transition to a low-carbon economy, posing an economic challenge to their owners.

Supply Chain: The system of organizations, people, activities, information and resources involved in moving a product or service from point of origin to point of consumption. Supply chains underlie value chains because, without them, no producer can provide customers what they want, when they want it, and at a price they will pay.

Sustainability: The pursuit of a business growth strategy that creates long-term shareholder value by seizing opportunities and managing risks related to the company's environmental and social impacts. Sustainability includes conventional environment, health, and safety (EHS) management; community involvement and philanthropy; labor and workplace conditions as well as elements of corporate citizenship, corporate governance, supply chain, and procurement.

Sustainability Principles: Various ways of characterizing the concept of sustainability. One example would be the four system conditions of The Natural Step.

Sustainability Ratings and Rankings: Those independent sustainability ratings and rankings that major companies across industry sectors and geographies typically view as the most influential or worthy, including:
o   Bloomberg
o   CR Magazine 100 Best Corporate Citizens
o   CDP
o   Dow Jones Sustainability Index (DJSI)
o   Fortune's *The World's Most Admired Companies*
o   *FTSE4Good Index Series*
o   Global 100 Most Sustainable Companies
o   Newsweek Green Rankings
o   Oekom Corporate Ratings

Sustainability Report: An organizational report that gives information about ESG positioning and performance. This can be a stand-alone report (often a companion to the Annual Report); it can be included with the financial information in a fully Integrated Report; or can be the equivalent information available on a company's website.

Sustainable Development Goals (SDGs): A set of 17 "Global Goals" with 169 targets between them, adopted by 193-member countries of the United Nations, intended to galvanize and guide the world's efforts to eradicate poverty, end hunger and address climate change by 2030.

TCFD (Task Force on Climate-Related Financial Disclosures): This industry-led task force, established by the Financial Stability Board (at the request of the G20 Finance Ministers and the Central Bank Governors) issued its final report in June 2017. The report includes recommendations to industry for disclosure to investors, following a simple structure (that incidentally is almost identical to our Corporate Sustainability Scorecard):
  - o Governance
  - o Strategy
  - o Risk (the Scorecard has separate sections for Environmental and Social)
  - o Metrics (the Scorecard folds this under Governance)

Unwritten Rules of the Game: How a cross-section of employees would describe "the way things work around here."

Value Chain: The process by which a company adds value to an article, including during production, transportation, marketing, and the provision of after-sales service.

Water-Neutral: Refers to a situation where an organization is returning to surface water or ground water the volume of water it uses—across the full supply chain—at a level of purity that is of the same or higher quality of the receiving body or aquifer.

Workplace: The physical and social environment where employees do their work and interact with peers.

---

i The International Integrated Reporting Council, The International <IR> Framework 13 December 2013, p. 5. http://integratedreporting.org/resource/international-ir-framework/

Index

DOI 10.1515/9781547400423-030